# In search of the Iron Age

*Proceedings of the Iron Age Research Student Seminar*
*2008, University of Leicester*

# In search of the Iron Age

*Proceedings of the Iron Age Research Student Seminar 2008, University of Leicester*

*Edited by*
**Martin Sterry, Andy Tullett and Nick Ray**

Leicester Archaeology Monograph 18


ISBN 978-0-9560179-3-2




Published by the
School of Archaeology & Ancient History,
University of Leicester

Typeset and printed by
4word Ltd, Bristol

# Table of Contents

# List of Figures

# INTRODUCTION

## Andy Tullett

*University of Leicester*

The tenth Iron Age Research Student Seminar (IARSS) held at the University of Leicester in 2008 was the latest in the illustrious history of this remarkable forum. The origins of the conference are publicized in each of the volumes of the proceedings that have been published to date but it is appropriate that we briefly note them once more here.

The first IARSS was held in 1998 at University of Wales, Newport, with the proceedings being published in 2003 in conjunction with those of the subsequent conferences at Southampton and Leicester (Humphrey 2003). Since that time IARSS has been held all around Britain: Durham (2001), Glasgow (2002), York (2004), Edinburgh (2005), Cardiff (2006) and Southampton (2007). Unfortunately the only other volume of proceedings to make it into print from all these conferences is that from the excellent 2006 Cardiff conference (Davis *et al.* 2008). The Seminar has a prestigious heritage and many of the early presenters have gone on to take places in academia, chairing sessions and guiding their students to participation in the IARSS tradition.

One of the aims of the first IARSS was to broaden the base of Iron Age studies and involve a wide range of individuals and interests from within British Archaeology. This has continued within recent years and the Leicester 2008 conference in particular managed to attract a very broad base of interest. The scope of the conference has expanded now to cover Europe not just in terms of attendees but also of studies. It shows the range and community of Iron Age archaeology has continued to grow, and that it is truly a European forum in which we operate.

The range of topics presented also reflected the expansive spectrum of research that our discipline now pursues. Whilst the conference saw a lot of contributions researching the continental Iron Age, this has unfortunately not followed through into the publication; something that following volumes will hopefully achieve. This range was also matched in terms of chronology, with papers stretching from the English Late Bronze Age through to the end of the 'long' Iron Age in Scotland (that might conceivably be labelled early medieval elsewhere in Europe).

The conference and its name remain close to that of the Iron Age Research Seminar (IARS) that produced the seminal 'Understanding the British Iron Age: an agenda for action' (Haselgrove *et al.* 2001). IARSS is very much the 'student arm' of Iron Age research and indicates the direction that future studies will head. It is not surprising therefore that all papers follow the strands of inquiry that IARS highlighted as essential to the progress of Iron Age studies.

One of the key points raised by IARS was to develop a more nuanced chronology for the changes witnessed during the Iron Age. Guy de Mulder's paper demonstrates the application of new dating methods to the continental material and how advances in scientific understanding and techniques can overthrow established typological chronologies and challenge quite entrenched beliefs. The continual improvement of chronological finesse in the study of the Iron Age, especially in areas outside of Wessex, remains a key challenge to future research.

The second section addressed by the IARS committee ('Settlements, Landscapes and People') has attracted the most attention over the years and did so again in 2008. The East Midlands, typically one of the underrepresented regions of the UK, received much attention, benefiting from the location of the conference with papers, from John Thomas and Gavin Speed. The latter shows in his work how some of the observations made from the Wessex material remain valid when transposed to another area of the UK. The spatial grammar contained within the structure of enclosed settlements in the East Midlands holds as true here as it does in Wessex. Thomas' paper however focuses on a much more poorly understood area of the settlement record, that of open settlements. The scale of habitation in these locations again raises concerns as to how valid our current models of Iron Age society are. These are heavily based upon our understanding of either small enclosed farmsteads (e.g. Hill 1995) or upon hillforts (Cunliffe 1984), and either statements of isolation and independence, or dependence upon power bases. Two papers in this volume start to question these dominant narratives that have been largely unchallenged in the last ten years. Community is a term often used in later prehistoric literature but authors often prefer to leave its definition vague, and so it is rarely defined. The first paper by Andy Tullett explores what we mean by the term and posits that as community is the social unit that links wider society with more organic units, such as the household, it represents the most appropriate level to study Iron Age society. This is a trend followed by Oliver Davis as he explores the varying scales at which society operated. Both papers acknowledge that 'the settlement' does not encompass the entirety of social interaction and as a result we have to look beyond these boundaries to a landscape-wide study when looking at society. The second paper by Andy Tullett further explores the scales at which interaction takes place and how affinity and community can be constructed through one aspect of life, that of journeys, travel or movement. It moves away from the strictly site based narratives that assume that the gamut of social life was contained within the sphere of the settlement, upholding the argument of the preceding papers for a landscape approach to social studies. These three papers have a more traditional Wessex focus showing that the wealth of archaeological data available in this region means that it remains an important area for the development of theories that can be extrapolated across a broader area. This large scale approach to social studies is further advanced by Greta Anthoons' paper that focuses on long distance elite networks made visible in the burial evidence from north-western Europe. She considers how as small contacts are added, changes in network systems can reflect changes in societal makeup.

Connected to the study of people in a more fundamental way, two papers seek to understand Iron Age life through physical human remains. Whilst human remains are almost ubiquitous on Iron Age sites, the presence of identifiable burial rites remains notoriously elusive. As human remains are the most direct contact that we have with Iron Age peoples, their study remains fundamental to the discipline. IARS highlighted the need to link burials and funerary rituals to their place in the surrounding landscape and the conduct of 'off-site' rituals (Haselgrove *et al.* 2001: 14). This is a theme picked up by Fiona Tucker in her summary of the Scottish material which presents a varied and difficult to interpret set of data, along with a greater chronological depth than faced by many of us. The second paper dealing with human remains is Sarah King's study of violence in prehistory, though it is challenged by interpretative issues surrounding the 'conflict' versus 'warfare' debate (James 2007). Vicky Score and Jen Browning also examine the negotiation of power relationships through the manipulation of material culture in their investigation of Hallaton, the site of the East Leicestershire hoard. The site suggests that rather than the large tribal group assumed to exist in this region, there existed much smaller political groups that were much more dynamic, producing small circulations of coinage and enacting ritual acts away from formal buildings and structures. It therefore potentially provides a key to understanding other similar deposits in areas that lack the same scale of excavation.

The reassessment of the 'massacre' deposits from South Cadbury by Sue Jones and Clare Randall shows the potential for returning to previously excavated sites for a reassessment of the data using modern methods; a topic again highlighted by IARS (Haselgrove *et al.* 2001). Their work suggests that far from a single act resulting from continental invasion, the deposits relate to a broader pattern of changing social practice concerning the deposition of humans, animals and metalwork. They posit that society was already in a state of flux by the time of the arrival of the Romans, showing the ongoing importance of such studies.

Finally Jeanette Wooding's work on the occurrences of bovine tuberculosis in domestic fauna displays the symbiotic relationship between people and their stock. It demonstrates the potential for studying the pathologies in archaeofaunal assemblages to understand animal husbandry practices and the transmission of diseases.

Whilst the conference and proceedings volume owe much to those that presented and authored papers, a great deal of thanks must go to the other parties that played their part in making the conference a success and led to this publication. Thanks must go to the University of Leicester Research Training Innovation Fund who were prepared to fund the conference and the publication of this volume. Without their help the conference would have been a much more expensive and poorly attended affair. Appreciation must go to Prof. Colin Haselgrove who gave his full support and provided an excellent closing address. Prof. Sir Bob Burgess, Vice-Chancellor was kind enough to host and fund a wine reception at the end of the first evening. We are also very grateful to the four chairs, Dr. Simon James, Dr. Jeremy Taylor, Dr. Patrick Clay and Dr. Rachel Pope, who facilitated a lively discussion of the papers and also the referee's who donated their valuable time to review the papers and provided excellent feedback. We are indebted to ULAS for providing permission for the use of images and support during the conference. Dr. David Edwards gave invaluable advice throughout the preparation of this publication and his patience is much appreciated. Finally thanks must go to the PhD community at the University of Leicester who helped organize and support the conference.

# Bibliography

Cunliffe, B. (1984). Iron Age Wessex: continuity and change. In B. Cunliffe and D. Miles (eds.) *Aspects of the Iron Age in Central Southern Britain*: 12–45. Oxford: Oxford University Committee for Archaeology.

Davis, O., N. Sharples and K. Waddington (eds.) (2008). *Changing Perspectives on the First Millennium BC: proceedings of the Iron Age Research Student Seminar 2006*. Oxford: Oxbow Books.

Haselgrove, C., I. Armit, T. Champion, J. Creighton, A. Gwilt, J. D. Hill, F. Hunter and A. Woodward (eds.) (2001). *Understanding the British Iron Age: an agenda for action*. Salisbury: Trust for Wessex Archaeology.

Hill, J. D. (1995). How should we understand Iron Age societies and hillforts? A contextual study from southern Britain. In J. D. Hill and C. G. Cumberpatch (eds.) *Different Iron Ages: studies on the Iron Age in temperate Europe*: 45–66. Oxford: British Archaeological Reports, International Series 602.

Humphrey, J. (ed.) (2003). *Re-searching the Iron Age: selected papers from the proceedings of the Iron Age Research Student Seminars, 1999 and 2000*. Leicester: Leicester Archaeology Monograph 11.

James, S. (2007). A bloodless past: the pacification of Early Iron Age Britain. In C. C. Haselgrove and R. E. Pope (eds.) *The Earlier Iron Age in Britain and the Near Continent*: 160–173. Oxford: Oxbow Books.

## CHAPTER 1

# The Village People? Origins and Development of 'Aggregated' Settlement in the East Midlands

*John Thomas*

*(University of Leicester Archaeological Services)*

## Abstract

Although traditional models of settlement in the Iron Age landscape highlight the proliferation of small enclosed farmsteads and defended hillforts it has become widely accepted that considerable differences existed between, and even within, regions of the British Isles. Recent excavations in central and eastern Britain have led to the recognition of substantial settlements dated to the late first millennium BC that seem strikingly different to 'traditional' settlement types. These sites are distinguished by their large size, the co-existence of both open and enclosed elements, and longevity of occupation. Now commonly described as 'aggregated' or 'agglomerated' settlements, their distinctive characteristics have caused many to think of them as 'proto-villages', raising the possibility of population groupings significantly beyond the level of the extended family unit. However, despite becoming increasingly recognized as a distinct settlement phenomenon of the region, they are poorly understood and there has been little detailed work into their origins, development and social role.

As a result of large-scale development, several extensive excavations of 'aggregated' settlements have taken place in the East Midlands, which have added detail to other evidence resulting from aerial and geophysical survey and fieldwalking. This paper will assess the results of these excavations with the aim of integrating the various strands of evidence to provide a better understanding of this type of settlement site. It will consider the origins, growth and development of such settlements, as well as examining their internal characteristics, purpose and position within the settlement hierarchy of later prehistoric society.

## Introduction

Since the introduction of PPG16 to British archaeology after 1990, there has been a dramatic increase in the discovery of Iron Age sites as a result of developer-funded work. In the East Midlands the results of this work have revealed the wide variety of settlement morphology that existed across the Iron Age landscape (Willis 2006: 89). Although traditional models of Iron Age settlement highlight the proliferation of small enclosed farmsteads and defended hillforts, it has become widely accepted that considerable differences existed between, and even within, regions (Cunliffe 1991; Hill 1999: 186). Whilst small enclosed farmsteads, presumably dwellings of extended family groups, are one of the more common settlement forms across much of Iron Age Britain, it is clear that other settlement types existed.

Recent work in central and eastern Britain has led to the recognition of large-scale 'aggregated' settlements of the later first millennium BC which seem strikingly different to 'traditional' settlement types, ostensibly appearing 'village-like' in size and morphology (Clay 2001: 13), and raising possibilities of population groupings significantly beyond the level of the extended family unit. Although apparently co-existing with smaller, enclosed farmsteads and hillforts in the landscape, 'aggregated' settlements are characterized by their greater size, the existence of both open and enclosed elements, the apparently greater longevity of occupation and diversity of function within the settlement (Kidd 2004: 56; Willis 2006: 109).

A wider examination of the landscape and its archaeology has been enabled as a result of large-scale surveys and excavations in advance of large development projects. It is now recognized that examples of aggregated settlement can be found across much of the region and were probably more common than previously thought. This increasing awareness of aggregated settlements in the East Midlands has prompted a reappraisal of what might be expected from the evidence for Iron Age settlement in the landscape (Clay 2001: 13; Willis 2006: 110).

## Problems with the data

The nature of aggregated settlements, however, poses many problems which hinder their recognition and interpretation. In terms of recognition, as is the case for most periods across the region, the evidence for settlement in the later first millennium BC is entirely dependent on the visibility of the archaeological record (Willis 2006: 89). Although it is clear that some aggregated sites have been identified as a result of aerial photography and geophysical survey, such methods are also open to misinterpretation. The common characteristics associated with aggregated settlement such as the loose clusters of 'open' or unenclosed domestic remains such as pits and post holes may not be readily apparent from the air under certain conditions, especially when not accompanied by an imposing ditch circuit (Deegan 2007: 90). In rural areas the extent of arable cultivation also plays a crucial part in the discovery or concealment of archaeological remains, depending on whether or not an area is subject to ploughing, thus producing cropmark evidence and artefact scatters. It is worth pointing out that the three case studies presented below were all found beneath pasture fields so there was no prior knowledge of their existence. Excavation on these sites is also reliant on factors such as the incidence of modern development and the level of archaeological input in particular areas which, given the overall size of aggregated sites, can result in partially revealed plans that may be open to misinterpretation.

Until fairly recently excavation methodologies may also have hindered the discovery of aggregated settlement by concentrating resources solely on well-defined enclosures without looking beyond the extremities of the boundary ditch for less obvious, open settlement remains (Haselgrove *et al.* 2001: 10). With the now widespread adoption of sophisticated geophysical survey and trial trench evaluation techniques, coupled with the increasing recognition that late first millennium BC life did exist beyond the confines of the enclosure ditch, detection of aggregated sites is increasing (Willis 2006: 92). Reliance on aerial survey and partial evidence from restricted excavations may provide misleading evidence to suggest either open or enclosed settlements (Kidd 2004: 56). An example of this occurrence is known at Great Doddington, Northamptonshire where excavations focussed on the known cropmark of a D-shaped enclosure (Windell 1981). More recently geophysical work and excavation have revealed the enclosure to be only a part of a much larger aggregated site (Thomas and Enright 2003).

The development of clear chronologies for later prehistoric sites in the East Midlands has also been a major problem, partly exacerbated by the conservative nature of the regional pottery traditions that witnessed little change over several centuries (Elsdon 1992; Knight 2002; Willis 2006: 89). In addition, the period coincides with problems in the radiocarbon calibration curve resulting in broad and vague dates for excavated sites and developmental phases (Stuiver and Reimer 1993; Willis 2006: 90).

At a site-specific level, there are many problems associated with the description and interpretation of aggregated sites, some of which reflect the broader problems described above. In particular there is uncertainty over the origins of this type of site and of their subsequent development over time (Willis 2006: 109). Their sheer size also makes it difficult accurately to define their edges, especially as excavation is likely to occur as a piecemeal response to episodes of development. In spite of the apparent 'village-like' proportions of aggregated settlements, suggesting large-scale contemporary activity, outward appearances may conceal subtle site dynamics (Kidd 2004: 56). A closer investigation may reveal the sites to be the product of seasonal settlement activity, or the product of a mobile settlement pattern similar to Anglo Saxon sites (Willis 2006: 110; Hamerow 1993; 2002). These suggestions also raise questions as to the overall size of each settlement at different periods of their development: how many buildings were standing at any one time? how many of the buildings were residential? and, what are the implications for the size of the individual household and wider community? (Haselgrove 2001: 58).

This paper presents three case studies of aggregated settlement from Leicestershire and Northamptonshire (Figure 1.1) and is based on a wider study of this phenomenon across the East Midlands, undertaken as research for an MA dissertation (Thomas 2005). The chosen sites all display similar characteristics, highlighting the origins and development of aggregated settlement in this part of the East Midlands. Collectively the three sites were also occupied throughout the Iron Age and comparison between them offers a view of the broad structural and social changes that occurred over the course of the first millennium BC.

## The Case Studies

### Beaumont Leys, Leicester

The Beaumont Leys settlement lies *c*.4km to the north of Leicester city centre and was excavated in advance of warehouse and office development (Thomas 2008a; forthcoming). The core of the settlement occupies an area of *c*.1.25ha located on a boulder clay ridge at a height of *c*.90m OD, to the west of the River Soar. Radiocarbon dating suggests that the settlement was mainly occupied during the Middle Iron Age between the fifth and third centuries BC, with activity potentially lasting up to 260 years.

Settlement remains consisted of a linear spread of roundhouses, post-built structures, fences and pit clusters adjacent to a long-lived linear boundary (LB) (Figure 1.2). Although essentially 'open' in character the relationship between the occupied area and its southern 'boundary' appears to have been strong and clearly defined. Virtually no evidence for transgression of this boundary was revealed, although activity had resulted in dense clustering of settlement remains alongside its northern edge. The development of the linear boundary consisted of at least three distinct phases indicating its longevity and the importance of maintaining the feature to the site's inhabitants. The original form of the boundary is difficult to judge on the basis of ploughed out evidence but it seems fairly likely that its creation would have made imposing, if not monumental changes to the landscape. The creation and maintenance

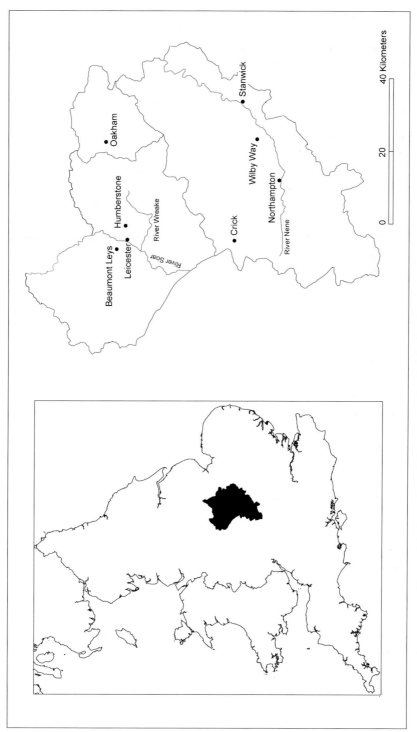

Figure 1.1: Location of the case study sites and other sites mentioned in the text

Figure 1.2: The Early Middle Iron Age settlement at Beaumont Leys with roundhouses, rectangular and four-post structures highlighted

of this boundary would have involved a considerable commitment to labour over long periods of time, and for the groups responsible its creation may have been more important than the end result. The ditches may have been the result of the combined labour of several different family groups, each responsible for a defined stretch, ultimately becoming the result of a community project and testimony to shared resources. Maintenance and re-cutting of the boundary over time would have served to reinforce this community identity and would have added legitimacy to claims on land.

At least ten roundhouses represented the main foci of occupation although it is difficult to say how many of these buildings were standing at any one time, or indeed if all of them were used as domestic dwellings. The roundhouses were relatively small and insubstantial, varying in size from *c.*5m to *c.*9m in diameter, and largely represented by arcs of postholes and curving wall slots forming fragmentary structural remains. A number of rectangular structures were also represented, presenting quite an unusual contrast with the circular buildings. It is difficult to determine the nature of these structures although larger examples may have been used as byre houses and the smaller ones as enclosures or pens for livestock (Moore 2003).

A linear arrangement of nine four-post structures, possibly raised granaries or other storage facilities, formed a line across the centre of the site, while others were positioned closer to particular roundhouses in other areas of the site. The apparently structured location for the majority of the four-post structures implies that certain areas or 'zones' of activity existed within the settlement, but as with the roundhouses it is far from clear how many of these structures would have been contemporaneous and it is possible they were replaced fairly regularly.

The occupants of Beaumont Leys appear to have been involved with mixed farming, although the suggestion is that their main concern was pastoralism. The animal bone recovered from the site shows that a narrow range of domesticated species was kept on the site including cattle, sheep/goat, pigs and horses, with cattle being the dominant species. In addition, dogs were kept as evidenced by several bones as well as characteristic gnawing patterns on other animal bones. The presence of red deer bone and antler in small quantities suggests that limited hunting of wild animals took place although, equally, the antler could have been collected after it had shed. Charred plant remains were recovered from the site but only in very limited quantities. Remains of cereal grains (barley and probable spelt wheat) and chaff were largely concentrated on the main roundhouses but even then were only representative of thin domestic waste scatters, probably the result of waste from domestic food preparation and consumption. In contrast to the meagre evidence for plant remains the site did produce a large assemblage (22 pieces) of quernstones. These were found in a variety of contexts across the site including examples from the linear boundary, pits, post holes and in association with particular roundhouses. One of the imported querns was of Millstone Grit and was a particularly well-worked item in contrast to the rest of the group. As an import from some distance this may well have been a prized household possession, not only of functional worth but as an indicator of wider contacts. A blue glass bead was another 'exotic' item from the site, perhaps also seen as an indicator of importance for the owner. Evidence for small-scale craft activities on the site included slag from iron working and perhaps more surprisingly evidence for shale working. The raw materials for such activity must have arrived at the site down the line from Kimmeridge in Dorset and provides further evidence of the wider network of communication within which the site existed.

## Humberstone, Leicester

The extensive aggregated settlement at Humberstone occupies a boulder clay ridge approximately 5km east of Leicester city centre, and has been revealed as a result of several pieces of work involving excavation (Elms Farm – Charles *et al.* 2000, Manor Farm – Thomas 2008b; forthcoming) and geophysical survey (Butler 1999; Thomas 2004 – see Figure 1.3). The known extent of the site covers approximately 8ha although it is clear from the evidence that the settlement extends further, certainly to the west and potentially to the south of that already exposed. Radiocarbon dating results suggests that the settlement was occupied throughout the Iron Age, with the main phases of activity potentially lasting between 220–330 years. Essentially, excavation on the site has been achieved in three distinct areas which offer similar, yet also contrasting evidence for the development of the settlement. These areas will be used here to describe the site.

The earliest settlement at Manor Farm consisted of a small open settlement made up of a cluster of buildings in Area A. Establishing a date for this settlement is problematic although on the basis of surrounding evidence a Late Bronze Age or Early Iron Age date seems likely. Settlement on the site developed further with the construction of a single roundhouse within a square enclosure in the Early Iron Age.

In the Middle Iron Age the main area of settlement at Manor Farm was represented by a linear spread of roundhouses, small enclosures, pits and other features adjacent to a linear boundary (LB) (Figure 1.4). The development of the settlement has strong similarities to that at Beaumont Leys, clearly respecting and following the alignment of the boundary that defined the northern edge of occupation. Also in common with Beaumont Leys, there was little evidence of activity beyond the boundary, suggesting that it marked a clear division between activities. The attraction of the boundary appears to have been strong enough to have caused a distinct, but invisible, southern

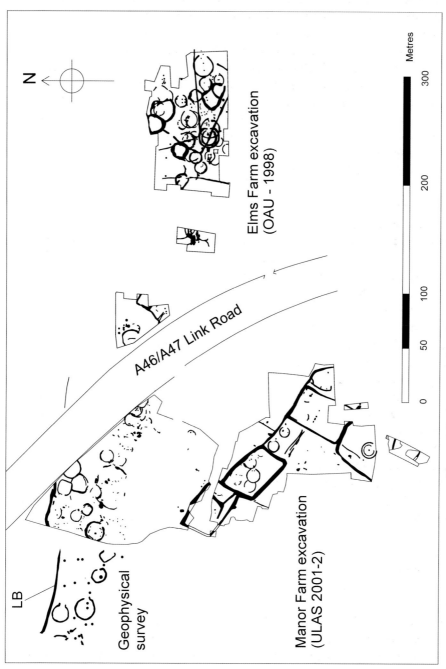

Figure 1.3: Aggregated settlement at Humberstone

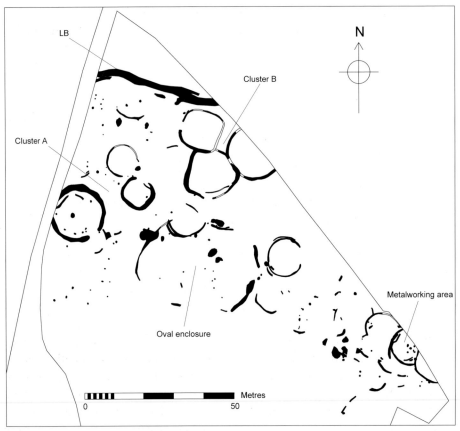

LB

Cluster B

N

Cluster A

Metalworking area

Oval enclosure

Metres

0

50

Figure 1.4: Mid-Late Iron Age settlement features at Humberstone Manor Farm, Area B

limit to the occupied area. Whilst this side of the site might feasibly have been constrained by hedging, it seems likely that this phenomenon was caused by a desire to maintain proximity to the northern boundary.

Occupation in Area B was characterized by distinct clusters of roundhouses and small enclosures with associated groups of post holes and pitting. Two main clusters, each consisting of a roundhouse and associated enclosures, occupied the western area of the site (Clusters A and B). With the exception of a single roundhouse, the central area of the site was apparently less densely occupied, which might possibly be explained by the presence of a large semi-enclosed space within which small-scale pitting was evident. A cluster of buildings on the eastern side of the excavated area represented two phases of use: the first related to domestic occupation and the second indicating a focus on metalworking. In contrast to the western side of the stripped area, this part of the site was also characterized by a distinct clustering of pits and short gullies, perhaps reflecting a series of fences demarcating activities in this part of the site. The evidence for metalworking in this area corresponds with similar evidence from a nearby area revealed on the Elms Farm site to the east, suggesting a degree of zoning for particular activities within the organisation of the settlement.

Broadly contemporary activity in Area A was characterized by three large rectilinear enclosures (Enclosures B, C and D) (Figure 1.5). Enclosures C and D were conjoined and of broadly similar size and orientation, and to the east of these, Enclosure B was slightly larger and oriented at right angles to the others. The last was attached to the largely infilled remains of Enclosure A, perhaps showing a reference to past activities on the site. The internal areas of all three were apparently empty and their ditches were relatively finds-free, suggesting they were located away from the main areas of occupation. The size and nature of these enclosures suggests they may have been used for corralling livestock, possibly during the winter periods when breeding and the culling of older animals could have taken place in a controlled area. The orientation of the enclosures, facing the occupation to the north, suggests that both areas were used contemporaneously and adds further evidence to the notion that specific areas or zones of the site were allocated to specific activities.

After the enclosures had gone out of use, the focus of activity in Area A was radically re-organized and it became the focus for domestic occupation based on a series of smaller, loosely enclosed areas containing three broadly contemporary roundhouses (Figure 1.6). A linear boundary ditch formed the spine of this new complex, which by its position, made explicit reference to the remains of the earlier enclosures and was perhaps indicative of a very visual link to past activities. Interestingly the organization of this new area of settlement had striking similarities with the layout of occupation in Area B although it is unclear if the two areas were occupied at the same time or if one replaced the other.

Settlement at Elms Farm was characterized by a dense pattern of overlapping phases, each consisting of clustered roundhouses, small enclosures and four-post structures with a gradual change in focus over time (Figure 1.7). A single large roundhouse on the east of the site was the focus for the earliest phase of occupation and was surrounded by associated small enclosures, pits and two four-post structures. Although essentially an unenclosed settlement, the buildings, enclosures and pits clearly respected what must have been the existing vestiges of a Late Bronze Age rectangular enclosure, within which they were located.

The second main phase of development lay to the east of the original focus, and was again dominated by a substantial roundhouse defined by a double circuit of imposing drainage ditches. By this time it appears that the earlier enclosure remains were no longer being respected, particularly given the location of the main roundhouse, which straddles the infilled ditch. In common

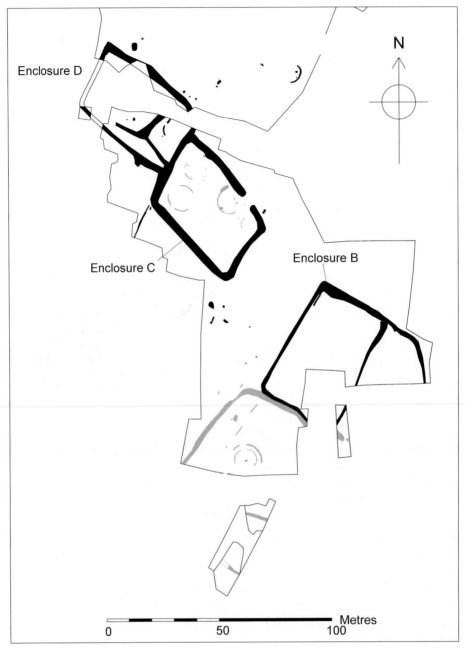

Figure 1.5: Middle Iron Age stock enclosures at Humberstone Manor Farm,
Area A (earlier phases in grey)

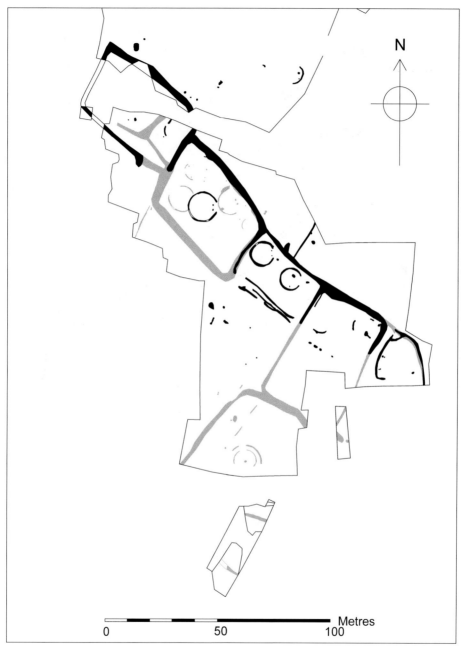

Figure 1.6: Late Iron Age settlement features at Humberstone Manor Farm,
Area A (earlier phases in grey)

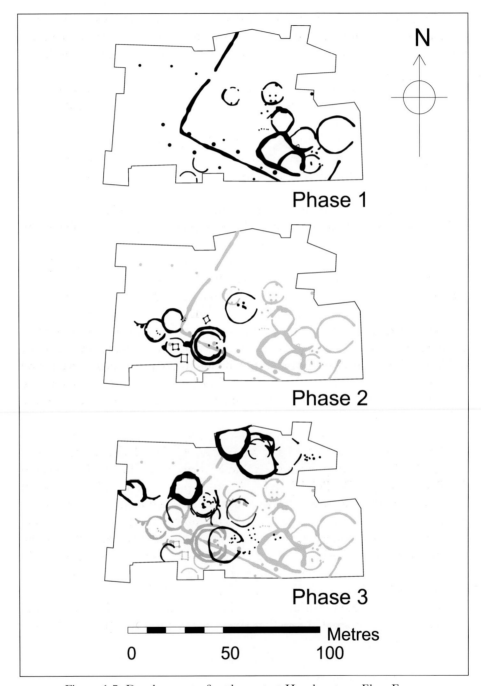

Figure 1.7: Development of settlement at Humberstone Elms Farm

with the previous phase the main roundhouse was associated with a cluster of smaller buildings and enclosures, all with east-facing entrances. Three four-post structures and a number of pits and post holes were also apparent during this phase of activity.

A final period of development instigated a further shift in focus, with activity predominantly clustering to the north of the earlier structures. A similar pattern of buildings was maintained in this phase and at least two buildings (including the main roundhouse) were clearly replaced, in each case shifting only slightly from their former locations. Two larger enclosures, also associated with possible structures, were constructed further to the north (Charles *et al.* 2000: 147).

As with Beaumont Leys the evidence indicates that mixed farming was carried out at Humberstone, but also with an emphasis on pastoral activities. In the earlier phases of occupation it appears that cattle were the dominant species and the large stock enclosures at Manor Farm tend to support this. The organization of the settlement suggests that particular zones were given over to specific activities. This is evident in the concentration of metalworking remains at both Manor and Elms Farm, but there is also an obvious distinction between 'living' areas and the large stock control features at Manor Farm in the early phases of occupation. In contrast there was greater evidence for arable farming from Elms Farm, with generally more processing remains and more storage provision in the form of four-post structures. This may be indicative of a distinction between farming regimes in the two areas of the settlement.

Indications are that occupation at Humberstone ended towards the end of the first century BC or early first century AD. At Elms Farm the latest date indicated by the pottery assemblage came from a fine bowl which copied the first century AD 'Belgic' style. A small purse group of two Roman Republican *denarii* may have been deposited in the Late Iron Age or post-conquest period as may a pair of copper alloy tweezers (Charles *et al.* 2000: 156). Fine Late Iron Age pottery was also recovered from the final backfilling of the last enclosure ditch in Area A at Manor Farm and from a large structure in Area B which also contained a Late Iron Age Thurrock-type potin coin (Thomas 2003: 54). As with Beaumont Leys, these finds give an indication of the network of contacts within which the Humberstone settlement existed, and also of the potential status that some of the site's occupants held as a result.

### Crick, Northamptonshire

The settlement at Crick, Covert Farm, lies on the Northamptonshire/Warwickshire border and, in contrast to the two Leicestershire sites, is situated on low lying ground occupying the lower slopes of a stream valley that forms a tributary of the River Avon. This site is also considerably larger, covering an area of approximately 16ha, yet despite these differences in scale and location the development of the site shares similar themes with Beaumont Leys and Humberstone. In common with Humberstone the overall pattern of occupation on the site has been steadily revealed as a result of several independent excavations (Figure 1.8).

A landscape boundary ditch (LB) on the northern side of the site formed the focus for the earliest occupation at Crick in the Early Iron Age (Woodward and Hughes 2007: 188) in a similar relationship to that at Beaumont Leys and Humberstone (Figure 1.9). Evidence for early occupation on the site was clearly focused on the southern side of the boundary and consisted of two clusters of roundhouses and associated four-post structures (A and B), as well as other scattered roundhouses and features (*ibid.*: 189).

In the early part of the Middle Iron Age settlement evidence showed a marked increase, although the occupation was more dispersed. The buildings of this phase were generally larger and more clearly defined than their predecessors, but the characteristic 'grouping' of structures was maintained. The boundary continued to define the main zone of occupation, although a single building and associated enclosure were constructed to the north of the boundary at this time.

Occupation at the Long Dole site also began during this period, further emphasizing the increase in settlement at Crick during this period (Andy Chapman *pers. comm.*). In marked contrast to the main settled area, however, occupation was focussed on a large rectilinear enclosure which contained several roundhouses. Clusters of roundhouses were also evident on the outside of the enclosure.

The second half of the Middle Iron Age witnessed a dramatic increase in the size of the settlement, with evidence for occupation more than doubling to approximately 44 roundhouses (Woodward and Hughes 2007: 191). Settlement continued to lie predominantly on the southern side of the boundary although further encroachment onto the northern side of the ditch was evident. Although the boundary was apparently still functioning during this period, there was some evidence that it had been allowed to silt up and had subsequently been redefined as a pit alignment (*ibid.*: 192), perhaps suggesting a changing role for the boundary. A further indication of a change in the perception of the boundary ditch was observed on the western side of the site. Here a D-shaped enclosure was constructed on the southern side of the boundary (C), using a section of the ditch for its northern edge (*ibid.*: 192). An isolated enclosure (D) was also constructed on the western side of the site. It had different characteristics to other structures on the site and possibly served the community as a ritual enclosure (*ibid.*: 192).

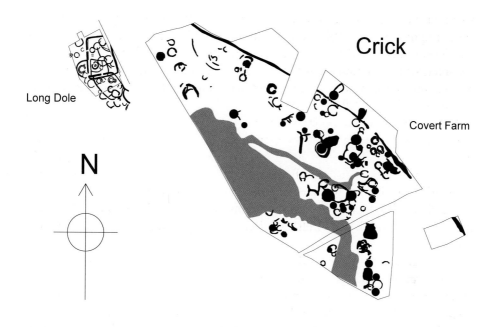

Crick

Long Dole

N

Covert Farm

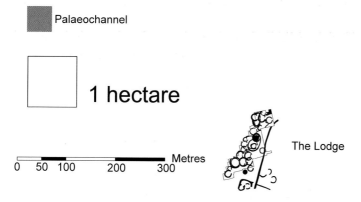

Palaeochannel

1 hectare

The Lodge

Metres
0   50   100      200      300

Figure 1.8: Aggregated settlement at Crick

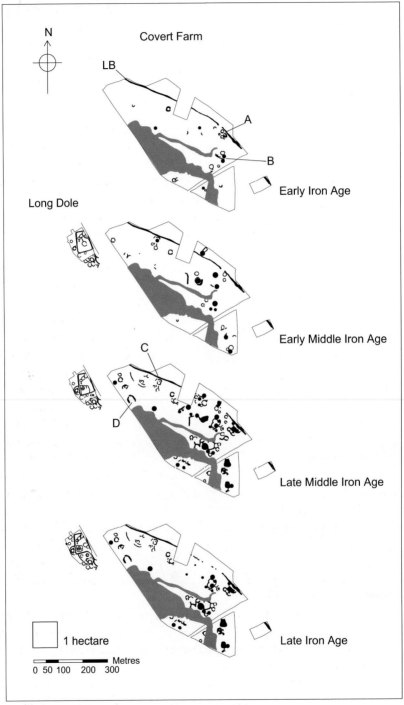

Figure 1.9: Development of settlement at Crick

Settlement also continued to expand at the Long Dole site during this period with further evidence for settlement on the outskirts of the enclosure. Increased subdivision of space within the enclosure is evidenced by the creation of a small enclosure in the south west corner, within which a west-facing building, interpreted as having a possible ritual function, was constructed (Chapman 1994: 6).

Occupation during this period shows a marked difference in character between the eastern and western sides of the site. This not only corresponds to a change in the site's geology, but may also reflect the apparent changes to the landscape boundary. The higher western side of the site has underlying clay, and evidence for occupation in this period, as with previous periods, is much sparser apart from the Long Dole site. In contrast, the evidence to the east, in an area of gravels adjacent to streams, is more abundant. Unlike the dispersed nature of occupation in the western area, settlement of the eastern area was considerably denser and consisted of conjoined groups of roundhouses with attached enclosures (Woodward and Hughes 2007: 192). It is possible that the Long Dole enclosure formed the main focus for activities on the western side of the site in this, and later periods.

The focus of settlement shifted in the Late Iron Age, with the evidence suggesting a contraction of occupation in the western area in favour of the more densely settled gravels to the east (*ibid.*: 192). Although there was little Late Iron Age pottery in the western features it is clear that some occupation persisted, in particular within the D-shaped enclosure attached to the boundary. On the eastern side of the site the dense area of settlement adjacent to the streams was maintained, with many of the clusters established in the later Middle Iron Age remaining in use, and some being enlarged. Across the settlement as a whole the evidence indicates a decline in population with only 23 roundhouses represented for this period (*ibid*: 195). Occupation at the Long Dole site is characterized by further increase in enclosure attached to the southern side of the original ditch.

As with the previous case studies, mixed farming was evident at Crick, although a predominance of cattle may indicate a greater emphasis on pastoralism. Small-scale metalworking was also carried out and imported pottery, briquetage and querns of Millstone Grit all provided evidence of long-distance trade links.

A general absence of first century AD material from the Crick excavations suggests that the site was abandoned in the decades before or after the Roman Conquest. This view is supported by the positioning of a Roman road, which cuts through the main area of Late Iron Age occupation on the site (*ibid.*: 195). Second century Roman occupation is known at The Lodge site (Figure 1.8), some distance from the Iron Age settlement, indicating a complete relocation of activity during this period (Chapman 1994).

# Discussion

All three study sites described above seem to have been part of a similar phenomenon of aggregation, following similar patterns of organization and development over time. The settlements at Humberstone and Crick provide good examples of the long life-span and early origins of aggregated sites. Although the period of occupation at Beaumont Leys is slightly more restricted it presents a particular 'phase' in the growth of these sites that can be seen in the context of the wider development of aggregated settlement in the East Midlands. The common characteristic of the development of all three sites was the creation and continued importance of the boundary against which the settlement was founded. The boundaries not only provided an initial focus for the site origins, but also apparently defined one 'edge' to the settlement, beyond which it rarely developed. Although development of occupation on the sites was obviously fluid and highly dynamic, the original focus of settlement was respected and maintained, which appears to have had a profound influence on the growth of the site. Recent research has highlighted the importance that communities may have bestowed upon the construction and maintenance of boundaries as a way of affirming group identity or tenurial rights (Bowden and McOmish 1987; Hingley 1990; Chadwick 1999). Repeated maintenance of the boundaries would also no doubt have become part of the experience of those involved, helping to create a strong 'sense of place' and perhaps leading to the origins of settlement adjacent to them. The development of these sites coincided with a wider phenomenon of linear earthwork construction that led to an increasingly bounded landscape, clearly defining areas and perhaps effectively bringing into focus systems of 'ownership' that had previously been fairly fluid (Wells 2007). In East Yorkshire, communities may have associated linear boundaries with the remains of earlier monuments in order to confirm claims to land (Giles 2007: 114), an interesting point in comparison to Humberstone where earthwork remains of earlier occupation clearly had a bearing on the siting of the Iron Age settlement. In the Thames Valley the development of a more bounded landscape appears to have resulted in a 'fossilization' of traditional patterns of land use as settlement intensified. Here settlements with tightly clustered linear layouts such as at Gravelly Guy (Lambrick and Allen 2004), very similar to the sites discussed above, were located around the edge of an area of *c.*250ha within which shared access to grazing had been established (Hey 2007: 160). This area was once an important ceremonial landscape in the Neolithic and Bronze Age and gatherings at the monuments may well have led to the formation of communal patterns of land use that became more formalized as local settlement increased (*ibid.*: 160).

Although the ground-plans of aggregated sites can appear very 'village-like' when taken at face value, the three study sites have shown that each was a result of gradual development over several generations, characterized by small-scale shift of multiple settlement clusters, creating a pattern of overlapping phases. This apparently deliberate reference to the past may indicate a conception of the cyclical nature of time, and of continuity with the past (Bradley 2005: 56). As such, the referencing of earlier generations may also represent an extension of the ideas associated with repeated boundary maintenance and rebuilding may have further served to reinforce a feeling of group or family identity and attachment to a particular place.

The overall pattern of settlement on aggregated sites offers a relatively unique view of later prehistoric communality, a closer look at the internal dynamics of occupation over time reveals evidence of possible tensions between concern for the lineage of the wider community and concern for kinship lineage. Repeated use of particular areas, apparently by the same family groups, created the patterns of clustered buildings which characterize the early phases of aggregated settlement, and may reflect a concern with establishing kinship rights within the site. Consequently, the overall picture of development on aggregated sites across the study area indicates a gradual shift away from the 'open' settlement that may signify a degree of communality, towards a more clearly defined pattern of enclosure, perhaps based on the definition of individual family groups. The shift in emphasis to a new area in the latter stages of occupation at Manor Farm, Humberstone, may illustrate this, as might the creation of the enclosure adjacent to the contemporary 'open' settlement at Long Dole, Crick. As a result of the long-lived nature of these sites this shift towards enclosure can be clearly seen over time, becoming more prominent towards the beginning of the first century BC. Similar trends can be seen at other aggregated sites in the East Midlands such as Wilby Way, Great Doddington and Stanwick. At Wilby Way a large D-shaped enclosure is constructed within an otherwise open settlement plan during the Later Iron Age phases (Thomas and Enright 2003: 30), and Later Iron Age phases at Stanwick witnessed the gradual introduction of enclosures and larger, more imposing buildings (Crosby and Muldowney forthcoming: 17). This pattern ties into a more generally observed pattern of restructuring and internal differentiation within settlements evident across the country in the first century BC (Haselgrove 2003: 24; Moore 2007).

Coupled with this general rise in evidence for enclosure and more substantial buildings in the later first millennium BC, was a corresponding rise in the range and amount of material deposited on settlement sites (Haselgrove 2003: 16). Whilst this may manifest itself in large deposits of domestic pottery or animal bone within ditches and roundhouse gullies, it may equally be evident in the rise of apparently 'prestige' objects, particularly coinage, or small items of individual significance such as brooches or toilet instruments (Haselgrove 2003: 16; Hill 1997). Just as the predominance of enclosure and more elaborately defined roundhouses is reflected during the later phases of the aggregated settlements described above, the evidence also reflects a rise in the deposition of material culture.

The apparent 'village-like' nature of aggregated settlement across the region has been shown to have been a creation of many generations of shifting occupation on the same site, but there is no doubt that populations at any one time on these sites were significantly larger than on other contemporary settlements, such as the enclosed farmsteads. The existence of larger sites within the landscape has complicated existing models of settlement hierarchy, and it has become unclear as to what levels of difference existed between various forms of settlement (Willis 2006: 110). Clay for example has suggested that aggregated sites were essentially the same as hillforts, without the hills or defences (2001: 13). However, it is difficult to make such comparisons, given the current level of excavated information and limited understanding of how hillforts functioned in the East Midlands (Willis 2006: 118). Instead, these sites could be interpreted as filling a gap in the hierarchy of settlement (should one have existed), but this is far from clear based on current understanding. We should also be wary of applying models of settlement hierarchy based on modern perceptions of what might constitute 'higher' or 'lower' status (Haselgrove 2003: 18). In fact, the architectural 'grammar' of these sites (circular buildings, four-post structures, clusters of pits) is not substantially different from other types of contemporary settlement, such as the smaller enclosed farmsteads; the differences lie in the way they were organized. Given the apparent emphasis on cattle herding this particular settlement form may have grown in relation to particular ways of living and, as such, may also represent a different expression of social identity to other sites in the landscape.

Apart from size there appears to have been little to distinguish aggregated sites from others in the landscape. In fact, rather than indicating social difference from other sites, the evidence from aggregated settlement suggests they too were firmly embedded within the agricultural economy (Willis 2006: 110). On the basis of the three study sites the agricultural emphasis appears to have been on pastoralism, with a bias towards cattle. This provides an interesting contrast to sites from southern England that are usually characterized by the importance of sheep husbandry (Hambleton 1999). The difference that can be suggested is that populations must have been significantly larger than on smaller farmsteads, offering greater opportunity for social interaction between different families on a regular basis. At Humberstone, for example, the available evidence suggests that five or six household clusters may have been occupied at any one time, and at Crick the peak of occupation consisted of up to nineteen clusters (Woodward and Hughes 2007: 192).

Despite the apparent large size of aggregated sites, excavation has shown that they are a palimpsest of several generations of repeated occupation at the same place. It is possible that the sites were formed during seasonal, or part-seasonal visits as at Crick (Woodward and Hughes 2007: 195); however it is evident that repeated occupation on the sites fostered a distinct 'sense of place' for the groups involved. Although there is a sense of communality about the sites, there are also indications of the importance of individual family groups, evident in the repeated use of certain areas of the settlement over time. As the settlements developed this distinction became more apparent with the rise of enclosure, the development of substantially defined roundhouses and increased deposition of artefacts. The evidence for continued settlement into the later stages of the Iron Age and the early Roman period suggests that a 'sense of place' was still maintained by the communities; however the suggestion is that this was somewhat overtaken by a rise in the need to distinguish family groups.

The long-lived nature of aggregated sites provides a reflection of the wider social changes that occurred in the landscape during the end of the first millennium BC. No doubt future work on these settlements will shed more light on the issues raised in this study as it is clear that they offer a unique insight into important questions of the later prehistoric landscape, such as the persistence of boundaries, the existence of a clear hierarchy of settlement and the transition from an open to fully enclosed landscape.

# Acknowledgements

The Leicestershire sites at Manor Farm, Humberstone and Beaumont Leys were excavated by the University of Leicester Archaeological Services in 2002–3 and 2006 respectively, in advance of development. The site at Crick, Northamptonshire was excavated by Birmingham University Field Archaeology Unit (now Birmingham Archaeology) in 1997–8. Results of all three excavations will be subject to detailed publication in the future. The Elms Farm part of the Humberstone settlement was excavated, ahead of development, by Oxford Archaeology in 1997–8 and has been published in Transactions of the Leicestershire Archaeological and Historical Society (see Bibliography). I would like to express my thanks to Martin Sterry and Andy Tullett for giving me the chance to present this work at the IARSS 2008. I would also like to thank Anne Woodward and Gwilym Hughes for providing access to unpublished work relating to the Crick excavations and Andy Chapman at Northamptonshire Archaeology for phasing information from the Long Dole site. Thanks are also due to the anonymous referee who provided useful feedback and comment on the original draft of the paper. Finally I am grateful to Jeremy Taylor, Rachel Pope and Patrick Clay for their interest, encouragement and discussion during the original research and subsequent production of this article.

# Bibliography

Bowden, M. and D. McOmish (1987). The required barrier. *Scottish Archaeological Review* 4: 84–97.

Bradley, R. (2005). *Ritual and Domestic Life in Prehistoric Europe*. London: Routledge.

Butler, A. (1999). *A Geophysical Survey on land at Quakesick Valley, Humberstone, Leicester (SK 630 067)*. Unpublished ULAS Report, No. 2000/160.

Chadwick, A. (1999). Digging ditches, but missing riches? Ways into the Iron Age and Romano-British cropmark landscapes of the north Midlands. In B. Bevan (ed.) *Northern Exposure: interpretive devolution and the Iron Ages in Britain*: 149–172. Leicester: Leicester Archaeology Monograph 4.

Chapman, A. (1994). *Excavation of Iron Age and Roman Sites at the Daventry International Rail Freight Terminal, Near Crick, Northamptonshire*. Unpublished Northamptonshire Archaeology Unit Report.

Charles, B. M., A. Parkinson and S. Foreman (2000). A Bronze Age Ditch and Iron Age settlement at Elms Farm, Humberstone, Leicester. *Transactions of the Leicestershire Archaeological and Historical Society* 74: 113–222.

Clay, P. (2001). Leicestershire and Rutland in the first millennium BC. *Transactions of the Leicestershire Archaeological and Historical Society* 75: 1–19.

Crosby and Muldowney (forthcoming) *Phasing the Iron Age and Romano-British settlement at Stanwick, Northamptonshire (excavations 1984–1992)*. English Heritage: Centre for Archaeology Reports.

Cunliffe, B. (1991). *Iron Age Communities in Britain. An account of England, Scotland and Wales from the seventh century BC until the Roman conquest*. London: Routledge. 3rd edition.

Deegan, A. (2007). Late Bronze Age, Iron Age and Roman settlements and landscapes. In A. Deegan and G. Foard (eds.) *Mapping Ancient Landscapes in Northamptonshire*: 81–124. Swindon: English Heritage.

Elsdon, S. M. (1992). East Midlands scored ware. *Transactions of the Leicestershire Archaeological and Historical Society* 66: 83–91.

Giles, M. (2007). Refiguring rights in the Early Iron Age landscapes of East Yorkshire. In C. C. Haselgrove and R. E. Pope (eds.) *The Earlier Iron Age in Britain and the Near Continent*: 103–118. Oxford: Oxbow Books.

Hamerow, H. (1993). *Excavations at Mucking Volume 2: the Anglo-Saxon settlement*. London: English Heritage.

Hamerow, H. (2002). *Early Medieval Settlements*. Oxford: Oxford University Press.

Hambleton, E. (1999). *Animal Husbandry Regimes in Iron Age Britain*. Oxford: British Archaeological Reports, British Series 282.

Haselgrove, C. (2001). Iron Age Britain and its European setting. In J. Collis (ed.) *Society and Settlement in Iron Age Europe*: 37–72. Sheffield: J. R. Collis Publications.

Haselgrove, C. (2003). Society and Polity in Late Iron Age Britain. In M. Todd (ed.) *A Companion to Roman Britain*: 12–29. Oxford: Blackwell.

Haselgrove, C. C., I. Armit, T. Champion, J. Creighton, A. Gwilt, J.D. Hill, F. Hunter and A. Woodward (2001). *Understanding the British Iron Age: an agenda for action*. Salisbury: Wessex Archaeology.

Hey, G. (2007). Unravelling the Iron Age landscape of the Upper Thames Valley. In C. C. Haselgrove and T. Moore (eds.) *The Later Iron Age in Britain and Beyond*: 156–172. Oxford: Oxbow Books.

Hill, J. D. (1997). The end of one kind of body and the beginning of another kind of body? Toilet instruments and 'Romanisation' in southern England during the first century AD. In

A. Gwilt and C. C. Haselgrove (eds.) *Reconstructing Iron Age Societies*: 96–107. Oxford: Oxbow Books.

Hill, J. D. (1999). Chapter 9. Settlement, landscape and regionality: Norfolk and Suffolk in the pre-Roman Iron Age of Britain and beyond. In J. Davies and T. Williamson (eds.) *Land of the Iceni: the Iron Age in northern East Anglia*: 185–207. Studies in East Anglian Archaeology 4. Norwich: Centre of East Anglian Studies, University of East Anglia.

Hingley, R. (1990). Boundaries surrounding Iron Age and Romano-British settlements. *Scottish Archaeological Review* 7: 96–103.

Kidd, A. (2004). Northamptonshire in the first millennium BC. In M. Tingle (ed.) *The Archaeology of Northamptonshire*: 44–62. Northampton: Northamptonshire Archaeological Society.

Knight, D. (2002). A regional ceramic sequence: pottery of the first millennium BC between the Humber and the Nene. In A. Woodward and J. D. Hill (eds.) *Prehistoric Britain: The Ceramic Basis*: 119–142. Oxford: Oxbow Books,

Lambrick, G. and T. Allen (2004). *Gravelly Guy, Stanton Harcourt, Oxfordshire: the development of a Prehistoric and Romano-British community.* Oxford: Thames Valley Landscapes Monograph 21.

Moore, T. (2003). Rectangular houses in the British Iron Age? – "Squaring the circle". In J. Humphrey (ed.) *Re-searching the Iron Age*: 47–58. Leicester: Leicester Archaeology Monograph 11.

Moore, T. (2007). The Early to later Iron Age transition in the Severn-Cotswolds: enclosing the household? In C. C. Haselgrove and R. E. Pope (eds.) *The Earlier Iron Age in Britain and the Near Continent*: 259–278. Oxford: Oxbow Books.

Stuiver, M. and P. J. Reimer (1993). Extended C14 data base and revised calib 3.0 C14 calibration program. *Radiocarbon* 35(1): 215–230.

Thomas, J. (2003). *Manor Farm, Humberstone, Leicester, (SK6275 0652-centre): post-excavation assessment report and updated project design.* Unpublished University of Leicester Archaeological Services (ULAS) Report, No. 2003–200.

Thomas, J. (2004). *Fieldwork Report: geophysical survey on land at Manor Farm, Humberstone, Leicester (SK 6267 0660).* Unpublished fieldwork report produced for Landscape Studies MA, School of Archaeology and Ancient History, University of Leicester.

Thomas, J. (2005). *From 'our place' to 'my place': the origins and development of aggregated settlement in the East Midlands.* Unpublished University of Leicester Dissertation submitted for the MA degree in Landscape Studies.

Thomas, J. (2008a). *Excavation of an Iron Age Settlement adjacent to Beaumont Leys Lane, Beaumont Leys, Leicester.* Unpublished University of Leicester Archaeological Services (ULAS) Report, No. 2008–114.

Thomas, J. (2008b). *Excavation of an Iron Age 'Aggregated' Settlement at Manor Farm, Humberstone, Leicester.* Unpublished University of Leicester Archaeological Services (ULAS) Report No. 2008–133.

Thomas, J. (forthcoming). *Iron Age 'Aggregated' Settlements in the Environs of Leicester: excavations at Humberstone and Beaumont Leys.* Leicester: Leicester Archaeology Monograph.

Thomas, A. and D. Enright (2003). Excavation of an Iron Age Settlement at Wilby Way, Great Doddington. *Northamptonshire Archaeology* 31: 15–70.

Wells, P. S. (2007). Boundaries and identity in Early Iron Age Europe. In C. C. Haselgrove and R. E. Pope (eds.) *The Earlier Iron Age in Britain and the Near Continent*: 390–399. Oxford: Oxbow Books.

Willis, S. (2006). The later Bronze Age and Iron Age. In N. Cooper (ed.) *The Archaeology of the East Midlands: an archaeological resource assessment and research agenda*: 89–136. Leicester: Leicester Archaeology Monograph 13.

Windell, D. (1981). Great Doddington: an Iron Age enclosure. *Northamptonshire Archaeology* 16: 65–70.

Woodward, A. and G. Hughes (2007). Deposits and doorways: patterns within the Iron Age settlement at Crick Covert Farm, Northamptonshire. In C. C. Haselgrove and R. E. Pope (eds.) *The Earlier Iron Age in Britain and Beyond*: 185–203. Oxford: Oxbow Books.

## CHAPTER 2

# Everything in its Right Place?
## An unwritten architectural language of Late Iron Age enclosed settlements in the East Midlands

*Gavin Speed*

(University of Leicester Archaeological Services)

## Abstract

Architectural space is a deliberate method, created by people to make spaces become 'places'. This paper will show that human activities are attitudes that are fixed within the architecture of the settlement, and that through the study of the surviving evidence from Iron Age enclosed settlements, it is possible to attempt to understand a little of how Iron Age people lived and thought.

The most common form of Iron Age settlement in Britain is the individual farmstead; however, until recently it is this feature of the landscape that is most often overlooked in favour of the large hillforts or territorial oppida. Of the large-scale landscape studies that have taken place, most have only focused on Wessex or the upper Thames Valley. Recently, studies in other parts of the country have started to redress this imbalance in settlement analysis, with research into many parts of central and northern Britain.

This paper presents the results of research into the layout and composition of Iron Age enclosed settlements with a dataset of thirty-five fully or partly excavated enclosed settlements from two counties in the East Midlands: Leicestershire and Northamptonshire. The main aim of this paper is to use the architectural analysis of these settlements as a tool to interpret how and why the people of the Iron Age lived and organised their social space. It will demonstrate if there is an 'unwritten grammar' that the people of the first millennium BC created, and then adhered to, as a form of social acceptance in a dramatically changing landscape.

# Introduction

In all societies people recognise the need for space, and architectural space is a deliberate bounding of an area and one of the most basic ways of organising activities (Hall 1969: 103). Architecture is therefore a combination of both practical requirements and what is seen as the correct or normal order of things: a spatial syntax. The principle aim of this paper is to analyse Iron Age enclosed settlements in the counties of Leicestershire and Northamptonshire in an attempt to see if there are spatial syntaxes to which these settlements are constructed. This analysis draws upon previous research into the order of architecture in archaeology by Clarke (1977), Hodder (1977) and Parker Pearson and Richards (1994) amongst others. It seeks to identify if Iron Age enclosed settlements follow distinct patterns or rules, for example what areas or structures are positioned to the front of the enclosure, and what activities are at the rear or periphery of the settlement. The paper will also look at the relationship of the enclosure to the landscape, an area of research so far lacking in this region, which has been noted as a potential for research in the East Midlands Archaeological Research Framework for the first millennium BC (Willis 2006: 132).

The counties of Leicestershire and Northamptonshire were chosen to demonstrate the changing nature of our understanding of Iron Age settlements, because of the huge increase in excavated sites in recent years (14 of the 35 sites were excavated within the last 15 years). Both counties have a more substantial number of excavated examples than the other counties in the East Midlands region, and it is for this reason that it is now possible to conduct such a detailed investigation into settlement patterning of this specific type and date. Northamptonshire heavily outweighs Leicestershire in terms of known and published sites, but this is to some extent due to the varied level of archaeological input (Willis 2006: 89), though it may also indicate a distinct difference in settlement density. Many of the excavated sites have come as a result of developer-funded archaeology, following PPG16 (planning and policy guidelines). Indeed this paper incorporates the author's own research following a M.A. dissertation in 2005 (Speed 2005), along with directing a large-scale excavation of an Iron Age enclosed settlement north of Leicester at Birstall (Speed 2004 and *forthcoming*). The dataset used is from either published excavation reports, unpublished post-excavation assessment reports, or through personal communication with colleagues at the University of Leicester Archaeological Services (ULAS). The substantial level of knowledge that is now available has made it possible to bring together this information, analysing settlement trends using modern interpretations of the later prehistoric period. This paper aims to do more than simply quantify settlement data, by demonstrating that grey literature can offer highly rewarding information, and can be used to help understand how and why people of the Iron Age were living and arranging their space in certain ways. It is hoped that the issues raised will act as a step towards highlighting our improving understanding of the perceptions and ideologies of the people of the first millennium BC The key results from the research are listed in Appendix One.

## Case studies and methodology

If we refer to the textual evidence in the Iron Age, the area of Britain in which the case studies lie is described as part of the territory of the Corieltauvi: an area that reached from the river Nene to the river Trent. This approximately covers the modern counties of Lincolnshire, Nottinghamshire, and most of Leicestershire and Northamptonshire (Cunliffe 1991: 176). The boundary of the tribal territory should be seen as flexible, thus the case studies in Groups Two and Three (along the Nene valley) can be more accurately described as on the boundaries of the territories of the Corieltauvi, Catvellavni, and Iceni (Taylor 1996:103). All sites in the dataset are either fully or near-complete excavated examples of Iron Age enclosed settlements within the modern county boundaries of Leicestershire and Northamptonshire. Some 'agglomerated' settlements have also been included, as these contain elements of enclosed settlement. A total of 35 enclosed settlements are used as case studies: 10 from Leicestershire and 25 from Northamptonshire (Figure 2.1). The case studies have been grouped based upon local clusters formed by their geographical positions (Groups One to Four, see Figures 2.2–2.5).

## Settlement boundaries: social exclusion or inclusion?

The enclosure ditch has often been viewed in the past as purely a static categorised entity. It is necessary to treat them as such for the purposes of analysing the settlement forms; however, it is important to identify that the enclosure ditches were settlement boundaries that had both practical and symbolic meanings. Although many of the case study settlements had periods of open and enclosed occupation, the enclosure ditch still symbolises and physically defines the settlement (Hill 1996: 102). But why create a ditched boundary? The primary function of a boundary ditch is surely a practical, physical one, and in some way defensive, either from 'the threat of raiding or...the attack of wild animals' (Hingley 1990: 96). It also physically delimits activity

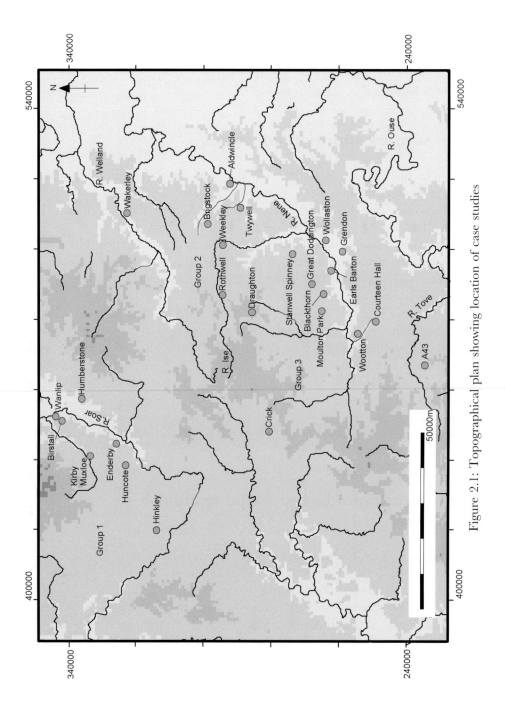

Figure 2.1: Topographical plan showing location of case studies

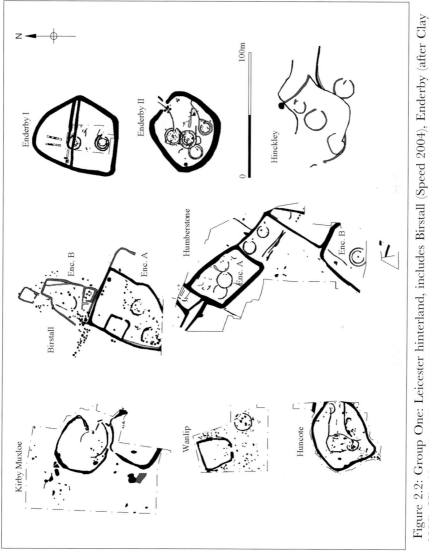

Figure 2.2: Group One: Leicester hinterland, includes Birstall (Speed 2004), Enderby (after Clay 1992), Hinckley (after Chapman 2004), Humberstone (after Thomas 2003), Huncote (after Clay *et al.* 2004), Kirby Muxloe (after Cooper 1994), and Wanlip (after Beamish 1998).

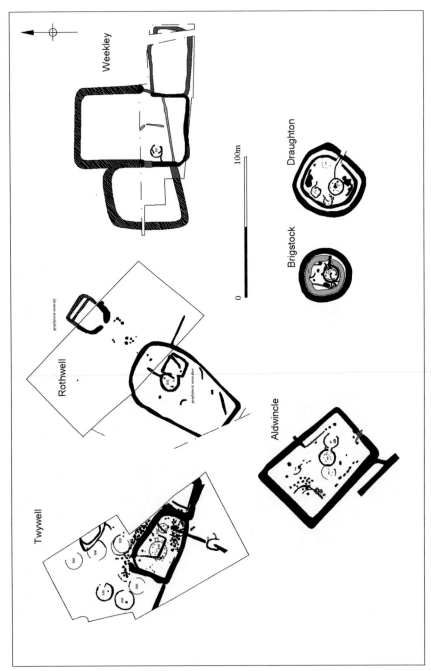

Figure 2.3: Group Two: Ise Valley, includes Aldwincle (after Jackson 1977), Brigstock (after Jackson 1983), Draughton (after Grimes 1958), Rothwell (after Priest 2003), Twywell (after Jackson 1975), and Weekley (after Dix and Jackson 1989).

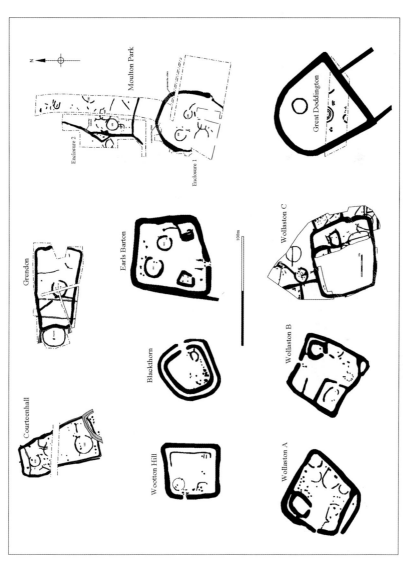

Figure 2.4: Group Three: Nene Valley, includes Blackthorn (after Williams 1974), Courteen Hall (after Buteux 2001), Earls Barton (after Windell 1981, 1984), Great Doddington (after Windell 1981, Enright and Thomas 2004), Grendon (after Jackson 1996), Stanwell Spinney (after Dix and Jackson 1989), Wollaston (after Chapman and Jackson 1993, Northampton Archaeology 1995), and Wootton (after Jackson 1991).

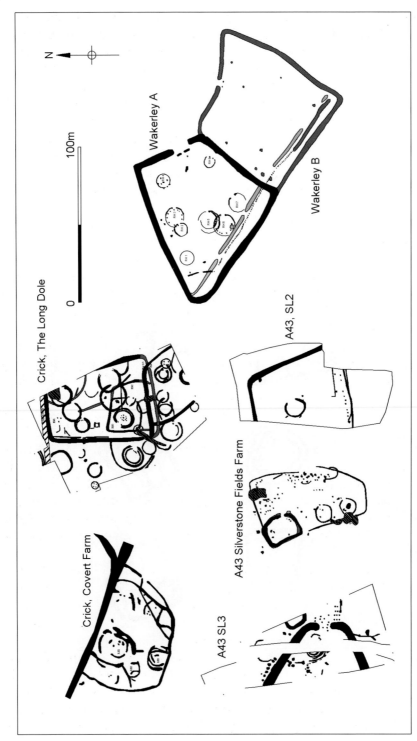

Figure 2.5: Group Four: Miscellaneous, includes A43 (after Northampton Archaeology 1994, Crick (after Mudd 2002), Woodward and Hughes *forthcoming*), and Wakerley (after Jackson and Ambrose 1978).

areas from the domestic activities within the enclosure, to the farming activities on the outside (Collis 1996: 89). Yet it can be argued that the boundary may have taken on a more symbolic role, as the boundary is the transition from the enclosed domestic space into the open landscape (Willis 1999: 93).

Hingley has argued that the boundary should be looked at in terms of the social conventions of those who lived within and built the settlements (1986, 1990). Taking this viewpoint, the enclosure can be seen as a form of social exclusion. Based on a study in the upper Thames Valley, social groups have been identified by the creation (and consistent maintenance) of boundaries, separating domestic groups (Hingley 1990: 96). Similar examples can be seen in the case studies analysed here. For example a similar 'social divide' can be seen occurring at Twywell in Group Two. Here the enclosure boundary is formed, and constantly re-dug, separating and excluding internal activities from within the enclosure, to the domestic buildings on the outside. Boundaries can also act as a form of social *inclusion*, for example in the Middle Iron Age at Wakerley the unenclosed settlement used an uninhabited enclosure (Wakerley B) for group activity by digging numerous pits along a boundary which were '…marked by the structured deposition of fineware pottery and infant burials' (Gwilt and Haselgrove 1997: 4).

The enclosure boundary can also act as a symbol of display and status, thus forming a 'corporate identity' (Ferrell 1997: 234). For example in Group Three, many of the Nene Valley settlements display distinctive defensive characteristics such as large ditches and elaborate entrance-ways. These defended settlements have been termed 'Wootton Hill' style enclosures by Dix and Jackson (1989). It is suggested that these elaborate small settlements may have been an overt form of social status as displayed through architecture, perhaps a reflection or imitation of the substantial defences seen at hillforts. The argument for status can be further enhanced by the deposits found within the fills of the enclosure ditches. For example at Weekley, the La Tène decorated pottery found within the substantial enclosure ditches indicates wide ranging exchange networks (the pottery was produced in Cornwall), and may also indicate a level of high status (*ibid.*: 71).

The third main theme for enclosure boundaries is that of ritual. There is extensive evidence that boundaries had an important role for ceremonies, which were marked by 'the deliberate deposition of certain materials' (Fitzpatrick 1997: 79). On many occasions disarticulated human remains are found in enclosure ditches; complete burials are also found in ditches, for example five infant burials were found regularly spaced within the sub-enclosure at A43 Silverstone Fields Farm (Mudd 2002: 14). Other 'special deposits' such as currency bars and swords are also known to be deliberate deposits in ditches and entrances (Hingley 1990: 100). Hill has used the enclosures at Winnall Down and Gussage All Saints in Wessex to analyse the spatial distribution of deposits in the enclosure ditch (1994, 1995). He identified that human remains were more concentrated to the 'front' of the enclosure, including a complete human skull which faced towards the entrance at Winnall Down (1995: 80). The reasons for these special deposits are not understood, however, it could be argued that these are deposits made to emphasise or mark the transition from one area into another: '...from the *inside* of households to the *outside* of fields or other social groups' (Parker Pearson 1996: 123, original emphasis). The use of human remains may also have been used to demonstrate that this part of the settlement is 'dead' or peripheral. The deposits of animal bones in ditches might instead have marked a major event, such as feasting (Maltby 1985: 33).

In some instances there is evidence to suggest that the enclosure is used to link the past with the present. For example the sub-rectangular enclosure at Grendon was built adjacent to a Bronze Age burial mound (Jackson 1996). The ditch surrounding the mound was even re-dug in the Iron Age, and this is therefore a good example of how an enclosure ditch was used to express the importance of past activities.

The enclosure ditch, therefore, was clearly an important and (almost vital) element of the Iron Age settlement: one which acted as both a functional and symbolic role for people living within the domestic settlement. Based on nationwide studies (which supports the evidence from this dataset); the enclosure boundary becomes more common throughout the first millennium BC because of the 'agricultural intensification (that) led to land becoming more valued as a form of property' (Thomas 1997: 211). The enclosures are therefore partly a product of the changing kinship relationships and symbolise the importance of dividing the insider from the outsider.

## Enclosure morphology

A study of the enclosure morphology is an important aspect to attempt to identify what similarities and differences there are across the study area. Do certain areas exhibit only one type of enclosure, or many differing forms? There are certainly many enclosure forms, but in general they can be broadly categorised as rectilinear, curvilinear, or D-shaped. They have been analysed in this way as it is argued that the geographical location, geology, and landscape surrounding the settlement will heavily influence the enclosure morphology; and that these three categories reflect the three main types of landscape use. The rectilinear form is generally seen in landscapes that have been heavily developed into field systems, often occurring along boundaries. D-shaped enclosures are more likely to be positioned in the corner of fields, as these enclosures have two straight sides (along the field boundaries). The third form, another curving, but more irregular enclosure – the curvilinear settlements – are more often seen in areas that do not have large field systems; they are generally oval or rounded.

Of the 35 case study sites, 22 are rectilinear, 8 are curvilinear, and 5 are D-shaped (Figure 2.6). The morphology of Group One enclosures, in the Leicester hinterland is (with the exception of Humberstone) either curvilinear or D-shaped, most examples are from the Middle Iron Age, and so the dominance of this type of enclosure may simply reflect issues of chronology. The later examples (such as Birstall, Enderby, and Humberstone), display more rectilinear forms of enclosure.

The morphology of enclosures in Northamptonshire is quite different to that of Leicestershire. 20 sites (80 percent) are rectilinear, whilst three (12 percent) are curvilinear, and only two (8 percent) are D-shaped. The rectilinear form reflects the nature of the surrounding landscape, as evidence was revealed for an extensive system of rectilinear ditches, indicating a large open area of landscape, cleared of forest trees. Despite the dominance of the rectilinear form, within Groups Two and Three there are still distinct general differences to one another. Group Two, in the Ise valley area has four rectilinear examples, three of them (Rothwell, Aldwincle, and Weekley) display quite similar characteristics, forming a sub-rectangular shape, close to the river. There are two curvilinear enclosures in Group 2 (Brigstock and Draughton). Both are situated on high ground away from the river valleys, they display a markedly different morphology to the rectilinear lowland settlements found elsewhere in the study region. The chronology reflects that of Leicestershire, with the curvilinear forms generally earlier than the Late Iron Age rectilinear forms.

Group Three offers the most consistent enclosure form. Once again the dominant form is rectilinear (84 percent) with only one curvilinear enclosure and one D-shaped. The most common form is more square in shape, rather than rectangular as seen in Group Two. The square form is seen at Earls Barton, Wollaston, and Wootton Hill Farm; all of these square enclosures are located close to each other along the Nene valley, close to the river, and are contemporary to one another. Given this close proximity and striking similarities in morphology each may be part of the same social group, built along large boundaries in areas that have very little or no earlier prehistoric monuments upstanding. Where there are earlier monuments the enclosure takes on a slightly different form: for example Grendon is more rectangular in form, built adjacent to a Bronze Age ring ditch (Jackson 1996: 1). The boundary from which the Wollaston sites are built up against stops at Grendon, and then continues on after it, thus avoiding the area containing numerous earlier monuments from the Neolithic and Bronze Ages. The only curvilinear site was at Moulton Park, though this is based only on fragmentary evidence (Williams 1974).

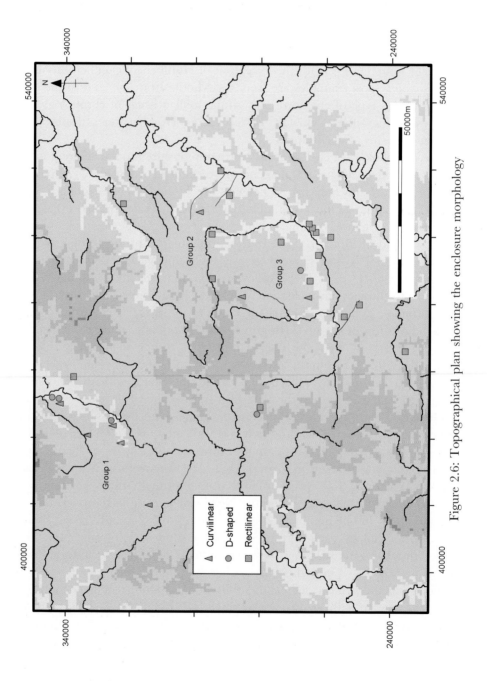

Figure 2.6: Topographical plan showing the enclosure morphology

The research has indicated that the more permeable soils (river gravels) are being more heavily exploited with large areas of woodland cleared, allowing enclosures to become part of a large managed landscape. Whereas in the higher ground (often on clay subsoil), enclosures are much more irregular, suggesting that they do not need to fit into a larger organised landscape and that perhaps it is more wooded in these areas. The settlements are therefore likely to be more hidden and less accessible..

## Enclosure size

The size of the enclosures has been calculated based on the amount of enclosure space in square metres. Taking all 35 case studies together, the median space enclosed by an Iron Age enclosure settlement is 2250m². If a comparison is made between the morphology and size of the enclosure, then we can begin to see some patterns emerging. The seven curvilinear enclosures in the data set range in size from 360m² (Brigstock) to 2400m² (Moulton Park I), with a median of 1531m². The five D-shaped enclosures range from 2500m² (Birstall I) to 4030m² (Great Doddington), with a median of 3058m². Finally, the 22 rectilinear settlements range from 915m² (Birstall II), to 4900m² (Wakerley B), with a median of 2413m². Figure 2.7 illustrates that curvilinear sites have a narrow range, whereas rectilinear sites are much more varied in size, but are generally larger. D-shaped sites have the narrowest range, and are, on average, a much larger size than the other two enclosure forms. The evidence suggests, therefore, that the larger settlements are most often either rectilinear or D-shaped, and the smaller settlements are more likely to be curvilinear in form.

## Enclosure entrance

The entrance is a crucially important area of any building or settlement. For the enclosed settlements of the Late Iron Age it represented the point where the outside becomes the inside; a crossing of a physical boundary, defining areas of culturally defined space (Hingley 1990: 96; Woodward and Hughes *forthcoming*). Generally, access into the enclosure was through a single entrance, though in some cases there are two (Weekley), and in some cases three (Long Dole, Crick). The most common form of entrance is simply a break in the ditches, generally about three to five metres in width. Some enclosures have no evidence surviving for an entrance, suggesting that the ditch was either crossed by a bridge, or by a causeway. Evidence for entrance gateways exists at only eight sites, one from Group One (Enderby II), two from Group Two

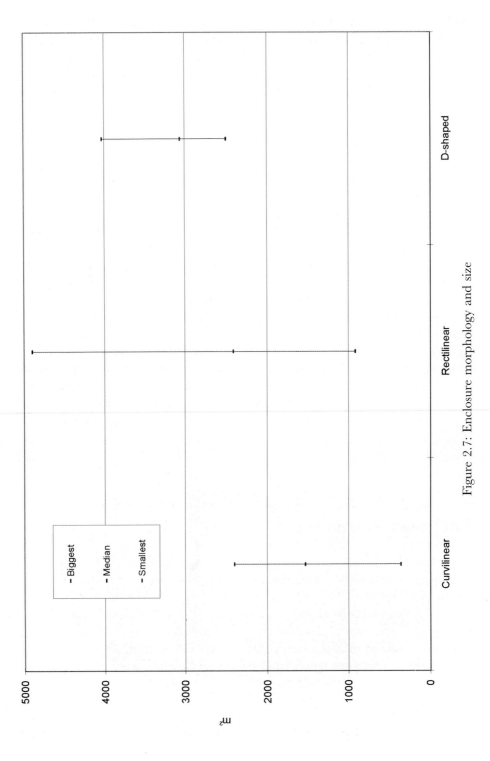

Figure 2.7: Enclosure morphology and size

(Aldwincle, Weekley), three from Group Three (Earls Barton, Stanwell Spinney, Wootton), and two from Group Four (A43 SL3, Wakerley A). The form is almost universal, consisting of a single (timber?) gateway approximately two metres in width. The internal postholes indicate that the gates were hinged, and generally open on the left hand side as entered (Dix and Jackson 1989: 163).

The majority of enclosures within the dataset are orientated in an easterly direction (55 percent, see Figure 2.8). The preference for an easterly-orientated enclosure entrance in this dataset matches what has been identified in wider studies across central and southern Britain (Hill 1995: 6). Only nine enclosures faced a different direction to this, and six entrances are unknown. The predominance of the east-facing enclosure lends itself well to the extensive research that has been undertaken on meanings behind Iron Age roundhouse orientation (Fitzpatrick 1997; Giles and Parker Pearson 1999; Oswald 1997; Parker Pearson and Richards 1994; Pope 2007). Some of the case studies appear to have had earlier unenclosed origins (such as Enderby II, Huncote, and Grendon), therefore when the enclosure ditches were dug, because the roundhouses were orientated east, the enclosure entrances may have simply mirrored these, in what could have been seen as the 'correct way'. They may have also been dug in that location so that the roundhouse entrances faced towards the enclosure entrance, which is seen in many sites in the dataset (including Humberstone, Enderby II, Grendon, and Courteenhall). In the small number of examples where enclosures do not face east, there are good contextual reasons for this. At Wollaston the enclosure

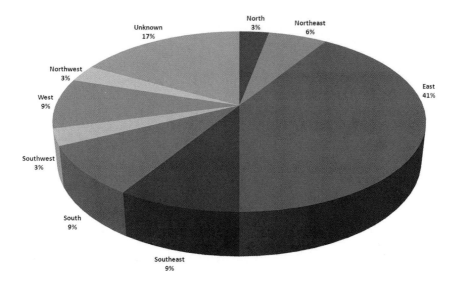

Figure 2.8: Enclosure entrance orientation

settlements are built at regular intervals along a pre-existing ditch boundary (Northamptonshire Archaeology 1995: 3). The entrances, therefore, either open onto this 'route-way' (such as the west-facing enclosure A), or face its neighbour (the north-facing enclosure B). A similar respect for pre-existing boundaries can also seen at enclosure 13 in area 6 from the extensive excavations at Courteenhall in Group Three (Buteux S. (ed.) 2001; Buteux *et al* 2005).

If the 'required' direction was to face east, then the evidence should show that curvilinear enclosures are almost exclusively orientated to the east because they do not need to fit into pre-existing boundaries and track-ways. The dataset is small and therefore interpretation is quite limited, though the evidence does hint at supporting this interpretation. For example there is certainly a lot less variation in orientation in curvilinear settlements, than there are in rectilinear examples, which are much more variable in direction (though the easterly direction is still most common). It must be noted that there are more rectilinear settlements in the dataset, and therefore more variation is likely because of this. From this small dataset there does not appear to be a clear link between the orientation of enclosures and roundhouses. There are some examples of roundhouses predating the enclosure (e.g. Enderby II), and the subsequent enclosure added on the same entrance orientation. However, other examples show no correlation.

The analysis has thus far indicated that there appears to be areas of both regional and localised syntaxes in terms of the enclosure morphology, size, and entrance orientation. Regionally, the morphology of the settlements is quite different between Leicestershire and Northamptonshire. The differences reflect where these enclosures are positioned in the landscape, as the curvilinear forms are more often seen in the upland areas, and the rectilinear forms in the river valleys. The morphology of the settlement affects the size of the settlement, as the case studies indicate that curvilinear sites are generally smaller than the rectilinear sites. The only overwhelming similarity across all settlements is the orientation of the settlements, as most have easterly orientated entrance-ways unless local landscape features dictate otherwise. Within these broad similarities there are more localised syntaxes for example the square enclosures in the Nene Valley, and the large, almost empty enclosures in the area of the Welland valley. The results therefore do indicate strong morphological patterning, depending on the geographic location and geology of the enclosure, which in turn affect the type of settlement that is likely to form there. For example, the settlements situated in lowland river valleys are almost without exception larger and rectilinear in form; whereas the settlements located on higher ground are far more likely to be much smaller and more curvilinear, reflecting differing methods of farming practices and landscape use.

# Roundhouses

The roundhouse was the most common house form in Iron Age Britain from the Middle Bronze Age through to the Late Iron Age (Parker Pearson 1994: 47). The evidence that remains for roundhouses in the 'ploughzone' of Leicestershire and Northamptonshire is generally a shallow curving gully that would have acted as either a water drainage gully, or in some cases, a post beam-slot. Having assessed the broad regional and localised settlement syntaxes, it is important to also look at the internal characteristics of each enclosure settlement, to see if similar patterns emerge. This part of the paper analyses the number of roundhouses within the settlements, their location with the enclosure, the average roundhouse size, and the orientation of the roundhouses. Tying into the latter half of this is a critique of the numerous studies into roundhouse orientation, and the relevance of spatial awareness the Iron Age people may have had.

# Number of roundhouses

The case studies indicate that the average number of roundhouses within an enclosure is either one (15 sites) or two (10 sites); this is widespread across the whole study area (Figure 2.9). Five sites had three roundhouses, Long Dole Crick was the only settlement to have four roundhouses (due to lack of phasing the actual number of contemporary roundhouses may be higher), and Wakerley was the only settlement to have six roundhouses within the enclosure at any one time (a much larger settlement).

Given the low number of roundhouses within each enclosure, it is suggested that the majority of settlements probably contained one family unit. The occurrence of paired buildings, often with one large, centrally placed roundhouse, and another smaller roundhouse located to the edge of the enclosure, suggests that the buildings may have had differing functions. At Enderby I, Clay suggests that 'The...building of a large size may be interpreted as a house for a family or families, whereas the smaller structure...appears to have been used as a kitchen or workshop' (1992: 33). A similar idea can be suggested for Draughton, but with three buildings rather than just two. Again their relative size and position suggests there is one larger main 'house', with two smaller ancillary buildings. The two-house unit is a good example of a deliberate spatial organisation, separating differing domestic activities. Some of the larger enclosures with four or more buildings indicate that these were occupied by larger family groups, or larger communities as at Long Dole Crick (BUFAU 1998) and Wakerley (Jackson and Ambrose 1978).

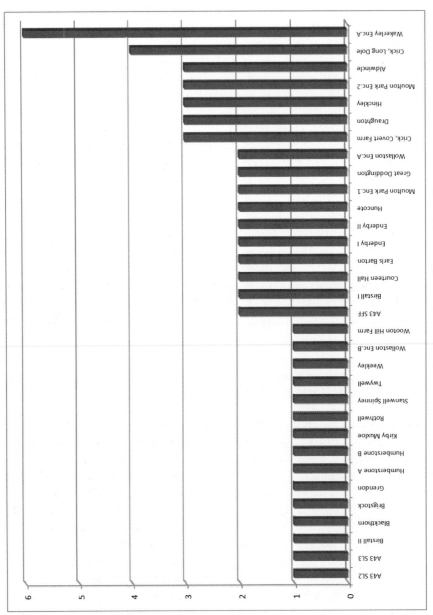

Figure 2.9: Number of roundhouses (phased)

# Location of roundhouses

The location of the roundhouse(s) within the enclosure is an important indication of the function of these buildings. The position of the roundhouse has been analysed by describing the location of the buildings using a subjective description of the location based upon viewing the roundhouse at the entrance of the enclosure; 63 examples were available for this analysis. While a relatively small number, this sample highlights some key themes. Again the predominant position of the roundhouse was in the middle of the enclosure (54 percent including middle-front and -back). A preference for the back of the enclosures (32 percent) rather than the front (22 percent) is noted. There appears to be a slight preference for the right (27 percent), rather than the left (19 percent). The buildings that were not centrally placed may have been an ancillary building.

The average diameter of the curvilinear drip-gully is around 10 metres; generally the roundhouse located in the middle of the enclosure is larger than those situated at the periphery of the settlement. For example at Draughton the centrally-placed roundhouse is 9.8m in diameter, whereas the buildings located at the back were both around 6m in diameter. At Wakerley the centrally-placed roundhouse is 14m in diameter; whereas the buildings located around the enclosure ditch are 6–8m in diameter. Again the size and location of the building have been chosen specifically to reflect the function of the building.

# Orientation of roundhouses

The study of the orientation of roundhouses has been a central theme in Iron Age studies in Britain for the past twenty years (especially by Fitzpatrick, Oswald, and Parker Pearson). Essentially, the studies have focused on the observation that: 'The great majority of entrances to Iron Age roundhouses are orientated to the east' (Fitzpatrick 1997: 77). The case studies here support the more widespread studies; of the 66 roundhouses in the dataset, the majority (90 percent) are orientated to the east, southeast, or northeast (Figure 2.10). There are only single examples of north, northwest, and southwest facing roundhouses, and only two examples of west-facing roundhouses.

The first paper to discuss the standardised orientation of roundhouses was by Graeme Guilbert. In this he noted that at the Iron Age hillfort at Moel y Gaer in Wales, all roundhouses faced either in an easterly or south-easterly direction as part of a rigid planned settlement (Guilbert 1975: 203). He noted that in some instances buildings would be east-facing even when this direction would make little sense to the location of the building within the settlement as

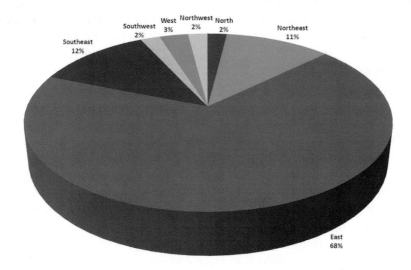

Figure 2.10: Orientation of roundhouses within the dataset

a whole. This is also seen at Wakerley, where one building is facing east towards the enclosure ditch and away from the main settlement (Jackson and Ambrose 1978). This led Guilbert argued that practical reasons accounted for such standardisation in orientation. Firstly, the easterly direction provides the best protection from prevailing westerly winds; secondly, it provides the best sunlight (Guilbert 1975: 205).

Until recently, Guilbert's explanations have been widely accepted as determining factors for the orientation of roundhouses from Lambrick's Upper Thames Valley survey to Knight's survey in the Nene and Great Ouse Basins (Knight 1984). However, the standardised orientation covers such a large area (throughout Britain), and timescale (some 1000 years, from the Late Bronze Age through to the early Roman period), that purely environmental reasons began to be questioned. The reasoning for easterly orientated roundhouses was seen as being not particularly disadvantageous, or advantageous; also if functional reasons were the sole factors in determining the orientation then we would expect to see more variation in the numerous known examples (Oswald 1997). For example, because the wind direction and amount of sunlight differs from place to place, surely this would be reflected in regional patterning of building types, rather than a more universal form. Studies since have identified a further degree of variation in the east-southeast norm, with a north to south trend from southeast-facing to east-facing (Pope 2007). Despite this, the preference for this direction could also be seen as a reflection of human behaviour. The earliest studies by Wait (1985), and Boast and Evans (1986) linked the potential of ritual to roundhouse orientation by demonstrating that ritual traditions from the Bronze Age had transferred into the domestic sphere in the Iron Age. The 'cosmological model' emphases that the entrance orientation corresponds with '...significant points on the solar calendar: sunrise at the equinoxes and the midwinter solstice' (Gwilt and Haselgrove 1997: 3).

The cosmological model was then developed by Fitzpatrick (1994; 1997) and Parker Pearson and Richards (1994) who began looking at the use of domestic space within the roundhouse. The latter argued that space could have been 'concentrically ordered within the roundhouse, with the main tasks being undertaken in the central 'public' area...and other activities, such as sleeping and food storage, located in the more 'private' outer area' (*ibid.*: 54). Fitzpatrick linked the roundhouse to time by arguing that the large landscape features such as henges and stone circles of the earlier prehistoric periods were now being reproduced in the domestic sphere. These monuments may have been used to record time, therefore he proposed that different activities occurred within the roundhouse at different times of the day, as a way of marking time (1997: 77). An excavation at Dunston Park, in Berkshire, preserved sufficient evidence to indicate what activities may have taken place within the building. Fitzpatrick interpreted the data to indicate that there was a living and working area in the light southern half and a sleeping and storage area in the dark northern half (1994: 68). Oswald used the idea of time, through reference to ethnographic examples, to demonstrate that this standardisation in orientation towards the rising sun reflects what activities are done around the house, in a clockwise direction around the building throughout the day, thus perhaps indicating 'a universal sun-cult' (Oswald 1997: 94).

The simple rejection of possible environmental considerations, in favour of a ritual explanation has now begun to receive some criticisms. Webley (2003) has demonstrated that over a large area domestic buildings can look architecturally identical, but, this does not mean that each had the same social meanings (*ibid.*: 59). He uses three-aisled longhouses in northern Europe as case studies for a comparison to Iron Age roundhouses in Britain, arguing that despite the recurring theme of easterly-orientated roundhouses, the cosmological theory should not be applied universally to all 'roundhouse-using groups' (*ibid.*: 66). This is a useful argument, demonstrating the complexity and danger of linking similarities between the layout of architecture to the same social beliefs. Giles and Parker Pearson (1999) do deal with this argument by emphasising that exchange networks act as a means of maintaining social relations, and forming and sharing social beliefs and ideas. These ideas and acts were then to become traditions, which became expressed though the repeated way space was used and maintained (*ibid.*: 228). These architectural elements then became what were perceived as the necessary and correct way of doing things.

Pope has been the most vocal in criticising the cosmological model. Reassessing much of Oswald's and Fitzpatrick's work, she argued that some data, conflicting with the main evidence, were ignored in order to further develop the cosmological model (Pope 2007). She argues that there is good evidence to suggest a use of both front and back space within the roundhouse, as well as central and peripheral space, (*ibid.*). These themes have also been picked up in this study, though based within the enclosure, rather than simply the roundhouse.

Buildings that are orientated to the west are not common, but do exist. Giles and Parker Pearson state that these buildings have been deliberately arranged to indicate that the building is different in terms of both status and social categorisation, though they do note that in some cases the evidence has been revealed showing that: '...activities were still the same, but simply reversed' (Giles and Parker Pearson 1999: 224). Parker Pearson emphasises the importance of west-facing buildings, suggesting that 'the west was considered as the opposite (to the east); profane, dark, associated with death and burial' (1996: 127). Building 5 at Wakerley is a good example of a west-facing building within an enclosure settlement full of east-facing roundhouses. In his re-appraisal of the excavation report, Gwilt (1997) argues convincingly that this building presents good evidence for a 'ritual' area of the settlement. The area had evidence for both 4 and 6–post structures for which he interpreted as excarnation platforms or food stores with communal roles. The importance of the place was later re-emphasised with a west-facing building. The deliberate choice to build around an area of special significance with a building deliberately positioned from the opposite of the 'living' east-facing roundhouses to the 'dead' west-facing building, could thus be seen as a 'house of the dead'. Essentially, '...this was a deliberate and symbolic opposition to the cultural norm and signified its different use and meaning from most of the other buildings' (*ibid.*: 164). A final interesting point regarding this building is that when a sight line analysis is undertaken, it is outside the human primary field-of-view, whereas all the other east-facing roundhouses are within this view. This further suggests that this area may have been seen as a sacred place, but one that need not be seen upon entering the settlement.

This research of 66 roundhouses has shown that across the Iron Age of the study area the roundhouse maintains a repetitive and predictable form. It seems quite clear that there are long-term practices which people are constantly repeating, perhaps as a way of social acceptance. As Giles and Parker Pearson state 'Knowing how to act appropriately with others is a means by which social identity is effected' (1999: 220).

# Sub-enclosures

The main enclosure ditch is often internally sub-divided into smaller areas. The shape of these sub-enclosures is generally rectangular, but the function can vary greatly. The most common uses are interpreted as:

- An animal pen
- A metalworking area (for example in the corner of the enclosure at Birstall II the sub-enclosure appears to have been used as a small-scale metal production area)
- Food storage area (evidence of four-post structures within these areas suggest that a raised building may have acted as a granary)
- A look-out-tower/entrance gatehouse (Earls Barton).
- A ritual area (for example at A43 SFF five child burials are located within the middle-fills of the ditch at regular intervals)

18 of the enclosure settlements (51 percent) had a sub-enclosure within them, the majority are rectilinear enclosures (only two are curvilinear: Huncote and Enderby I). The location within the enclosure was then analysed, firstly by cardinal direction, and then by the subjective location, as viewed at the enclosure entrance. When the location is looked at subjectively, some patterns begin to emerge. The majority of sub-enclosures are positioned at the front, either to the left or right, or at the back in the middle or to the right. In general, the position of the enclosures perhaps reflects their function, as they tend to be located on the periphery of the enclosure settlement, as a means to separate domestic activities within the settlement. They are also far more likely to be present in rectilinear enclosures, perhaps reflecting different farming practices.

# Pit groups

Pits are common throughout all Iron Age settlements. Their primary function was for the storage of grain, and when no longer needed were allowed to fill, or deliberately backfilled with domestic waste (Cunliffe 1992: 73). The pits are often found in groups, located in certain areas within and outside of the enclosure. Eleven of the thirty-five case studies had evidence for pit groups of these types. The majority were located to the back of the enclosure (78 percent), with only a very small number located elsewhere. The evidence therefore indicates that pits were dug on the periphery of settlements, in what may have been seen as the correct place for this to take place. When excavated, pits sometimes contain more than simply domestic rubbish or grain residues; they frequently contain 'special deposits' (Cunliffe 1992: 75; Fitzpatrick 1997: 79), examples of which are known across (mainly southern) Britain, and into northwest Europe as far as central France (Bradley 2003: 19). Pits are also often built along boundaries, forming a pit alignment (Thomas 1997), or close to the entrances. Perhaps, therefore, the 'special deposits' within pits were used to symbolise an important event such as the end of an agricultural cycle, or as a symbol of fertility and rebirth (Barrett 1989, cited in Fitzpatrick 1997: 80).

## A 'view from the ground'

The final part of this paper is an attempt to experience a 'view from the ground', as so far the analysis has been based from an archaeologist's point-of-view – viewing the settlements objectively from a plan-view of the settlement. The idea here is to look at what would be visible to a visitor to the enclosure settlement to assess what similarities there are across the dataset. The view from five metres outside of the enclosure entrance is analysed, followed by the view within the settlement, at the entrance. The angles of human sightlines is based on Tadahiko Higuchi's work on *The Visual and Spatial Structure of Landscapes* (1983). Essentially there are two fields-of-view: the total field-of-view is 160–200°, and the binocular field-of-view is around 120°. There are numerous determining factors affecting what can be seen or not seen (such as the topography for which the settlement is built upon, or the height of the individual). However, this approach shows generally what was visible and what was hidden to the visitor upon entering the settlement.

The sightlines at Aldwincle are used as an example of a rectilinear enclosure (Figure 2.11). It shows what would be visible if one was standing outside the enclosure and then within the entrance, during both structural phases. When on the outside, if the gate was closed the entire settlement (presuming it had an internal bank) would have been virtually hidden from the outside; even if the gates were open then very little would actually be visible, with only part of a building in both phases. On the inside it is the roundhouse which dominates both phases, with pit groups and the sub-enclosure hidden at the rear of the settlement. The figure illustrates that the view from inside and outside changes little between phases 1 and 2 as the new roundhouses in phase 2 occupy a similar space to the roundhouse in phase 1 (though not identical as the first enclosure may have stood briefly in phase 2 (Jackson 1977: 29)).

The sightlines at Draughton (Figure 2.12) are used as an example of a curvilinear enclosure. It shows that when approaching the settlement (presuming any gateway was open) then most of the settlement would have been hidden from view, with perhaps only part of the roundhouse visible. From the inside, the roundhouse is within the binocular field-of-view; though it does not

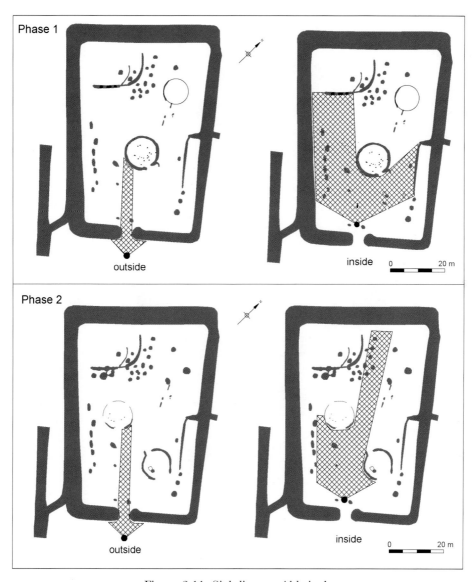

Figure 2.11: Sightlines at Aldwincle

dominate the sightline as much as the Aldwincle example, as some pit activity at the back right is also visible within this primary field-of-view.

The two examples used are a fair representation of both enclosure forms (no entrances are known from D-shaped enclosures, so sightline analysis could not be undertaken). It certainly demonstrates the visible presence (importance?) of the roundhouse within these settlements, and the more hidden (unimportance?) of other domestic activities. On a study of Iron Age enclosures in North-East England, Willis noted that generally it was enclosures

51

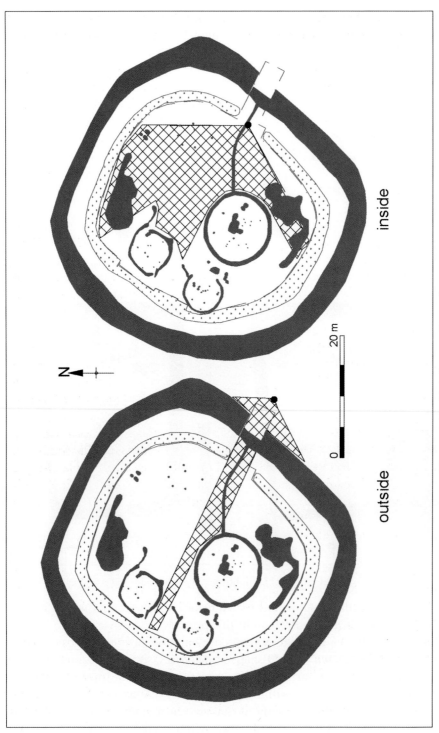

inside

outside

N

20 m

0

Figure 2.12: Sightlines at Draughton

from the earlier first millennium BC that were hidden from the outside, and that it was not until the later first millennium BC that enclosures became less hidden (1999: 92). The dataset here is in complete contrast to these findings; from this research it seems that the earlier settlements are actually more visible (many have unenclosed origins) than the later examples. This is clearly an interesting point, perhaps emphasising differing social relationships in this part of the East Midlands compared to that in the North-East, though it should be noted that the dataset here is only based on 35 examples.

## An idealised farmstead?

'The idealised Iron Age farm of southern Britain, with its roundhouses, farm-yard compound, and storage pits is well known' (Fitzpatrick 1997: 75). There is certainly not a standard model for which all enclosures abide by, however, the components that make up a small Iron Age enclosed settlement are certainly extremely similar, and this paper has attempted to analyse these components in an attempt to establish how and why settlements were organised in such a standard way.

The analysis of inter-site patterning has demonstrated that across the study area there are distinct similarities within certain groups. This is because the morphology of the settlements is essentially a reflection of their immediate environs. The majority of the rectilinear forms are located in river valleys (and therefore on more permeable soils), it is in these areas that the landscape in the Iron Age appears to be more heavily exploited with evidence for large field systems. The smaller curvilinear forms are, instead, generally located on higher ground, on less manageable soils, in possibly more wooded landscapes. They are more irregular in form because they do not need to fit into established field systems and boundaries and perhaps had the freedom to have a more flexible settlement shape. This would lead us to believe that the curvilinear settlements are likely to be more hidden and less accessible because of their location. For this reason, we should also expect the intra-site patterning of these settlements to also be much more varied. However, the study has shown this need not to be the case, with evidence clearly indicating that there are distinct rules and patterns within all Iron Age enclosed settlements, irrespective of enclosure morphology.

The intra-site analysis has shown that generally all settlements have either one or two roundhouses, this is especially true in curvilinear settlements, whereas in rectilinear settlements there is much more variation in numbers (though this is probably a reflection of the larger number of rectilinear settlements in the dataset). The roundhouses are predominantly positioned in the middle of the settlement; and generally it is the smaller buildings that are positioned to the back and sides of the settlement. The evidence demonstrates that there is a general preference for easterly orientated roundhouse and enclosure entrances across the entire dataset, irrespective of morphology or location. This clearly indicates that building the domestic structure in this way was seen as the 'correct' way to do things, the cosmological significance to this should not be underestimated because Iron Age society was a 'non–complex' society (Hill 1994: 6). The other main architectural elements (pit groups and sub-enclosures) were also found to be positioned in similar places within the differing settlements. These were almost always positioned on the periphery of the enclosure, with pits generally at the back and sub-enclosures (predominantly in rectilinear settlements) either at the front or back.

Whilst the research has identified these key similarities between all settlements, other, more local areas have also been identified as having context-specific similarities, which in turn helped to establish what became regarded as a 'correct' architectural layout for settlements. Two distinct types of settlements have been identified within the dataset that have formed as a result of social groupings: the river valley settlements and the uplands settlements. The layout of each settlement is unique, but all share such striking similarities in what they contain and the way in which the settlements are organised, that a schematic plan, suggesting the basic spatial organisation, can be proposed for the two forms of settlement.

The settlements in these areas, especially in the Later Iron Age, are situated in a bounded and organised landscape, dominated by field systems, with each settlement clearly defined by substantial boundary ditches and entrance-ways (rectilinear enclosure, Figure 2.13). These settlements were limited by where they could be built (only in the corner of fields), and once the boundaries had been set the organised settlement was then limited to strict spatial limits for which the inhabitants could then construct and live in a way that became accepted as the 'norm'. These settlements display a stark distinction between the enclosed domestic settlement, and the shared networked landscape beyond. Key sites from this group are the Wollaston, Earls Barton, and Wootton Hill enclosures in the Nene Valley.

Settlements situated on higher ground, often on less permeable subsoil, are found to be predominantly curvilinear (Figure 2.13); and given their location and form these settlements can be considered to be part of a more wooded landscape. There was less need for the boundary ditches to conform to rectilinear shapes as these did not need to fit into such field systems, indeed some of these settlements had evidence for an earlier unenclosed phase (Enderby I and II, Huncote), which was then later enclosed by a ditch. It could be suggested that these settlements may have only constructed enclosure ditches after seeing the settlements in the river valleys, perhaps as an attempt to attain a level of social status. The internal components of these settlements are very

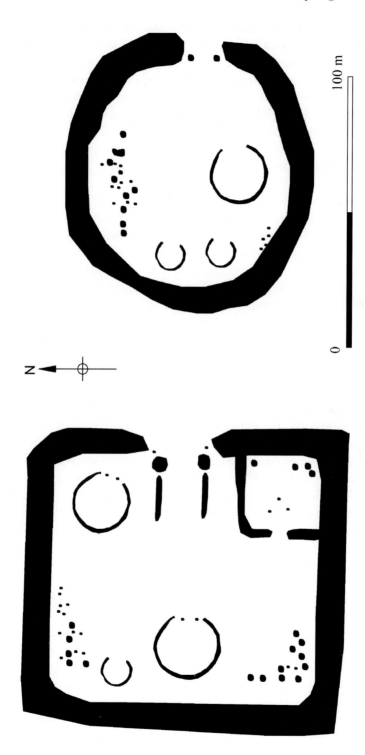

Figure 2.13: Schematic plan of a typical river valley settlement (left), and upland settlement (right)

100 m

0

similar to those in the lowland areas. In some, aspects of the architecture —conform to a rigid social syntax, the orientation of roundhouses being a prime example. The Leicestershire enclosures are all predominantly of this type, perhaps reflecting the nature of the society in this region. These settlements are thus more hidden and (perhaps) more independent, with a strong inside-outside dichotomy. The key sites include Enderby (I and II), Huncote, Brigstock, and Draughton.

## Conclusion

In summary, all the enclosed settlements within the study area do have many similarities in the layout of each settlement, though there are subtle differences within some local groups, who clearly tried to emulate one-another through the use of architecture. Once a particular form had been established it was continually maintained. This clearly demonstrates that 'spaces' became 'places' which the inhabitants maintained in such strikingly similar ways across the region.

As far as the two counties are concerned, the research has highlighted that both contain wide ranging settlement forms, however, there are broad (and in some cases close) similarities within these that have been formed as a result of the local landscape to which the settlement is placed. It is during the first millennium BC that land becomes increasingly used for agriculture, and this intensification thus affected how people view land. It is argued therefore, that more settlements may have become enclosed as a result of the changing views of land and ownership. As part of this process settlements became structured in a certain way that would become acceptable to society, and therefore acknowledge the settlement's place in the managed landscape.

This research is based only on a limited number of case studies, however, if further research were to be conducted it would be interesting to test the findings here with a wider dataset, thus allowing a more comprehensive and accurate analysis. An attempt to tighten the chronologies of settlement, and a development of the sightline analysis (perhaps by looking at views between family groups and communities) may help to establish what kind of social syntaxes were present within Iron Age society. This paper has illustrated how the study of often overlooked aspects of the archaeological record can help us learn more about how, and why, the people of the British Iron Age lived and manipulated their domestic space in the way that they did. The work has highlighted the importance and usefulness of reassessing excavation reports as there is now a wide range of both excavated evidence and surveyed areas in both counties which allowed this research to take place. The settlement evidence is ever increasing, with the constant urban growth around the major towns in the region, for example Great Doddington was a poorly understood and isolated enclosed settlement, but has now been placed within a much larger 'agglomerated' settlement following recent excavation (Enright and Thomas 2004). Therefore, the study of Iron Age settlements should be constantly reassessed, without need for complacency, in order to fully account for the changing and differing settlement forms and communities in the region.

# Bibliography

Beamish, M. (1998). A Middle Iron Age site at Wanlip, Leicestershire. *Transactions of the Leicestershire Archaeological and Historical Society* 72: 1 91.

Boast, R. and C. Evans (1986). The transformation of space: two examples from British pre-history. *Archaeological Review from Cambridge* 5: 193–205.

Bradley, R. (2003). A life less ordinary: the ritualization of the domestic sphere in later prehistoric Europe. *Cambridge Archaeological Journal* 13 (1): 5–23.

BUFAU. (1998). *The excavation of an Iron Age settlement at Covert Farm (DIRFT East) Crick, Northamptonshire.* Birmingham University Field Archaeology Unit unpublished post-excavation assessment and updated research design.

Buteux, S. (ed.) (2001). *Grange Park, Courteenhall, Northamptonshire. Archaeological Investigations 1999.* Birmingham University Field Archaeology Unit unpublished post-excavation assessment and updated research design.

Buteux, S., L. Jones and A. Woodward (2005). *Country life on the margins. Iron Age, Roman and Saxon occupation at Grange Park: excavations at Courteenhall, Northamptonshire, 1999.* Birmingham University Field Archaeology Unit unpublished draft report.

Chapman, P. (2004). Iron Age settlement and Romano-British enclosures at Coventry Road, Hinckley, Leicestershire. *Transactions of the Leicestershire Archaeological and Historical Society* 78: 35–80.

Chapman, A. and D. Jackson (1993). Wollaston Bypass, Northamptonshire, Salvage Excavations (1984). *Northamptonshire Archaeology* 24: 67–76.

Clarke, D. L. (1977). *Spatial Archaeology.* London: Academic Press.

Clay, P. (1992). An Iron Age farmstead at Grove Farm, Enderby, Leicestershire. *Transactions of the Leicestershire Archaeological and Historical Society* 66: 1–82.

Clay, P., J. Meek, and M. Shore (2004). Iron Age Enclosures at Enderby and Huncote, Leicestershire. *Transactions of the Leicestershire Archaeological and Historical Society* 78: 1–34.

Collis, J. (1996). Hill-forts enclosures and boundaries. In T.C. Champion and J.R. Collis (eds.) *The Iron Age in Britain and Ireland*: 87–94. Sheffield: J.R.Collis Publications.

Cooper, L. (1994). Kirby Muxloe, A46 Leicester western by-pass. *Transactions of the Leicestershire Archaeological and Historical Society* 68: 162–165.

Cunliffe, B. (1991). *Iron Age Communities in Britain* (3rd edition). London: Routledge.

Cunliffe, B. (1992). Pits, preconceptions and propitiation in the British Iron Age. *Oxford Journal of Archaeology* 11(1): 69–84.

Dix, B. and D. A. Jackson (1986). Late Iron Age and Roman settlement at Weekley, Northamptonshire. *Northamptonshire Archaeology* 21: 41–93.

Dix, B. and D. A. Jackson (1989). Some Late Iron Age defended enclosures in Northamptonshire. In A. Gibson (ed.) *Midlands prehistory, some recent and current researches into the prehistory of central England*: 158–179. Oxford: British Archaeological Reports, British Series 204.

Enright, D. and A. Thomas (2004). Excavation of an Iron Age settlement at Wilby Way, Great Doddington. *Northamptonshire Archaeology* 31: 15–69.

Ferrell, G. (1997). Space and society in the Iron Age of north-east England. In A. Gwilt and C.C. Haselgrove (eds.) *Reconstructing Iron Age Societies*: 228–238. Oxford: Oxbow Books.

Fitzpatrick, A. P. (1994). Outside in: the structure of an Early Iron Age house at Dunston Park, Thatcham, Berkshire. In A. P. Fitzpatrick and E. L. Morris (eds.) *The Iron Age in Wessex: recent work*: 68–72. Salisbury: Trust for Wessex Archaeology.

Fitzpatrick, A. P. (1997). Everyday life in Iron Age Wessex. In A. Gwilt and C. C. Haselgrove (eds.) *Reconstructing Iron Age societies*: 73–86. Oxford: Oxbow Books.

Giles, M. and M. Parker Pearson (1999). Learning to live in the Iron Age: dwelling and praxis. In B. Bevan (ed.) *Northern Exposure: interpretative devolution and the Iron Ages in Britain*: 217–231. Leicester Archaeology Monograph 4.

Grimes, W. F. (1958). Settlements at Draughton, Northants., Colsterworth, Lincs., and Heathrow, Middlesex. In S. S. Frere (ed.) *Problems of the Iron Age in Southern Britain*: 21–28. London: University of London Institute of Archaeology, Occasional Paper No. 11

Guilbert, G. C. (1975). Planned hillfort interiors. *Proceedings of the Prehistoric Society* 41: 203–221.

Gwilt, A. (1997). Popular practices from material culture: a case study of the Iron Age settlement at Wakerley, Northamptonshire. In A. Gwilt and C. C. Haselgrove (eds.) *Reconstructing Iron Age societies*: 153–166. Oxford: Oxbow Books.

Gwilt, A. and C. C. Haselgrove (1997). Approaching the Iron Age. In A. Gwilt and C. C. Haselgrove (eds.) 1997. *Reconstructing Iron Age societies*: 1–8. Oxford: Oxbow Books.

Hall, E. T. (1969). *The Hidden Dimension*. New York: Anchor Books.

Hartley, F. (1989) Aerial archaeology in Leicestershire. In A. Gibson (ed.) *Midlands prehistory, some recent and current researches into the prehistory of central England*: 95–105. Oxford: British Archaeological Reports, British Series 204.

Higuchi, T. (1983). *The Visual and Spatial Structure of Landscapes*. London: MIT Press (Translated by C. S. Terry).

Hingley, R. (1986). The archaeology of settlement and the social significance of space. *Scottish Archaeological Review 3*: 22–31.

Hingley, R. (1990). Boundaries surrounding Iron Age and Romano-British settlements. *Scottish Archaeological Review* 7: 96–103.

Hill, J. D. (1995). How should we understand Iron Age societies and hillforts? A contextual study from southern Britain. In: J. D. Hill and C. G. Cumberpatch (eds.) *Different Iron Ages: studies on the Iron Age in temperate Europe*: 45–66. Oxford: British Archaeological Report, International Series 602.

Hill, J. D. (1996). Hill-forts and the Iron Age of Wessex. In T. C. Champion and J. R. Collis *The Iron Age in Britain and Ireland*: 95–116. Sheffield: J. R. Collis Publications.

Hodder, I. (1977). Some new directions in the spatial analysis of archaeological data at the regional scale (macro). In: D. Clarke (ed.) *Spatial Archaeology*: 223–352. London: Academic Press.

Jackson, D. A. (1975). An Iron Age site at Twywell, Northamptonshire. *Northamptonshire Archaeology* 10: 31–93.

Jackson, D. A. (1977). Further excavations at Aldwincle, Northamptonshire, 1969–71. *Northamptonshire Archaeology* 12: 9–54.

Jackson, D. A. (1983). The excavation of an Iron Age site at Brigstock, Northants, 1979–81. *Northamptonshire Archaeology* 18: 7–32.

Jackson, D. A. (1991). An Iron Age enclosure at Wootton Hill Farm, Northampton. *Northamptonshire Archaeology* 23: 1–21.

Jackson, D. A. (1996). Archaeology at Grendon Quarry, Northamptonshire. Part 2: other prehistoric, Iron Age and later sites excavated in 1974–75 and further observations between 1976–80. *Northamptonshire Archaeology* 26: 3–32.

Jackson, D. A. and T. M. Ambrose (1978). Excavations at Wakerley, Northants, 1972–75. *Britannia* 9: 115–242.

Knight, D. (1984). *Late Bronze Age and Iron Age Settlement in the Nene and Great Ouse basin*. Oxford: British Archaeological Reports, British Series 130.

Maltby, M. (1985). Patterns in faunal assemblage variability. In G. Barker and C. Gamble (eds.) *Beyond Domestication in Prehistoric Europe*: 33–74. London: Academic Press.

Mudd, A. (2002). *A43 Towcester to M40 dualling project*. Northamptonshire County Council, Northamptonshire Archaeology, unpublished post-excavation assessment and updated project design.

Northamptonshire Archaeology (1994). *Excavation of Iron Age and Roman sites at the Daventry International Rail Freight Terminal, near Crick, Northamptonshire*. Northamptonshire County Council, Northamptonshire Archaeology, unpublished report.

Northamptonshire Archaeology (1995). *Archaeological Evaluation: stage 1. Land south of Hardwater Road, Wollaston*. Northamptonshire County Council, Northamptonshire Archaeology, unpublished report.

Oswold, A. (1997). A doorway into the past: practical and mystic concerns in the orientation of roundhouse doorways. In: A. Gwilt and C.C. Haselgrove (eds.) *Reconstructing Iron Age societies*: 87–95. Oxford: Oxbow Books.

Parker Pearson, M. (1996). Food, fertility, and front doors in the first millennium BC. In T. C. Champion and J. R. Collis (eds.) *The Iron Age in Britain and Ireland*: 117–132. Sheffield: J. R. Collis Publications.

Parker Pearson, M. and C. Richards (1994). *Architecture and Order: approaches to social space*. London: Routledge.

Pope, R. E. (2007). *Ritual and the roundhouse: a critique of recent ideas on the use of domestic space in later British prehistory*. In C. C. Haselgrove and R. E. Pope (eds.) *The Earlier Iron Age in Britain and the Near Continent*: 204–228. Oxford: Oxbow Books.

Priest, V. (2003). *Archaeological Excavations: site 9 (Rothwell), A6 Rothwell and Desborough Bypass*. University of Leicester Archaeological Services unpublished report 2003–040.

Speed, G. (2004). *An Archaeological Evaluation at Hallam Fields, Birstall, Leicestershire*. University of Leicester Archaeological Services unpublished report 2004–016.

Speed, G. (2005). *An Unwritten Architectural Language? A comparative analysis of the spatial syntax of Iron Age enclosure settlements in Leicestershire and Northamptonshire*. Unpublished M.A. dissertation, University of Leicester 2005.

Speed, G. (forthcoming). *An Archaeological Excavation at Hallam Fields, Birstall, Leicestershire*. University of Leicester Archaeological Services unpublished report.

Taylor, J. (1996). *Iron Age and Roman landscapes in the East Midlands: a case study in integrated survey*. Unpublished PhD thesis. Department of Archaeology, University of Durham.

Taylor, J. (1997). Space and place: some thoughts on Iron Age and Romano-British landscapes. In A. Gwilt and C. C. Haselgrove (eds.) *Reconstructing Iron Age societies*: 192–204. Oxbow: Oxbow Books.

Thomas, J. (2003). Excavation of an extensive Iron Age settlement at Manor Farm, Humberstone, Leicester. Post excavation assessment and updated project design. University of Leicester Archaeological Services unpublished report 2003–200.

Thomas, T. (1997). Land, kinship relations and the rise of enclosed settlement in first millennium B.C. Britain. *Oxford Journal of Archaeology* 16(2): 211–218.

Wait, G. A. (1985). *Ritual and religion in Iron Age Britain*. Oxford: British Archaeological Report, British Series 149.

Webley, L. (2003). Iron Age houses and social space. A case study of the three-aisled long-houses of northern Europe during the pre-Roman and Early Roman Iron Age. In J. Humphrey *(ed.) Re-searching the Iron Age*: 59–68. Leicester: Leicester Archaeology Monograph 11.

Webley, L. (2007). Using and abandoning roundhouses: a reinterpretation of the evidence from the Late Bronze Age-Early Iron Age Southern England. *Oxford Journal of Archaeology* 26(2): 127–144.

Windell, D. (1981). Great Doddington: an Iron Age enclosure. *Northamptonshire Archaeology* 16: 65–70.

Windell, D. (1984). Clay Lane: Interim Report. *Northamptonshire Archaeology* 18: 33–42.

Williams, J. H. (ed.) (1974). *Two Iron Age sites in Northampton*. Northampton: Northampton Development Corporation Archaeological Monograph 1.

Willis, S. (1997). Settlement, materiality and landscape in the Iron Age of the East Midlands: Evidence, interpretation and wider resonance. In A. Gwilt and C. C. Haselgrove (eds.) *Reconstructing Iron Age societies*: 205– 215. Oxford: Oxbow Books.

Willis, S. (1999). Without and within: aspects of culture and community in the Iron Age of north-eastern England. In B. Bevan (ed.) *Northern Exposure: interpretative devolution and the Iron Ages in Britain*: 81–110. Leicester: Leicester Archaeology Monograph 4.

Willis, S. (2006). The later Bronze and Iron Age. In N. Cooper (ed.) *The Archaeology of the East Midlands. an archaeological resource assessment and research agenda*: 89–136. Leicester Archaeology Monograph 13.

Woodward, A. and G. Hughes (forthcoming). *Deposits and doorways: patterns within the Iron Age settlement at Crick Covert Farm, Northamptonshire*.

## CHAPTER 3

# COMMUNITY – FINDING THE MIDDLE GROUND IN STUDIES OF PREHISTORIC SOCIAL ORGANISATION

### Andy Tullett

*(University of Leicester)*

## Abstract

Community as a term is much-used, if poorly defined, within papers on British prehistory, displaying a variety of more-or-less explicit physical or emotional connotations. This paper looks at sociological and anthropological work on 'community' to see how an unambiguous concern for the fundamental attributes of community can enhance our narratives of life in the Iron Age.

The community is constructed from an individual's interaction within a number of interconnected cross cutting structural groups that creates a shared affinity between participants. Communal identities are in turn central to the creation of individual identities and provide the basis for social practice. In turn it is crucial to biological and social reproduction as well as economic production, making it a fundamental unit of society.

The current ascendant model of Iron Age social organization focuses on the independent household as the primary unit of social analysis. This paper will highlight how this focus on a largely independent unit, inhibits our understanding of a variety of larger-scale social interactions which constituted key aspects of life in the Iron Age. It explores how a landscape approach, mapping activities spatially and functionally, can be used to investigate community through movement and interaction between structural groups. Finally it reviews evidence from the Earliest Iron Age midden sites in the Vale of Pewsey to show how a community framework can be used to create a more nuanced understanding of the historical conditions of life.

# Introduction

Recently J.D. Hill (2006) highlighted the lack of research on Iron Age social organisation over the last 25 years. This paper is partly a response to such concerns as well as the growing use of the term 'community' – although commonly undefined – in current archaeological papers. On a large scale, community is often attributed overriding tenure in the landscape for common resources such as woodland and rough pasture (Hill 1996: 105) and even for land farmed at the household level (Bradley and Yates 2007; Sharples 2007: 175). On a smaller scale authors also link the daily subsistence activities of the household to those of the community (Fleming 1985, Brück 2000: 290). However, although widely cited in works on British prehistory, few authors have attempted to investigate community as a social entity (Andrew Fleming is a notable exception, 1985, 1988, 1989) or establish the scale of activities in which we may recognise intra-communal as opposed to household activities. In other contexts, archaeological studies of community have become increasingly important in, for example, New World archaeology (Kolb and Snead 1997, Canuto and Yaeger 2000) and have started to include European prehistoric archaeology (Knapp 2003; Gerritsen 2003, 2004). Such works consider research on community to be essential to the study of social archaeology (Knapp 2003: 559), primarily because it forms the medium between small biological units and larger social formations (Kolb and Snead 1997: 609). As noted above, for prehistoric Britain we continue to focus on studies of the household (Hill 1996; Brück 1999) and whilst the existence of communities is acknowledged, their impact is largely ignored.

This paper will first explore some of the fundamental features of community, how they may be structured, how they structure the lives of their members and the world in which they exist. It will then review existing models of social organisation for the Iron Age to show how they currently inhibit an understanding of the scales at which the lives of people within prehistory operated. Lastly, it will review how we can investigate community in prehistory and look at a case study based upon the Earliest Iron Age in the Vale of Pewsey.

# Themes in community studies

Sociological and anthropological research has identified a number of themes that are core to the concept of community as a social institution. Interaction, locality, morality, tradition and practice are highly interrelated components that together immerse the individual within a framework of behaviour and identity to create a sense of belonging framed within the idea of the community (Cohen 1982a, 1982b). Due to the constraints of this paper, this will not be an exhaustive study of community, but will dwell on the points that are considered most pertinent to the study of prehistory.

Interaction is fundamental to the creation and maintenance of community and thus in pre-modern societies is inextricably linked to locality. People that share a locality will regularly encounter each other providing the opportunity for interaction and the exchange of knowledge. As a detailed interpersonal knowledge is accrued, complex relationships are able to develop to create shared perceptions of empathy and affinity (Amit 2002: 18). It is important to note that locality alone is insufficient for the creation of community and Appadurai distinguishes between locality, which is considered as primarily relational and contextual, and neighbourhood which represents locality where social relationships are realised (1996: 179). Interaction between individuals is ordered through performance, informed by the customs of that community. Whilst the exchange of information between members allows or maintains affinity, actions are continually judged against the group's customary modes of practice and the community's moral code (Sarup 1994: 103). So individuals may be bound to suppress their individuality and suppress and conceal their actions (Cohen 1978: 450). The moral ethos and community code of practice are rarely expressed as concrete rules but result from the accretion of decisions and value judgements made by the community over a long period of time (Sarup 1994: 103). This does not restrict individuals to a single path of action but defines a range of acceptable practice (Cohen 1978: 468). The modern western mind, obsessed as it is with individuality, might at first sight see this as stifling (Scherer 1972: 5), whilst it in fact it provides the individual with a framework that allows them to interpret the world around them and acts as a reference for action (Delanty 2003: 47).

For patterns of action, material culture and socialised space to be reproduced over time spans exceeding that of generations, a common knowledge must be transmitted over and above that of the individual and household (Goodman 1999: 151). It is the code of practice and behaviour that lies at the heart of what the community is and explains how it reproduces itself socially. Whilst daily and routine actions are performed by individuals, together they are characteristic of a larger social grouping. This does not deny the agency of individuals who may personalise their actions but these actions are only meaningful and natural within the wider context of the community (Bourdieu 1977: 159–171). In part, a customary way of practice evolves from individuals within a community finding a method of action that functions within their social and environmental surroundings. This way of doing things suits them, and whilst the conditions that gave rise to these forms continue there will be little impetus for them to change (Cohen 1982a: 5). This is not to assume that customary practice is inflexible, as already mentioned there will be a range of acceptable performance, but every deviance will be judged. If the deviation is castigated the social norm will be reinforced but if it goes unpunished precedence is set for future transgression and a possible shift of the boundaries of performance (Sarup 1994: 103). It is therefore through practice that the agency of the individual is linked to the structuring of larger social institutions (Barrett 2000). Transgression of the community's customs without ratification will initially cause the individual to be considered 'odd' by their fellows and if social castigation is insufficient to rectify their behaviour they will tend to be ostracised (Tuan 1980: 175).

## Communal structures

Household, neighbourhood, kinship, lineage, knowledge, hereditary status and activity groups are all social institutions that are commonly seen as structuring both the character of individuals and the larger communities that they are part of. They play variable roles in the construction of what may be considered to be a wider community which doubtless exists however difficult it may be to define.

These groups may have an identifiable association with certain locations like a kin group with a certain valley or shepherds with upland pasture, have a particular morality or code of behaviour, and share information through interaction. Each group may also have their own notions of affinity and hence belonging, leading some to see these as types of community. However, unlike a real community these structural groups are not self sufficient entities and so do not meet the full requirements for actual community status (Amit 2002: 18). By self sufficient we are referring to the ability of a group to reproduce itself socially and biologically over several generations. The localities of these structural groups will be encompassed by the territory of the community, whilst specific moralities and behavioural codes fall within the realms of those of the wider community.

An example of such a misinterpretation can be seen in Knapp's work on a Bronze Age mining area on Crete which he envisages as worked by a seasonal mining community (Knapp 2003). This organisation would be better described as a mining activity group whilst his 'real imagined' community would be better described as a community.

The household represents the co-habiting members of a house, although interpretations are usually based around narratives of an extended nuclear family, perhaps with several generations living under the same roof. In general, household sizes fall into a narrow band as even in societies where the family may legally be polygamous at the household scale they tend to be monogamous (Goody 2000: 2). The lifecycle of a family, starting with two adults and growing as children are born and then falling as the children leave or members die, means that the size of the family and hence labour capacity fluctuates. However, the household need not strictly be constructed from the same family as families with 'excess' children may place offspring with certain households where they can learn subsistence skills (Arensberg and Kimball 1940; Rees 1950). These children are usually from related or neighbouring families and the circulation of children in this way has many purposes. It increases the bonds between families (Goodman 1999: 150), balances labour with production and facilitates the circulation of knowledge and skill.

Kinship is usually considered as biological relatedness to certain individuals or families within the community. However, this is an over simplification and kinship also has social and cognitive elements beyond that of basic biology (Cohen 1982b: 28). It has to be acknowledged that societies may only recognise certain degrees of kinship such as cousin after which individuals may be referred to as 'related'. Even in unilateral descent groups, there is always a reckoning of consanguinal ties through both parents (Goody 2000: 2), effectively uniting two kinship groups for that individual. Kinship ties must be kept alive through regular communication, failure to do so can in some cases lead to their relegation to "relatedness". Alternatively, distant relations that are particularly active in communication may be included in an acknowledged kin group. The same may be true for biologically unrelated individuals such as godparents or particularly close family friends who may sometimes be termed fictive kin (Goodman 1999: 150). As such, kinship relations outside of the nuclear family are usually grounded more in acknowledgement than actual biology. Members of kinship groups recognise the interdependent rights and obligations of physical, material and moral support that membership entails. As a result, households tend to look to their kinship groups for assistance, as a first line of recourse in times of trouble. Kin groups therefore form the primary medium for insurance policies as to subsistence and development. Lineage is closely related to kinship and relates the individual to past relations rather than present kin. The skills and characteristics of forebears are often considered to be inherited by, or at least claimed by later generations and in many communities these traits are usually thought more important in establishing a genealogical link than biological associations (Cohen 1982b: 46). Lineage is primarily concerned with the inheritance of status or property from a forebear as in some societies customs exist that prevent the alienation of property, such as land, outside of the kin group (Goody 2000: 48).

Neighbourhood is the result of locality and regular actualised social involvement between nearby households. Because of their proximity, households in neighbourhood groups are ideally placed for the pooling of labour and resources for economic purposes that are beyond the ability of the individual household (Fleming 1985: 132). As neighbourhood groups are based upon proximity, each household will be the centre of their own neighbourhood group. This means that they will in turn be members of neighbourhood groups based upon other households leading to the creation of a polythetic system of overlapping groups (Rees 1968: 94; Fleming 1985: 132). For children leaving their family's household it is desirable to establish their own houses near to the family domicile, so that active communication and assistance can be maintained (Cohen 1982b: 30; Fleming 1985: 132). The result is that neighbourhoods usually contain a high degree of kin and relations, although this is not always exclusively so (Cohen 1982b: 29). As with kinship, neighbourhood groups commonly have an ideological element that entails rights and obligations of assistance and usually form the second source from which a household will seek assistance from in times of trouble.

Knowledge groups are generally limited to certain members of the community who have specialist knowledge in certain activities such as metalworking, medicine or religion. Here the bond between members is not so much in shared activity or even a physical relationship but in actual knowledge that separates them from the remainder of the community and they may indeed be very different and in fact hard to integrate in any way within a wider community. By definition they may be outsiders to the main body of the community, as for example is commonly the case with various craft-castes in Africa (D. Edwards pers. comm.). Entry into such groups is usually the result of a long process of initiation or apprenticeship and may be limited to certain age, gender or kin groups. The elderly may also form such a group in societies that value the knowledge that these individuals have collected over many years (Chadwick 2004: 236). Their importance is usually connected to judgements on inheritance claims, land disputes and other areas concerning lineage, oral tradition and lore.

Status groups refer to hereditary elites and class systems and are closely associated with kinship and lineage. Where inheritance of status occurs it is usually inferred that the abilities by which this group is differentiated, such as leadership, are themselves also inherited. Such a structural group need not exist in every community as in some societies leaders may emerge through their own abilities and in such cases status is achieved rather than ascriptive (Bell and Newby 1971: 24). In these cases they are elevated from activity or knowledge groups because of the abilities that they have displayed in certain roles and their position is likely to be passed on to the next worthiest member rather than an heir. Leadership roles are different to status groups and though they may exist or emerge they may not be inheritable. Most societies will have leadership positions though these may be activity based roles which can lead to changes in status and power throughout the year as emphasis shifts with the turn of the agricultural cycle (Galaty and Johnson 1990: 24; Netting 1974: 29).

Activity groups consist of individuals that come together to undertake certain tasks and achieve certain defined goals (Bell and Newby 1971: 36). These range from full time employment to seasonal events such as fruit picking or sheep shearing. As such, factors that affect the profiles of these groups include the duration, regularity, location, risks, rewards and separation of the tasks (Brück 2007: 31). These groups typically involve the greatest variability in terms of mobility, seasonality and age/gender divisions of any of the structural groups within a community (Chadwick 2004: 202). This variation in distances travelled, locations visited and timing of the visits would lead to distinctly different experiences of the landscape and community that would only be exacerbated by age and gender differences (Brück and Goodman 1999: 12). The variability in these factors would also have shaped the people that they met across the community and the degree of contact and hence ties that were formed.

From this, we can see that a community will be constructed from many smaller structural groups all of which will have demands on the individual that are sometimes in conflict. Individuals will be aware of their membership of these different groups and their continued membership of the wider community depends on acceptance of the norms of behaviour which are demanded by the band of the community's moral ethos (Bell and Newby 1971: 24; Cohen 1982b: 33). This code will in turn provide individuals with guidance on priorities in inter-group interaction. In essence the community's moral code mediates the plurality of group membership which in turn mediates their experience of the community (Cohen 1982a: 16). The structural associations will also necessarily shape their identity and how other people view and interact with them (Cohen 1978: 454). They are often imparted with the characteristics that are publicly attributed to these groups and so the individual is treated as the product of their social structural associations (Cohen 1982b: 24).

Archaeologists have been good at identifying some of these structural groups but have usually failed to trace their intersections and how plural membership is reflected by the manipulation of the space in which they operate and the material culture that is used. It is impossible to contemplate these manifestations and intersections whilst Iron Age studies remain focused on households and individual settlements. Archaeology therefore has to be studied at the appropriate scale, that of the community, to appreciate these dimensions of society.

## Identity, the individual and community

The characteristics of a community will be defined by a range of factors such as the interaction of its component social groups, the identities of its members, its moral code, history, subsistence patterns, landscape and interaction with neighbouring communities. Whatever the particular qualities that characterise a certain community, the group itself may not be overtly conscious of them as they are intimately tied into the daily conduct of the members' lives. It is only when a community is confronted by another community with different values or characteristics that they become conscious of their own identity (Cohen 2002: 167). This process includes an act of assessment where they make value judgements between the relative qualities of each community and in turn to a reassessment as to what is the essence of their community (Cohen 1982a: 5). The identity that the community then projects will be a simplification of the actual character experienced by its members (Cohen 1982a: 8). The core values may be projected as part of this identity, but in order to maintain uniqueness they may project characteristics that are considered exclusive. Therefore a communal identity is never a simple recognition of its members' cultural similarity but is constructed around concepts of exclusion and otherness (Gupta and Ferguson 1997: 13).

Identity is constructed through a process of interaction between people, institutions, places and practices (Sarup 1994: 102). The community being the core of these provides the individual with a source of identity and a frame of reference (Cohen 1985: 118; Yaeger 2000: 124). Identity is intimately linked to performance and is a self reflexive process where actions and their outcomes are constantly assessed (Giles 2007: 105). It is therefore highly contextual with temporal consequences (*ibid.*). But we should remember that the individual does not view themselves as a set of characteristics but as a unique entity composed and confronted by elements peculiar to them which provide them with their behavioural terms of reference (Cohen 1978: 450). A person's identity is shaped by their structural associations such as kinship, neighbourhood and activity groups with the ensuing differential experiences of landscape, interaction and performance that membership entails (Gerritsen 2004: 147). Their individuality will therefore be recognised and legitimised within strict limits according to the community's core values and will be explained with reference to their structural associations (Cohen 1982b: 24). The individuals will be credited with certain characteristics or attributes based upon these social associations, often regardless of their actual abilities. This will increase the uniqueness of their identity within the community but it may appear unfaithful to the individual's personal perception (Cohen 1978: 453). The community therefore strives to preserve the impression of the individuality of its members, yet as these identities are reflective of the community's idealised core values, it sustains its own collective identity whilst subordinating that of its members to it (*ibid.*: 455).

# An archaeological definition of community

Marx rightly stated that 'a community has no actual existence except in the assembly of its members' (1979: 98) and this lack of quantitative substance has resulted in continual problems over definition. In 1955 Hillery reviewed the 94 definitions that had been forwarded for community at that time, finding that the only common ground to be found was that they all involved people (1955). There was however general if not unanimous consensus that community concerned social interaction, had a connection with specific areas of land and involved common ties between its members (*ibid.*). In particular, Arensberg put forward a definition of community as a minimal territorially based aggregate, which is able to maintain itself and reproduce its key cultural traits over time (cited by Lipe 1970: 86). Later work no longer considered community as a bounded entity but as an overlapping and cross cutting network of social interaction (Gerritsen 2004: 141). That is, a series of dynamic processes that draw people together into a system of belonging rather than something that can be physical identified and counted. If we return to Hillery's work we can see that most consensus was reached over social interaction within certain areas of land that led to common ties developing between its members. Retaining a spatial dimension is therefore important even if community can no longer be seen as a bounded institution with members of different communities sharing affiliations, albeit unequally, with members of more than one community due to their structural associations. The suggestion made by Arensberg that communities need to be able to reproduce themselves socially and biologically over generations means that they need to be self sufficient entities even if in practice they are not isolated from wider realms of interaction.

From this, we can see that community is the product of its parts. It is a social institution made up of many different structural groups for whom it is a source of identity and referent to behaviour. It is situated within a territory that satisfies the economic requirements of its structural groups whose interaction reproduces the community socially and biologically. The self sufficiency of the community does not always entail that it acts in isolation from the communities that surround it, but that it has the ability to reproduce itself over time without wider interaction if required to do so. Having defined what community is, its key themes and how it may be structured we should compare these ideas with those of the dominant social model for the British Iron Age.

# Iron Age communities in southern Britain

The study of social organisation in later prehistory for southern Britain is dominated by two leading strains of thought. Those that look at society organized through concepts of power and domination (Rowlands 1980; Cunliffe 1984) or those that focus on households and independence (Hill 1995, 1996; Brück 1999). It is fair to say that over the last ten years that the latter have held the most sway and that the study of independent households is currently the ascendant model.

During the mid 1990's Hill laid out a theory that was juxtaposed to Cunliffe's highly ranked societies. Hill's model, is of a society based upon locality rather than kinship with the result that it is only held together through weak social bonds (1995: 51). The consequence of this weak kinship system is an absence of strict rules governing marriage alliances preventing the success of certain lineages over generations (*ibid.*: 52) none of which are visible archaeologically. In this model the household is a largely independent social unit that controls its own land and resources and hence its own relations of production (Hill 1996: 105). This independence is physically stated through the enclosure of the settlement, creating a barrier between the household and other households (Hill 1995: 51). Whilst communal resources such as water meadows are acknowledged as necessary these are considered almost superfluous to the needs of the household, the icing on the cake of the household's subsistence needs (1995: 51). However the requirement for social and biological reproduction means that households can never be wholly independent and as a result Hill acknowledges that independence may have been more of a desire than the reality of the situation (Hill 1995: 51; 1996: 105). The requirement for biological and social reproduction is solved through periodic communal assemblies at locations such as hillforts (Hill 1996: 105). The result of Hill's model has been to focus enquiry around the household/settlement and inter-household interaction limited to hillforts.

More recently Hill has modified this model slightly to produce a more community friendly picture but one very much still focused on the household (2006). Hill acknowledges community as a network of interaction between different groups that construct it as a social institution although at one point he does note that the inter-related component groups and the contradictions that these caused could mean that 'no single fundamental social unit ever existed' (*ibid.*: 174). It is therefore perhaps ironic that he later suggests that the community may have had a strong ideological emphasis on the group rather than the individual to prevent social/political inequality (*ibid.*: 176). Kinship is also given more weight but marriage patterns again prevent the creation of powerful lineages (*ibid.*: 173–4). It would be fair to say that, Hill's 2006 paper is still obsessed with refuting Cunliffe's model and is structured around the denial of social elites or status groups and providing a social framework for the current trend in settlement archaeology. Current evidence does appear to suggest the absence of elites in southern Britain during the Early and Middle

Iron Ages but does Hill's model of society based upon the household stand up to what we know of community?

## 'What if?'

- What if households did not control their own means of production?
- What if households were happy to belong to wider communities?
- What if community provides a more useful level of analysis than the household?
- What if we are studying social organisation during the Iron Age at the wrong scale?

The household is poorly suited to the mixed agricultural regime that is suggested for most settlements in this region/period because of its lifecycle. This mismatch between household labour supply and demands of subsistence means that the household at certain points will need assistance from their neighbours. To receive assistance a household must be prepared to offer assistance, tying it into a web of reciprocal obligations that in turn, over time, locks them into relationships emotionally (Glasser 1977: 67). In essence households may initially help each other because of the economic reality of their situation, but this creates bonds that means after a while they help because they want to. Whether assistance is lent for economic or emotional reasons, it is fundamentally in the interests of households to be willing participants in the community and in reality it is difficult to find any society in which households do in fact act as independent agents.

Hill's theories work on the basis that the household forms the fundamental unit of prehistoric society and that these were the people that created, lived and structured the world within the domain of their small settlement. This takes a very basic view of the household (compare with Goodman 1999) considering, as it does, households as unitary isolates without the structuring implications of wider social contact and landscape. It is appropriate to study sites of all sorts in terms of the people who structured their lives at these locations. As we have seen, biological and social reproduction are dependent on the communities beyond the household/close familial unit and factors such as the household lifecycle and the agricultural cycle mean that individual households are very unlikely if ever able to support themselves economically throughout the entirety of their lives. The household therefore cannot form the fundamental unit of society, for which, a larger community that varies in constitution/makeup in every historical context is much better suited.

To date, the study of insular households does not tend to investigate the interaction between households, nor wider symbolic systems which extend across broad geographical and temporal areas. Neither does it take into account the broader implications of these wider contacts upon household organisation and hence settlement structure. The result is that continuing to study the Iron Age using a model based on households fails to establish wider social contexts or indeed how societies functioned within landscapes as a whole.

## Investigating Iron Age communities

One of the main problems when looking at communities in the archaeological record is that we are trying to study a social concept or entity with no physical existence using the material traces that were left behind (Knapp 2003: 570). As has been seen, it is hard to impose fixed definitions, as a community is defined by its own historical existence, as a contextual/situational construct. A community consists of networks of relationships between individuals and their structural groups that vary spatially and so create spatial cultures based upon regional networks of interaction. They create material culture and shape the landscape around them and these things in turn feed back into the core social code of the community. The result is that these relationships can be revealed in the way that space is structured and material culture is manipulated (Cheney 1992: 40).

Scale appears to be the principle entry point to identifying communities archaeologically. By scale I am referring to phenomena which are too large to have been purely created by a single household. Most obviously this suggests large sites or features, most obviously on the scale of hillforts but also includes geographically and temporally dispersed phenomena. The manifestations of larger scale activities and larger activity scales would be exemplified by the recurrence of a specific artefact type, practice or feature over a large geographical area during the same period or temporally over a period exceeding that of several generations.

In past archaeological studies, the 'site' has become the standard unit of study and its inhabitants equated with communities even though the fit between these is at best dubious (Kolb and Snead 1997: 612). Inevitably communities utilise space beyond the boundaries of sites as currently defined (Neustupný 1998). Sites should not be studied in isolation but with reference to the surrounding landscape and seen as elements that define the inhabitants' relationship within the broader structure of the community (van Dommelen *et al.* 2005: 58). Recent landscape studies such as the Danebury Environs Programme (Cunliffe 2000), Wessex Linear Ditches Project (Bradley *et al.* 1994) and Hillforts of the Ridgeway Project (Miles *et al.* 2004) have helped to redress the landscape-scale that we study but have still perhaps failed to explore the full consequences of their findings for community. To do this, I would suggest, that we must investigate all the activities that structured the landscape and provided a sense of community however intangible these may be, from subsistence practices, movement and seasonality to domestic activities and the burial record (Gerritsen 2004: 147). To do so it is important to define the chronology, range of activities that were undertaken at sites, how space was structured and how they related spatially and functionally to other sites in the area, crucially to work at a wider landscape scale. From this we can start to see how activities were distributed across the landscape to uncover patterns of movement and interaction. Defining these relationships we can start to draw out the internal organisation of the community, the experiences of its members and ultimately the meaning that they bestowed upon locations in the landscape (Knapp 2003: 566).

A further opportunity to investigate community is presented through the study of material culture and its roles in the creation or maintenance of identity. In his ethnographic study, Hodder noted that material culture is often used symbolically to represent the identity of communities and/or structural groups (1982). Certain aspects of material culture may be overtly manipulated as a construct of identity, as a symbol of inclusion or of opposition, and in turn may point to underlying tensions such as a plurality of group membership. For instance, Barber highlights the example of the Maa speaking pastoralists of East Africa where the form of spearheads is used to communicate age grades and hence, economic and social status (Barber 2003: 144). Archaeologically speaking, there are a number of issues that we must remain aware of when dealing with material culture. It can be difficult to define the group that is manipulating a certain type of artefact and why they are doing so. Hypothetically, a number of distinct communities may use similar artefacts such as ceramics to denote a loose confederation between them. Alternatively a symbol may only be overtly used by a particular structural group within the community. The use and symbolic manipulation of material culture is therefore highly complex. As a result we must be careful not to confuse a distribution plot of artefact types or ceramic forms with the territory of a community.

# The Vale of Pewsey

In this final section I will look briefly at a case study based in Wiltshire to show how a community based approach to social organisation can help provide a better understanding of Iron Age life. The Vale of Pewsey is a valley situated between the chalk downlands of Salisbury Plain and the Marlborough Downs. Over the last 25 years a series of large midden deposits have been excavated in and around the Vale, at Potterne (Lawson 2000), East Chisenbury (McOmish 1996), All Cannings Cross and Stanton St. Bernard whilst further potential middens have been identified at several other locations in and around the Vale of Pewsey such as Bishops Cannings Down, Erlestoke, Steeple Ashton, Blackpatch and Westbury (McOmish 1996).

These sites are characterised by a black earth deposit that reaches up to 2m in depth and covers several hectares. The Early All Cannings Cross wares that form a major component of the middens, dates them firmly to the Earliest Iron Age, though the midden at Potterne appears to have formed on a Late Bronze Age soil containing Plain wares (Needham 2007: 55). The site at East Chisenbury is particularly interesting as it appears to have formed over as little as 100 years (Brown *et al.* forthcoming). Artefacts from these sites all suggest that a number of craft activities were taking place at them. All have turned up artefacts connected with spinning, weaving and metal working in greater quantities than their neighbouring, slightly later but longer lived settlements (Brück 2007: 31). For instance 58 spindle whorls were recovered from All Cannings Cross and 62 from Potterne compared to 19 from Swallowcliffe Down, 11 from Little Woodbury, 17 from Gussage All Saints, 59 from Maiden Castle and 18 from Danebury phase 1–6 (Marchant 1989). This is merely one form of craftwork but goes some way to showing the quantity of material within the middens and potentially a comparison between the volumes of craftwork undertaken there.

The Early All Cannings Cross wares are a dramatic change from earlier Plain wares, with more decoration and new forms such as bowls and cups. The development in forms and decoration is usually considered to be synchronous with an increase in the emphasis on the preparation and service of food (Barrett 1989: 312). The midden assemblages vary from standard assemblages of the Earliest Iron Age in the number of vessels with perforated bases which are considered rare until the Late Iron Age (Gingell and Morris 2000: 153). It is thought that these acted as strainers and relate to a specialized aspect of food processing (ibid.). In this instance these vessels would be well adapted to straining the curd for cheese production. Fabric analysis at Potterne suggests that some ceramics were being brought to the site from some distance away (Morris 2000: 166) a situation that was mirrored at All Cannings Cross (Cunnington 1923: 29–30).

Extrapolations of animal bone data from East Chisenbury suggest that over the course of a century 3,800 sheep/goats, 600 cows and 450 pigs could have been slaughtered annually, supporting a possible full time population of up to 2000 over a 100 year period (Serjeantson *et al.* forthcoming). The numbers of animals slaughtered annually at these sites implies truly massive, possibly communal, herds to support such a large kill off. Sheep dominate all the assemblages with 60% at East Chisenbury (Serjeantson *et al.* forthcoming) and 65% at Stanton St. Bernard (Tullett and Harrison 2008). Comparison of sheep mandible wear stages (per Payne 1973) for these sites show a high degree of seasonality with 30.2% at stage B (2–6 months) at East Chisenbury (Serjeantson *et al.* forthcoming) and 25% at stage B and 30% at stage C (6–12 months) at Stanton St. Bernard (Tullett and Harrison 2008). Both of these schemes compares well with Payne's hypothetical model for a meat and dairy regime for sheep (1973). Analysis of animal lipid residues from prehistoric pottery has highlighted the importance of processed dairy products in agricultural regimes and of the vessels investigated from Potterne that contained lipids, 60% related to processed ruminant dairy fats (Copley *et al.* 2005: 900).

The main characteristic of the deposit is its dark earth component. Micromorphological and micro-chemical investigation of this deposit at Potterne and East Chisenbury, suggests that it consisted primarily of burnt and partially decomposed herbivore stabling residues (Macphail 2000: 70; forthcoming). This suggests that the dominant activity taking place at middens was concerned with animal management. Serjeantson has suggested that this build up of byre material reflects an intensive animal management programme where animals are brought into the settlement area for milking (Serjeantson 2007: 89). Whilst pits, chalk platforms and post holes have been identified within the middens suggesting that some structures were set within the middens there does not appear to be the quantity of structures that would be required to house the populations suggested by the animal bone data. The implication is that substantial villages existed besides the middens that have eluded our attention as archaeological focus has been attracted to the artefact rich midden deposits.

Looking at the surrounding landscape, linear earthworks were being constructed across the downs to the north and south of the Vale of Pewsey towards the end of the Late Bronze Age. In some cases these are constructed across earlier Middle Bronze Age field systems and it is apparent that they represent a reorganisation of the landscape both in terms of how it was perceived and functioned. The creation of this system, along with the evidence of field systems being abandoned around this time on the Marlborough Downs (Gingell 1992: 158) has been linked with a trend towards pastoralism on the downs as well as territorial and/or tenurial divisions (McOmish *et al.* 2002: 64; Cunliffe 2004). At certain nodal points in this system, early hilltop enclosures were constructed. These rarely show much settlement activity and the fact that they are so closely associated with linear earthworks suggests that both were part of an integrated system of stock management (Cunliffe 2004: 75). The early hilltop enclosure at Martinsell, itself near to a potential midden, was laid out with a linear earthwork forming its northern boundary (Cunliffe 2004: 72), whilst the East Chisenbury midden was deposited within an enclosure that is the focus of six linear earthworks (McOmish *et al.* 2002: 58). Rybury hillfort which overlooks All Cannings Cross and Stanton St. Bernard is another potential early hilltop enclosure.

In terms of scale these deposits are far too large to have been laid down by a single household. The amount of land and labour required to raise herds of this size would also preclude them from belonging to a single household. Whilst it appears that there was a fulltime population at the sites involved in a dairy regime, seasonality in the assemblages suggests that they were augmented at certain points in the agricultural calendar. In view of the pastoral evidence the most likely source of these visitors is from the downs where they were utilising the linear earthwork system to rear the large flocks of sheep. Management of these huge flocks would in turn create a large demand on labour at times such as lambing or fleecing, labour that could only be met by a concentration of the community. The middens therefore appear to represent the activities of a number of activity groups associated with different areas of the agricultural regime. On one side you have those resident around the midden whose dairying activities led to the large build-up of dung. On the other were groups that visited seasonally and could be linked to pastoral activities either with visiting herds or to help with an annual shearing. Ethnographically such activity groups tend to be drawn along age and gender lines (Brück 2007: 32) implying that when they were dispersed there was a dramatic fragmentation of these communities that was sometimes at conflict with their membership of other structural groups such as the household. The demands of the agricultural regime would therefore draw these disparate elements back together at the middens. These congregations would be a time of reunion with tensions over plurality of structural group membership reaching resolution. They provided the opportunity to share food and drink, news, stories and jokes with family and other members of the community from whom they had perhaps been separated for months. Also as site with a focus of craftwork they fulfilled a major role in the sharing of knowledge and expertise associated with these activities and thus the social reproduction of the community.

The Vale of Pewsey is worthy of an environs programme similar to those undertaken for some hillforts, that would allow us to develop a broad understanding of the intricacies of communities throughout the area and hence how peoples' lives were structured, at scales far beyond the individual household. That said, from the limited excavations that have taken place, we are able to make some observations. Like Hill's (1995) suggestion for hillforts, the midden sites were symbolic of community. Here however, the idea of communities may have been particularly framed around certain forms of subsistence with its own rhythms of activities, organization and practice and by implication one which may have been limited to certain parts of the country. This model with an integrated subsistence economy and social life, where different members of the community worked together on a regular basis, is far from Hill's model of highly independent households. Although the middens may have formed the forum for 'rituals that cross cut households' and ultimately the social reproduction of the community, it appears likely that the congregations were driven by the agricultural practicalities and demands of a community working together and the tensions that these involved.

## Conclusion

Although community is constructed from many cross cutting structural groups, it is the minimum self sufficient social unit and is therefore a fundamental though hard to define social institution. For the individual it is essential to concepts of practice, the creation of identity, and forms the basis for interpreting the world around them. Households are fragile and short-lived with culture transmitted and reproduced through the medium of the community thus it is more fitting that this is the scale at which we investigate prehistoric societies. Current models of social organisation, dominated by attempts to confirm or deny the existence of social elites, draw our attention away from areas of study that are equally if not more worthwhile. They fail to address some of the key themes of what it is to be human and inhibit our ability to understand the reproduction of society over generations. Community can be best understood by looking at evidence on a landscape scale but is not dependent upon new large scale environs type projects. For most areas of Britain there is a large body of published data which is being augmented by developer funded work. Together we have an ample body of data through which we can trace the possible networks and linkages that constituted communities.

## Acknowledgements

I would like to thank Prof. Colin Haselgrove and Dr. L. MacFadyen whose supervision has provided valuable insight during my PhD; Dr. David Edwards for his excellent comments on this paper; Prof. John Barrett and David McOmish for providing access to the Vale of Pewsey archives and to the Arts and Humanities Research Council who have funded my research.

## Bibliography

Amit, V. (2002). Reconceptualizing community. In V. Amit (ed.) *Realizing Community: concepts, social relationships and sentiments*: 1–20. London: Routledge.

Appadurai, A. (1996). *Modernity at large. Cultural dimensions of globalisation*. Minneapolis: University of Minnesota Press.

Arensberg, C. and S. Kimball (1940). *Family and Community in Ireland*. Cambridge, MA: Harvard University Press.

Barber, M. (2003). *Bronze and the Bronze Age: metalwork and society in Britain c. 2500–800 BC*. Stroud: Tempus.

Barrett, J. C. (1989). Food, gender and metal: questions of social reproduction. In M. L. S. Sorensen and R. Thomas (eds.) *The Bronze Age – Iron Age transition in Europe*: 304–320. Oxford: British Archaeological Reports, International Series 483.

Barrett, J. C. (2000). A thesis on agency. In M-A. Dobres and J. Robb (eds.) *Agency in Archaeology*: 61–68. London: Routledge.

Bell, C. and Newby, H. (1971). *Community Studies: an introduction to the sociology of the local community*. London: George Allen and Unwin Ltd.

Bourdieu, P. (1977). *Outline of a Theory of Practice*. Cambridge: Cambridge University Press.

Bradley, R., R. Entwistle and F. Raymond (1994). *Prehistoric Land Divisions on Salisbury Plain: the work of the Wessex Linear Ditches Project*. London: English Heritage.

Bradley, R. and D. Yates (2007). After 'Celtic' fields: The social organisation of Iron Age agriculture. In C. C. Haselgrove and R. E. Pope (eds.) *The Earlier Iron Age in Britain and the Near Continent*: 94–102. Oxford: Oxbow Books.

Brown, G., D. Field and D. McOmish (forthcoming). *The Late Bronze Age – Early Iron Age site at East Chisenbury, Wiltshire*.

Brück, J. (1999). Houses, lifecycles and deposition on Middle Bronze Age settlements in southern England. *Proceedings of the Prehistoric Society* 65: 145–166.

Brück, J. (2000). Settlement, landscape and social identity: the Early-Middle Bronze Age transition in Wessex, Sussex and the Thames Valley. *Oxford Journal of Archaeology* 19(3): 273–300.

Brück, J. (2007). The character of Late Bronze Age settlement in southern Britain. In C. C. Haselgrove and R. E. Pope (eds.) *The Earlier Iron Age in Britain and the Near Continent*: 24–38. Oxford: Oxbow Books.

Brück, J. and M. Goodman (1999). Introduction: themes for a critical archaeology of prehistoric settlement. In J. Brück and M. Goodman (eds.) *Making Places in the Prehistoric World: themes in settlement archaeology*: 1–19. London: UCL Press.

Canuto, M. A. and J. Yaeger (eds.) (2000). *The Archaeology of Communities: a New World Perspective*. London: Routledge.

Chadwick, A. M. (2004). Footprints in the sands of time. Archaeologies of inhabitation on Cranbourne Chase, Dorset. In A. M. Chadwick (ed.) *Stories from the Landscape: archaeologies of inhabitation*: 179–256. Oxford: British Archaeological Reports, International Series 1238.

Cheney, S. L. (1992). Uncertain migrants: the history and archaeology of a Victorian Goldfield Community. *Australasian Historical Archaeology* 10: 36–42.

Cohen, A. P. (1978). 'The Same – But Different': the allocation of identity in Whalsay, Shetland. *The Sociological Review* 26: 449–469.

Cohen, A. P. (1982a). Belonging: the experience of culture. In A. P. Cohen (ed.) *Belonging: identity and social organisation in British rural cultures*: 1–17. Manchester: Manchester University Press.

Cohen, A. P. (1982b). A sense of time, a sense of place: the meaning of close social association in Whalsay, Shetland. In A. P. Cohen (ed.) *Belonging: identity and social organisation in British rural cultures*: 21–49. Manchester: Manchester University Press.

Cohen, A. P. (1985). *The Symbolic Construction of Community*. London: Tavistock Publications.

Cohen, A. P. (2002). Epilogue. In V. Amit (ed.) *Realizing Community: concepts, social relationships and sentiments*: 165–70. London: Routledge.

Copley, M. S., R. Berstan, S. N. Dudd, S. Aillaud, A. J. Mukherjee, V. Straker, S. Payne and R. P. Evershed (2005). Processing of milk products in pottery vessels through British prehistory. *Antiquity* 79: 895–908.

Cunliffe, B. (1984). Iron Age Wessex: continuity and change. In B. Cunliffe and D. Miles (eds.) *Aspects of the Iron Age in Central Southern Britain*: 12–45. Oxford: Oxford University Committee for Archaeology.

Cunliffe, B. (2000). *The Danebury Environs Programme: the prehistory of a Wessex landscape, volume 1 introduction*. Oxford: English Heritage/Oxford University Committee for Archaeology Monograph 48.

Cunliffe, B. (2004). Wessex Cowboys? *Oxford Journal of Archaeology* 23(1): 61–81.

Cunnington, M. (1923). *The Early Iron Age Inhabited Site at All Cannings Cross Farm, Wiltshire*. Devizes: George Simpson and Co.

Delanty, G. (2003). *Community*. London: Routledge.

Fleming, A. (1985). Land tenure, productivity, and field systems. In G. Barker and C. Gamble (eds.) *Beyond Domestication in Prehistoric Europe: investigations in subsistence archaeology and social complexity*: 129–146. London: Academic Press.

Fleming, A. (1988). *The Dartmoor Reaves: investigating prehistoric land divisions*. London: Batsford.

Fleming, A. (1989). Coaxial field systems in later British prehistory. In H.A. Nordström and A. Knape (eds.) *Bronze Age Studies: transactions of the British-Scandinavian colloquim in Stockholm, May 10–11, 1985*: 151–162. Stockholm: Statens Historika Museum.

Galaty, J. G. and D. L. Johnson (1990). Introduction: Pastoral Systems in Global Perspective. In Galaty, J. G. and D. L. Johnson (eds.) *The world of pastoralism: herding systems in comparative perspective*: 1–31. London: Belhaven Press.

Gerritsen, F. (2003). *Local Identities: landscape and community in the Late Prehistoric Meuse-Demer-Scheldt Region*. Amsterdam: Amsterdam University Press.

Gerritsen, F. (2004). Archaeological perspectives on local communities. In J. Bintliff (ed.) *A Companion to Archaeology*: 141–154. Oxford: Blackwell.

Giles, M. (2007). Refiguring rights in the Early Iron Age landscapes of East Yorkshire. In C. C. Haselgrove and R. E. Pope (eds.) *The Earlier Iron Age in Britain and the Near Continent*: 103–118. Oxford: Oxbow Books.

Gingell, C. J. and E. L. Morris (2000). Form series, section 6 – the artefacts. In A. J. Lawson, *Potterne 1982–5: animal husbandry in later prehistoric Wiltshire*: 149–53. Salisbury: Trust for Wessex Archaeology. Wessex Archaeology Report 17.

Gingell, C. (1992). *The Marlborough Downs: a Later Bronze Age landscape and its origins*. Devizes: Wiltshire Archaeological and Natural History Society Monograph 1

Glasser, R. (1977). *The Net and the Quest: patterns of community and how they survive progress*. London: Temple Smith

Goodman, M. (1999). Temporalities of prehistoric life: household development and community continuity. In J. Brück and M. Goodman (eds.) *Making Places in the Prehistoric World: themes in settlement archaeology*: 145–159. London: UCL Press.

Goody, J. (2000). *The European Family: an historico-anthropological essay*. Oxford: Blackwell.

Gupta, A. and J. Ferguson (1997). Beyond 'culture': space, identity, and the politics of difference. In A. Gupta and J. Ferguson (eds.) *Culture, Power, Place: explorations in critical anthropology*: 33–51. Durham, North Carolina: Duke University Press.

Hill, J. D. (1995). How should we understand Iron Age societies and hillforts? A contextual study from southern Britain. In J. D. Hill and C. G. Cumberpatch (eds.) *Different Iron Ages: studies on the Iron Age in temperate Europe*: 45–66. Oxford: British Archaeological Reports, International Series 602.

Hill, J. D. (1996). Hill-forts and the Iron Age of Wessex. In T. C. Champion and J. R. Collis (eds.) *The Iron Age in Britain and Ireland: Recent Trends*: 95–116. Sheffield: J. R. Collis Publications.

Hill, J. D. (2006). Are we any closer to understanding how later Iron Age societies worked (or did not work)? In C. C. Haselgrove (ed.) *Celtes et Gaulois L'Archaéologie face à l'Histoire: les mutations de la fin de l'âge du Fer*: 169–179. Glux-en-Glenne : Bibracte, Centre archéologique européen, 12/4.

Hillery, G. A. (1955). Definitions of community: areas of agreement. *Rural Sociology* 20: 111–123.

Hodder, I. (1982). *Symbols in Action: ethnoarchaeological studies of material culture*. Cambridge: Cambridge University Press.

Knapp, A. B. (2003). The archaeology of community on Bronze Age Cyprus: Politiko Phorades in context. *American Journal of Archaeology* 107: 559–580.

Kolb, M. J. and Snead, J. E. (1997). It's a small world after all: comparative analyses of community organisation in archaeology. *American Antiquity* 62(4): 609–628.

Lawson, A. J. (2000). *Potterne 1982–5: animal husbandry in later prehistoric Wiltshire*. Salisbury: Trust for Wessex Archaeology. Wessex Archaeology Report 17.

Lipe, W. D. (1970). Anasazi communities in the Red Rock Plateau, southeastern Utah. In W. A. Longacre (ed.) *Reconstructing Prehistoric Pueblo Societies*: 84–139. Albuquerque: School of American Research, University of New Mexico Press.

Macphail, R. I. (forthcoming). A brief assessment of the soil micromorphology. In G. Brown, D. Field and D. McOmish (eds.) *The Late Bronze Age – Early Iron Age site at East Chisenbury, Wiltshire*.

Macphail, R. I. (2000). Soils and microstratigraphy: a soil micromorphological and microchemical approach. In A. J. Lawson, *Potterne 1982–5: animal husbandry in later prehistoric Wiltshire*: 47–71. Salisbury: Trust for Wessex Archaeology. Wessex Archaeology Report 17.

Marchant, T. (1989). The evidence for textile production in the Iron Age. *Scottish Archaeological Review* 6: 5–12.

Marx, K. (1979). Economic Manuscripts of 1857–1859. In K. Marx and F. Engels, *Pre-Capitalist Socio-Economic Formations*: 83–135. Progress Publishers: Moscow.

McOmish, D. (1996). East Chisenbury: ritual and rubbish at the British Bronze Age – Iron Age transition. *Antiquity* 70: 68–76.

McOmish, D., D. Field, and G. Brown (2002). *The Field Archaeology of the Salisbury Plain Training Area*. English Heritage: Swindon.

Miles, D., S. Palmer, G. Lock, C. Gosden and A. Cromarty (2004). *Uffington White Horse and its Landscape: investigations at White Horse Hill, Uffington, 1989–95 and Tower Hill, Ashbury, 1993–94*. Oxford: Thames Valley Landscapes Monograph 18.

Morris, E. L. (2000). Pottery – summary. In A. J. Lawson, *Potterne 1982–5: animal husbandry in later prehistoric Wiltshire*: 166–177. Salisbury: Trust for Wessex Archaeology. Wessex Archaeology Report 17.

Needham, S. (2007). 800 BC, The Great Divide. In C. C. Haselgrove and R. E. Pope (eds.) *The Earlier Iron Age in Britain and the Near Continent*: 39–63. Oxford: Oxbow Books.

Netting, R. M. (1974). Agrarian Ecology. *Annual Review of Anthropology* 3: 21–56.

Neustupný, E. (1998). The transformation of community areas into settlement areas. In E. Neustupný (ed.) *Space in Prehistoric Bohemia*: 45–61. Prague: Institute of Archaeology, Academy of Sciences of the Czech Republic.

Payne, S. (1973). Kill-off patterns in sheep and goats: the mandibles from Asvan Kale, *Anatolian Studies* 23: 281–303.

Rees, A. D. (1950). *Life in a Welsh Countryside: a social study of Llanfihangel yng Ngwynfa*. Cardiff: University of Wales Press.

Rees, A. D. (1968). *Celtic heritage: ancient tradition in Ireland and Wales*. London: Thames and Hudson.

Rowlands, M. J. (1980). Kinship, alliance and exchange in the European Bronze Age. In J. C. Barrett and R. Bradley (eds.) *The British Later Bronze Age*: 15–55. Oxford: British Archaeological Report, British Series 83i.

Sarup, M. (1994). Home and identity. In G. Robertson, M. Mash, L. Tickner, J. Bird, B. Curtis and T. Putnam (eds.) *Travellers' Tales: narratives of home and displacement*: 93–104. London: Routledge.

Scherer, J. (1972). *Contemporary Community: sociological illusion or reality?* London: Tavistock Publications.

Serjeantson, D. J. Bagust and C. Jenkins (forthcoming), 'Animal bone'. In G. Brown, D. Field and D. McOmish *The Late Bronze Age – Early Iron Age site at East Chisenbury, Wiltshire*.

Serjeantson, D. (2007). Intensification of animal husbandry in the Late Bronze Age? In C. C. Haselgrove and R. E. Pope (eds.) *The Earlier Iron Age in Britain and the Near Continent*: 80–93. Oxford: Oxbow Books.

Sharples, N. (2007). Building communities and creating identities in the first millennium BC. In C. C. Haselgrove and R. E. Pope (eds.) *The Earlier Iron Age in Britain and the Near Continent*: 174–184. Oxford: Oxbow Books.

Tuan, Yi-fu (1980). *Landscapes of Fear*. Oxford: Blackwell.

Tullett, A. S. and C. Harrison (2008). The Pewsey Middens – centres of feasting or symbols of community? In S. Baker, M. Allen, S. Middle and K. Poole (eds.) *Food and Drink in Archaeology 1*: 149–157. Totnes: Prospect Books.

van Dommelen, P. F. Gerritsen, and A. B. Knapp, (2005). Common places. Archaeologies of community and landscape. In P. Attema, A. Nijboer and A. Zifferero (eds.) *Papers in Italian Archaeology VI: communities and settlements from the Neolithic to the Early Medieval Period. Proceedings of the 6th Conference of Italian Archaeology held at the University of Groningen, Groningen Institute of Archaeology, The Netherlands, April 15–17, 2003*: 55–63. Oxford: British Archaeological Reports, International Series 1452.

Yaeger, J. (2000). The social construction of community in the Classic Maya countryside: strategies of affiliation in western Belize. In M. A. Canuto and J. Yaeger (eds.) *Archaeology of Communities: a New World perspective*: 123–42. London: Routledge.

## CHAPTER 4

# AN INVESTIGATION OF AN IRON AGE COMMUNITY ON WINNALL DOWN: HOUSEHOLDS AND NEIGHBOURHOOD GROUPS

*Oliver Davis*

*(Cardiff University)*

## Abstract

This paper examines how Iron Age communities maintained and negotiated space and place within an ordered and densely settled landscape. In particular it explores how households may have perceived their place within wider group identities. Dr Gerhard Bersu's excavations at Little Woodbury in the 1930s have been largely responsible for providing many of our familiar ideas concerning Iron Age social and economic structure. For Bersu (1940), Little Woodbury was a typical example of an entire social unit, in an enclosed self-sufficient settlement. In much of the literature, the settlement record is still dominated by the Little Woodbury type enclosure. Excavations by Wainwright (1979) at Gussage All Saints and Fasham (1985) at Winnall Down appeared to confirm this archetype; a single farming unit, representing the independent homestead of an Iron Age farmer and his family, who engaged in a mixed farming economy. Yet the cropmark evidence suggests that some enclosures in Wessex were often only one part of much larger complexes of settlement and other features. This paper (re)examines the evidence from a number of sites concentrated on and around Winnall Down and questions whether the settlement organisation does point towards independent and isolated communities.

## Introduction

Ideas of how Iron Age people constructed and maintained their communities have been regularly explored in recent years. Some of these have built upon a deeply rooted hierarchical 'Celtic' model. Cunliffe (1991: 303) for instance has defined the smallest socio-economic unit as the single family occupying a small farm set amongst its fields and pastures. In turn, these family groups were organised together into clans and tribes. The development of regional pottery styles in the Early Iron Age he suggests reflected the emergence of formalised tribal territories centred around hillforts, which were the homes of the aristocracy with coercive power over the clans (*ibid.*: 304). A widespread rejection of generalised 'Celtic' social models in the last 20 years has suggested potentially varied forms of social organisation even within areas such as Wessex that have previously been thought relatively homogenous (see especially Collis 1981; Hingley 1984; Hill 1993; 1996). Indeed, Hingley (1984) has argued that Iron Age society was primarily decentralised with an absence of a strong political and administrative elite class. Starting from an interpretation of the 'Germanic mode of production' Hingley (1984: 76) suggested that property and labour relations were organised through kinship.

Hill (1996) has developed these ideas further and emphasised the household as the basic building block of Iron Age society. The household he suggests was a small sized social unit, generally composed of a nuclear or extended family, which resided in an enclosed settlement and formed a complete productive unit. According to Hill (*ibid.*: 51) the individual household was the centre of production, owning specific land and resources, and possessing an existence distinct, self-sufficient, and spatially discrete from the larger clan, community or tribe. Household social, economic and biological reproduction however depended upon its involvement at the larger scale of community such as the construction and maintenance of hillforts. For Hill (*ibid.*: 52) households were linked by webs of kin and economic relations, but these did not form an organic whole, and the tribe was based on shared locality rather than kinship.

Fleming (1985, 1989) has explored notions of household cooperation through his analysis of the Dartmoor reave system. According to Fleming (1989: 153) the reave network was conceived by people who did not start from the small farm and work outwards, but began from the territory of a whole community and the land of its neighbours. Three levels of social organisation were postulated (Fleming 1985: 132). The primary level was the household, while the tertiary level was the large socio-political group or community that could organise manpower to defend a territory or construct a reave system. Intermediate between the household and community was a secondary level social unit composed of cooperative relationships between groups of households that existed in loose clusters spatially remote from other clusters. These Fleming named 'neighbourhood groups', which corresponded to social units of people linked by kinship, marriage ties and obligations toward their neighbours (1989: 153). In this sense, each household could be at the centre of a circle of cooperation that differed slightly from those of its immediate neighbours, while also overlapping with them for different purposes.

The idea of neighbourhood groups is a useful one to help understand collective community enterprise. Cooperation may have related to the collective holding of land or the pooling of labour and other resources. Households would have joined together with other households to form such neighbourhood groups. Can Fleming's model of social organisation on Dartmoor be transposed to Wessex, and in particular central Hampshire, from which the data set for this paper is derived? The cropmark evidence suggests that some enclosures in Wessex were often only one part of a much larger complex of settlement and other features. Others were arranged into clusters of two or more settlements, located within one to two kilometres of one another (Figure 4.1). This paper (re)examines the evidence from one of these clusters concentrated on and around Winnall Down, Hampshire and questions whether the settlement organisation does point towards independent and isolated communities.

It will be argued in this paper that the household, defined as an extended family sharing a living space, was unlikely to have been a complete productive unit. Rather, it would have been through collective land allotment and labour organisation that households would have perceived their place within wider group identities. Drawing from a recent excavation on Winnall Down, this paper will show the development of a specific sequence in which the pattern and changing structuring principles of the settlement layout reflected the integration of communities into wider scale networks of social and spatial relationships. This brings into question whether enclosures really did represent the autonomy of the individual, and therefore independent, household. In turn, I will consider whether enclosure ditches necessarily marked the outer limit of settlement, and I will suggest that such boundaries may have delimited only the nucleus of occupation. I will argue that digging a ditch or building a house would have been endowed with specific meanings that referred both to people and place and as such would have been a lived metaphor and a mechanism for a family or group to create a sense of place. Furthermore, it will be suggested here that the biographies of individual households or kin groups may have become intertwined with particular places, the ditches and houses acting as a metaphor for those ties and relationships.

## Winnall Down/Easton Lane

In 1974 Collin Bowen discovered by aerial photography an enclosure complex on Winnall Down, less than two kilometres north-east of Winchester in Hampshire (Fasham 1985). The proposals for the M3 motorway and its interchanges (Junction 9) meant that this enclosure (Winnall Down I) was to be completely destroyed. The threat of destruction offered the opportunity for

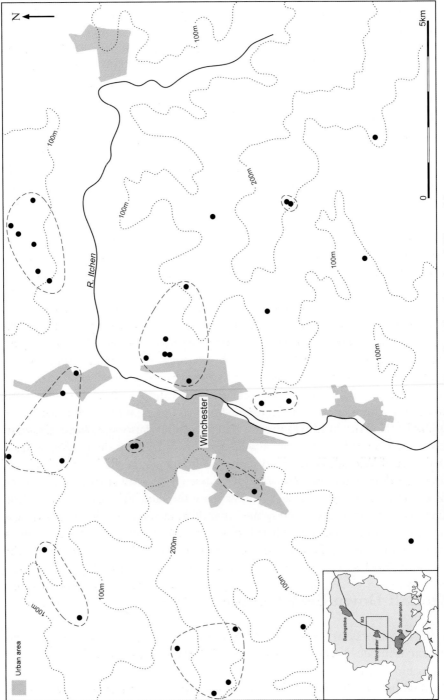

Figure 4.1: Clustering of Iron Age sites in central Hampshire.

the total investigation of a small enclosure, which would become a 'type-site' for the final decades of the twentieth century comparable to that of Bersu's (1940) Little Woodbury. Subsequently, a large area to the west of the enclosure, directly under the interchange itself, surrounding what was then known as Easton Lane, was also investigated (Fasham *et al.* 1989). This revealed extensive evidence of Bronze Age and Iron Age occupation, set within a rectilinear ditch system and extending over an area of 15ha.

The excavation of the enclosure, Winnall Down I, by Peter Fasham (see Fasham 1985) was a rare exercise insofar as only a few Iron Age sites in Britain have been excavated to such an extent that their entire plans could be recorded. Yet the enclosed settlement examined by Fasham (*ibid.*) was actually only one of a pair of enclosures located about 300m apart that were placed within the same complex system of fields and linear boundaries. However, there was no attempt by Fasham to examine the adjacent enclosure, Winnall Down II, although he indicated that the full story of occupation on Winnall Down could not be told while it remained unexcavated (*ibid.*: 143). Indeed, both enclosures appeared in plan to be of similar size and shape, with entrances orientated towards the west, and recent excavation of Winnall Down II (Davis 2008), suggests that both enclosures were occupied contemporaneously. The implication is that the settlement pattern represents a situation in which there would actually have been significant cooperation and interdependence between family and kin groups, rather than dispersed and isolated communities just 'doing their own thing'.

An analysis of crop mark features has revealed other Iron Age settlement on neighbouring downland (Figure 4.2). Around 1500m to the southeast of Winnall Down II is a banjo enclosure with an entrance orientated to the west. A further enclosure has also been identified by aerial photography 1000m northwest of Winnall Down II at Winnall Cottage Farm. This may also be of Iron Age date, and Iron Age pottery has been recovered from the vicinity (Fasham *et al.* 1989: 3). Collis (1978) has also recorded another enclosure, which he tentatively assigned to the early Middle Iron Age, identified during the construction of the Winnall Housing Estate 1000m southwest of Fasham's enclosure on Winnall Down. A small polygonal enclosure around 50m to the east of Winnall Down II has also been noted, and interpreted as a Romano-British shrine (Hill 1995: 84). Taken together, the evidence suggests a clustering of sites along the eastern valley slopes of the River Itchen.

## Occupation and activity on Winnall Down

Although Winnall Down I is one of the most thoroughly examined small enclosures in southern Britain that is not to say that the nature of the

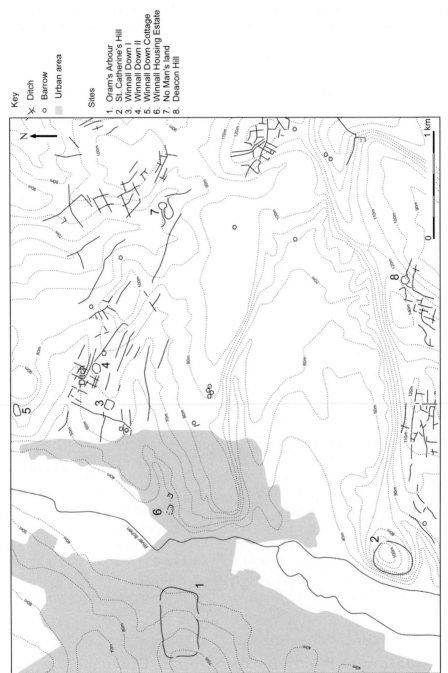

Figure 4.2: Cropmark survey of later prehistoric features on and around Winnall Down, Hampshire.

settlement is well understood (Sharples pers. comm.). In particular the precise structuring of space within the enclosure is open to question. The original excavator defined four areas within the Early Iron Age enclosure (Figure 4.3) that he suggested was the result of the activity of four distinct households (Fasham 1985: 127–30). The enclosure was abandoned at the end of the Early Iron Age and subsequently, the occupation was moved about 70–80m to the northwest to what was to become the Easton Lane interchange. This 'unenclosed' Middle Iron Age settlement was framed in the north and west by part of the Late Bronze Age ditch system (Figure 4.4).

This settlement was probably occupied for only a short period of time before there was a shift back to the site of the former Early Iron Age enclosure. This was set within the context of a settlement without prescribed limits. Fasham was unable to define specific activity areas for this Middle Iron Age

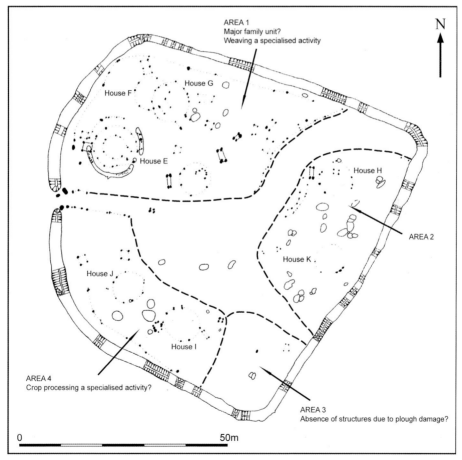

Figure 4.3: Four activity areas within the Early Iron Age enclosure, Winnall Down I (based on Fasham 1985: figure 84).

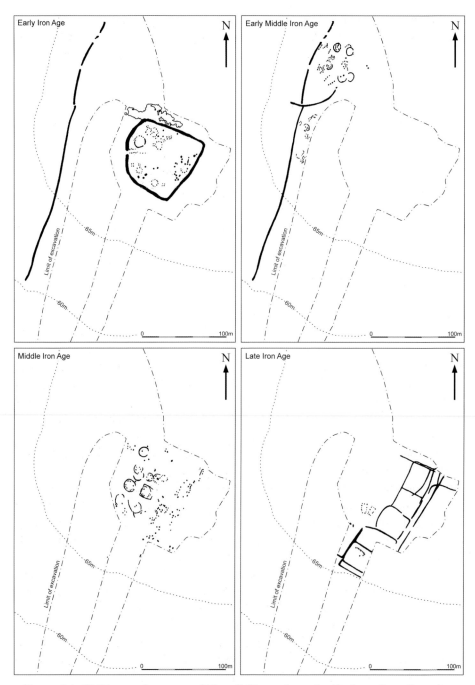

Figure 4.4: Shifting settlement on Winnall Down from the Early to Late Iron Age
(based on Fasham *et al.* 1989: figures 66, 67, 72 and 75).

settlement, although he emphasised the separation of the site into distinct zones of occupation (houses) and storage (pits), with four-post structures more widely dispersed. Fasham (*ibid.*: 130–4) suggested that the spatial arrangement of circular structures indicated that household units would have consisted of a pair of structures, one for accommodation, and the other as an ancillary building. At the end of the Middle Iron Age, at the time that the production and use of decorated saucepan pottery had declined, the settlement was abandoned. After a brief hiatus of activity, a series of three small enclosures connected by a track-way were constructed on the site.

The spatial patterns for the settlements on Winnall Down are not as clear-cut as Fasham suggests and they have been critically re-evaluated by Parker Pearson (1996; Parker Pearson and Richards 1994) and Hill (1995). According to Parker Pearson (1996: 124; Parker Pearson and Richards 1994: 52) the internal organisation of Early Iron Age Winnall Down I was divided into two, with houses on either side of an open space which extended from the entrance to the northeast corner. This precise structuring of space has been taken by Parker Pearson to represent the residential areas of two households each with two principal houses (1996: 124). Parker Pearson (*ibid.*) postulates that this two house unit would have been divided between one house for food storage, preparation and craft activities, and the other for food consumption and accommodation. The directional alignment of the houses would also appear to be important. Parker Pearson (*ibid.)* suggests that the two food consumption houses were aligned east-west, while the preparation areas were aligned north-south, with the two units separated by the open space running east-west from the main entrance into the enclosure.

Hill, on the other hand, has argued that the occupation within the Early Iron Age Winnall Down I enclosure was the result of the activities of only a single household (1995: 85). According to Hill (*ibid.*: 84) the enclosure ditch stressed the importance of the entrance, a front-back distinction, and the marking of the cardinal compass points. Hill (*ibid.*) postulates that some of these distinctions appear evident within the organisation of the interior, such as the distribution of large storage pits, which suggest that the enclosure was divided into two unequal halves from the entrance to the northeast corner. Hill (*ibid.*: 85) argues that the interior depositional patterns represent a coherent entity and were not divided into clear elements as might be expected if the enclosure contained two or more spatially distinct household units. For Hill (*ibid.*) the main residential unit was a primary porched house located in the north of the enclosure (house E), whereas the other circular structures were ancillary buildings for craft activities and food preparation.

Hill (*ibid.*: 87) argues that the shift in settlement during the Middle Iron Age represented a dramatic social and spatial reorganisation. However, if the shift in settlement was simply the result of increasing population, Hill (*ibid.*: 86) questions why was the existing settlement neither enlarged nor replicated? These questions will be considered in further detail below, especially given new evidence from the second enclosure Winnall Down II. Indeed, the new settlement at Easton Lane was comprised of two clusters of structures, which Hill (*ibid.*: 86) proposes could represent two social units coming from both Winnall Down I and II at the same time.

Hill (*ibid.*: 87) argues that the move back to the site of the Early Iron Age enclosure was probably a less dramatic spatial and social re-organisation. The new layout and orientation of the Middle Iron Age (CP7) settlement was determined by the (still visible) old enclosure ditch, since it had to be levelled up around where some of the houses were built (*ibid.*). Crucially for Hill however, the orientation of the settlement had been reversed. People would now enter the site from the east, through an open area between a grouping of pits and four-post structures, rather than through the west facing entrance of the Early Iron Age enclosure. The north and south boundaries of the settlement may also have been expressed through the deposition of human remains (*ibid.*: 89).

To summarise, the nature of the Iron Age settlement on Winnall Down/Easton Lane is not straightforward. Fasham (1985) argues that the Early Iron Age enclosure and early Middle Iron Age settlement at Easton Lane was occupied by four households with specific areas designated for certain activities such as crop processing and weaving. Parker Pearson (1996) has suggested that the enclosure was the residential space of two households, the internal space precisely structured to segregate areas of craft activities and food preparation from living accommodation. Hill (1995) has argued that the enclosure was the residence of a single household, the layout of space shaped by concerns with the cardinal points of the compass and a distinction between inside and outside, and front and back. He suggests that these structuring principles continued in some form throughout the occupation of Winnall Down.

## A (re)interpretation of activity and occupation on Winnall Down

Expansion, contraction and movement are the key elements in understanding the settlement evidence on Winnall Down. Fasham (1985: 142) has attempted to explain the sites in terms of continuums of development, such as increasing socio-economic centralisation and the emergence of a tribal society. Hill (1995) favours a social model in which settlement space and landscape are structured in reference to cosmology and symbolism. For Hill (*ibid.*: 91) the early Middle Iron Age occupation of Easton Lane should be seen as a short-lived episode to escape the ingrained structures reproduced by the Early Iron Age enclosure. It was a fresh start and location to escape the spatial tyranny of the enclosure and its past. However, it is argued here that to fully understand Iron Age activity on Winnall Down we must initially get past the notion that the settlements were self-contained units whose outer limits were marked by enclosure ditches. Indeed, Fasham *et al.* (1989: 56–8) recorded a number of pits containing Early Iron Age pottery to the northwest of Winnall Down I, suggesting activity beyond the limits of the enclosure. It is also important to mention that the Late Bronze Age ditch system was still used and subsequently modified during the Early and Middle Iron Age. Taken together, it is perhaps more useful to consider Winnall Down as a combination of different locales in which people repeatedly came together at various times to perform a range of activities. The ditches and boundaries should then be regarded as delimiting only the nuclei of occupation, which were only parts of a larger system of settlement and activity.

## Landscape biographies and the creation of place

In order to understand the settlements on Winnall Down as a whole, and not as separate entities, we need to consider the biography of this landscape within the consciousness of Iron Age people. In particular, it is through the interactions of individuals during their routine activities at particular places and times that constitute the contextuality of the landscape. Yet as Moore (2007: 90) has argued, Iron Age communities are unlikely to have perceived or constituted their place in the landscape within a vacuum from earlier landscape features and existing narratives or perceptions of place. Instead they would have developed upon existing traditions and perceptions. Winnall Down would appear to have a long history in the consciousness of local communities. During the Middle Bronze Age this location was marked out as a focus of occupation set within a system of fields and trackways. By the Late Bronze Age, a small cluster of houses, with prominent porches orientated to the southwest (Fasham 1985: fig. 7), were situated on the site of the subsequent Early Iron Age enclosure ditch. The settlement was still set amongst field ditch systems.

This was a landscape of everyday life and of routine praxis. Personhood and group identities would have been attained and maintained through engagement with the landscape and involvement in specific activities. The performance of tasks such as making pots, tending crops, herding animals or processing foods would have reinforced core senses of identity in which participation in such tasks engendered different constructions of personhood. Some activities may have required contact with external groups. The maintenance and construction of field boundaries probably took place at certain times of the year with neighbouring communities gathering together to undertake such tasks and affirm relationships. The recovery of fragments of a greensand quern, not locally sourced, from the postholes of one of the Late Bronze Age houses (*ibid.*: 126) suggests that the exchange of material culture was also likely to have been a key element of creating and mediating such relationships between communities.

Activities were likely to have been divided between several households each living separately within a single house. Each house possessed an elaborate porch orientated to the southwest marking the transition from outside to inside. Yet, by the Early Iron Age these houses, and presumably certain activities, had been brought into a compound defined by a ditch. This enclosure, Winnall Down I, was kite or 'D' shape in plan with two straight sides meeting at a right angle in the northeast corner, while two curving ditches defined the entrance in the west. The enclosure was positioned on the south-facing slope of a spur of chalk downland and the entrance was superimposed directly over the location of the Late Bronze Age houses. The position, shape and orientation of the enclosure were not coincidental. Sharples (pers. comm.) has suggested that the shape of the enclosure was determined by the pre-existing field system. This is very likely to have been the case and an examination of cropmarks (Figure 4.5) has revealed a number of lynchets and field boundaries surrounding the enclosure running northeast to southwest and northwest to southeast. This suggests that Winnall Down I was fitted into the northeast corner of a rectangular plot of land, although as Sharples (pers. comm.) notes these field boundaries, perhaps hedges or positive lynchets, have not survived to be recovered by archaeology. A similar situation can also be recognised at other enclosed settlements in Wessex such as Old Down Farm (Davies 1981).

The association of the enclosure with field boundaries was important because it directly linked the enclosure into a wider pre-existing landscape. However we need to consider why a field boundary was used to align two sides of the enclosure ditch. In particular we need to ask why a field boundary, perhaps a hedge, was used to mark the eastern edge of the ditch, since that precluded the entrance to the enclosure being in the east as the field boundary would have had to have been traversed. The common orientation of Early Iron Age enclosures is usually considered to be easterly (see Bowden and McOmish 1987; Hingley 1990; Hill 1995; Parker Pearson 1996) but this was deliberately reversed at Winnall Down I. Clearly the orientation of the enclosure was driven by a desire to continue to follow precisely the orientation of the Late Bronze Age houses, since it would have been easy to simply have built the enclosure 50m to the west so that the remains of those houses were on the east side. This suggests a concern with cosmological principles, but also a sense of attachment to place that referenced past experiences, activities,

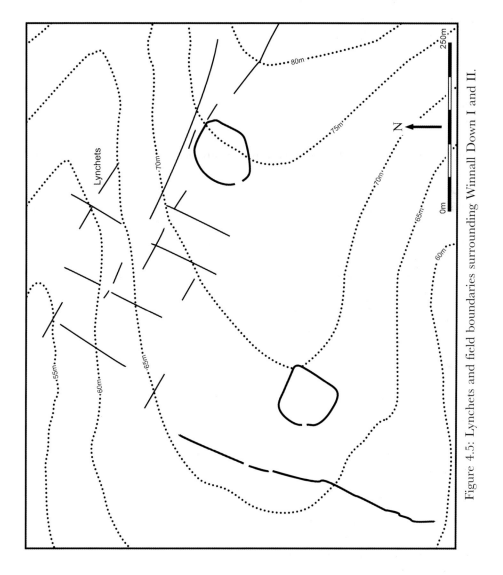

Figure 4.5: Lynchets and field boundaries surrounding Winnall Down I and II.

histories and relationships. In this sense the past, possibly still in living memory, was essential for how community identity could be created.

The Iron Age community on Winnall Down also helped to maintain a sense of place by fitting the enclosure into the existing field system pattern, which produced a place-relation between the community and the agricultural landscape. The use of a boundary of a field system to set out the enclosure was a means of establishing a collective and corporate identity that referred to both people and place. The community were involved in the exploitation and maintenance of the field system. Participation in specific tasks in these locales was a mechanism for creating the community's placedness. The enclosure was fixed into the field system and was therefore an element of the same phenomenon, including the nuances associated with the boundary, such as permanence, history, and daily routine.

Geophysical survey of Winnall Down II has shown that the enclosure was 'D' shape in plan with two broadly straight sides meeting in the northeast corner, while two curving ditches define the entrance in the west (Davis 2008). The enclosure can be divided into two roughly equal and asymmetrical halves by drawing a line drawn from the south-westerly entrance to the northeast corner. The enclosure may have been aligned upon a prehistoric field boundary observed running parallel to the north-eastern stretch of the enclosure ditch. This suggests that the shape of the enclosure ditch was probably determined by a pre-existing field system, and raises the possibility that this enclosure was also fitted into the north-eastern corner of a rectangular plot of land.

The ceramic assemblage recovered from Winnall Down II suggests that this adjacent enclosure was set out after Winnall Down I had been established (Davis in prep). If this was the case then it raises a number of interesting questions concerning the social relationship between the people that used the two enclosures. In particular, if the appearance of enclosures in the Early Iron Age was an expression of the independence of social groups, then why were two enclosures fitted into the same pre-existing field system? One answer could be that Winnall Down II did not function as a settlement, but was complementary to the activities undertaken at Winnall Down I, perhaps serving as an animal paddock. Yet the pottery and animal bone recovered by excavation (see Davis 2008) suggests domestic activity similar to other enclosed settlements in Wessex. More likely then is that the construction of Winnall Down II was the result of a group moving out from Winnall Down I. Such 'budding off' may have been a strategy to resolve a dispute (Hill forthcoming) or as a result of population pressure, which led to an attempt to replicate the Winnall Down I enclosure. The southwesterly orientation of the entrance to Winnall Down II was probably an attempt to conform to important cosmological concerns apparent at Winnall Down I, but it was also a clear visual reference to existing and historical relationships with people and place. By fitting Winnall

Down II into the same field system pattern as Winnall Down I it established a relation between place and community.

This arrangement also implies complex agreements over land apportionment and agricultural activities. It is too simplistic to consider enclosure boundaries as signifying economic or social isolation since as Moore (2007: 93) has argued, households clearly would have needed contact with external groups to facilitate biological and social reproduction and to carry out tasks beyond that of a small group. Enclosures therefore may have had more to do with emphasising the household as the primary social unit rather than community isolation. The spatial association of the enclosures on Winnall Down therefore suggests corporate interdependence of households, especially concerning the management of the field system surrounding them.

## Enclosures as landmarks

Inter-site visibility is also an interesting issue. The enclosures are positioned either side of a ridge of chalk downland from which the land initially slopes gently and then much more sharply. Topographic field study undertaken during the excavation of Winnall Down II established that at least part of the interior of both enclosures would have been visible from either settlement. However, the slope of the down would have meant that although the entrance to Winnall Down II, situated on the crest of the ridge, was visible from Winnall Down I, the northern half of the enclosure would have been obscured from sight. It might also have been possible to have seen the enclosures at Winnall Cottage Farm and Winnall Housing Estate from both of the settlements on Winnall Down, although at present modern tree cover and urban development obscure them. The banjo enclosure on No Man's Land would not have been visible and its relationship to the other enclosures is not known. However, the westerly orientation of the entrance to the banjo closely follows those of Winnall Down I and II, which may suggest some association. The large Middle Iron Age enclosure of Oram's Arbour to the west of the River Itchen may also have been visible from Winnall Down.

It appears therefore that intervisibility might have been an important consideration for this cluster of settlements on and around Winnall Down. However, perhaps equally as significant is that collectively these enclosures suggest an interest in locations that facilitated survey and access to the surrounding landscape. However, these settlements may have been more about looking 'towards' from the outside than looking 'out' from within. As such, they would have provided landmarks in specific locations that may have tied the biographies of people to the biographies and perceptions of the landscape.

## Building communities: neighbourhood groups

The clustering of sites on and around Winnall Down suggests cooperative relationships between groups of households that we can loosely define as a neighbourhood group. This community probably exploited a territory of no more than around three to four kilometres across that nonetheless had access to a range of resources such as rich arable and pasture and the reed beds of the River Itchen. This cluster of settlements may only have had a population of a few hundred people, but they would have been bound together as a neighbourhood community through kinship, marriage ties, locality and mutual obligations. This was a community of close cooperation although the emergence of enclosures points to a desire to define specific localities for activities that were to remain spatially distinct from the neighbourhood group. The creation of the enclosure Winnall Down II then was not by an incoming group of migrants, but by knowledgeable people who shared a sense of attachment and place through embodied and emplaced experiences. They knew where the enclosure had to be constructed, what shape it could be, and which way to orientate the entrance. They knew what pots they should use, and where to get the clay to make them. They knew what animals to farm. Essentially, they were knowledgeable of their specific historical and social circumstances, and of a shared sense of community with other groups.

Yet households would have come to rely on the support of other households to such an extent that they were no longer self-sufficient or complete productive units. Labour and resources would have been pooled for specific types of agricultural practices such as ploughing, harvesting, threshing and storage. Labour was likely to have been organised into small groups of family, kin and neighbours in which personhood was interwoven into participation with specific labour tasks in particular localities: women spun cloth near the house while men ploughed the fields.

Moore (2007: 91) has recently challenged the model of independent enclosure communities, and demonstrated that the evidence from many parts of the Severn-Cotswolds suggests that rather than seeking to be isolated from each other, enclosure communities clustered together in specific areas of the landscape. In some instances, enclosures were integrated into wider landscapes through field boundaries and trackways, the construction and maintenance of which reaffirmed 'ownership' and territories through mutual labour. In this way, apparently independent communities tied themselves into a web of mutually dependant relationships. Indeed, environmental evidence suggests that enclosures were not necessarily agriculturally or socially independent. As Moore (*ibid.*: 92) highlights, crop residues from the enclosure at Rollright, Oxfordshire, suggest that the enclosure may have been involved only in the later stages of crop processing, implying enclosure communities may have been co-operating at various stages of crop production. Similarly, Campbell (2000: 194) has argued that the absence of cereal and grass straw from the carbonised plant remains recovered from the enclosure at Suddern Farm, Hampshire, may suggest that threshing was not taking place at the site. On Winnall Down, carbonised plant remains recovered by Fasham (1985: 115) consisted principally of six row hulled barley and spelt wheat with relatively low weed contamination, which may suggest thorough cleaning and sorting of the harvest, or that such practices took place elsewhere.

## Creating place through co-operative labour organisation

Taken together, the evidence suggests widespread group inter-dependence, continually affirmed and reaffirmed through a web of social relationships (Moore 2007). People would have been closely linked by networks of exchange, kinship, marriage ties and the mutual obligations of their neighbours. In turn, communities would have been repeatedly created and recreated based on the experience of ethnicity and locality, and people's engagement with collective social and economic enterprises and activities. Indeed, Amit (2002: 18) has argued that people associate the idea of community with people they know, with whom they have shared experiences, activities, histories, and places. The link between community and place-making, or emplacement, is especially important. Community is social engagement, but a sense of attachment is felt, embodied, and emplaced through shared experiences and practices, which can create a 'placedness'. In Iron Age Wessex, one mechanism of creating 'placedness' may have been through mutual and cooperative labour projects such as house construction, enclosure ditch digging, animal husbandry, and primary food processing (*cf.* Sharples 2007; Fleming 1985). Recent reconstruction of the large Little Woodbury house at Butser Ancient Farm has shown that more than 16 tonnes of timber would have been required for its construction as well as a considerable quantity of straw for thatch. Clearly, this would have represented a significant investment of labour and resources for an Iron Age community, which suggests cooperative relationships between households and kinship groups.

Building a house or digging a ditch would have been endowed with specific meanings that referred both to people and place and as such would be a lived metaphor and a mechanism for a family or group to create a sense of place. Giles (2007: 240) has argued that architecture can have a mnemonic role, enabling people to trace the genealogy of their relationships in these places, sometimes across several generations. Taking part in construction projects would have been a way that networks of debt and obligation could have been created, and the ability of groups to procure the labour necessary would have depended upon both its position in wider exchange networks and their social status. Inclusions of the mineral glauconite within the fabrics of some pottery recovered from Winnall Down (Hawkes 1985) and Winnall Down II (Davis 2008), which does not occur naturally on the chalk downlands of central Hampshire, could point to relationships between groups that were external to the local community. Such exchanges of material culture over considerable distances may just have been 'one-offs', perhaps to influence short-term alliances (Moore 2007). However, recent stable isotope analysis of human bones from Winnall Down by Jay and Richards (2007) has shown that some individuals buried at the site had spent a significant part of their lives away from this location. It seems that people were embedding themselves, sometimes quite literally, at particular places. In this way, enclosure ditches and roundhouses could have stood as a kind of mnemonic for the names of the people who created them. The biographies of individual households or kin groups may have become intertwined with particular places, the ditches and houses acting as a metaphor for those ties and relationships.

However, the relationships between communities would have fluctuated over time as a group's social position fluctuated with the successes and failures of the individual lives of people. Many enclosure ditches in Wessex appear to go through periods of enhancement or maintenance, and it seems possible that such re-working of ditches provided occasions to bring people together and renegotiate kin ties to particular places. Indeed, such acts may have had a bearing on a group's access to land, where by giving or withdrawing cooperation may have served to reinforce or reduce claims to particular places. In effect, the relationship between people and place would have been repeatedly reproduced through the extent to which groups supported specific acts of construction and maintenance.

If ditch and house construction were political acts that affirmed alliances, and the ditches and houses themselves stood as metaphors for those relationships, then allowing a ditch to silt up or to be backfilled, or abandoning a house would have contested those alliances. The gradual silting of a ditch may have acted as a visual reminder that alliances had not been renewed. At Winnall Down I and II, the enclosure ditches appear to have been deliberately backfilled. The filling of the ditches, especially with particular material such as human bone, fragmented pottery and burnt flint, could suggest a kind of ceremonial death of past relationships and interests, but most crucially, the relationship with place and therefore community. I would argue that the people who lived within the enclosures of Winnall Down I and II shifted their occupation to Easton Lane in the fourth century BC. The settlement at Easton Lane is divided into two distinct groups of houses by a curving ditch. Clearly there was a desire for households to live together, which was perhaps a reflection of close kinship and shared histories, but their occupation areas were still to remain clearly separate. To move in these spaces would have drawn attention to people's knowledge of place. By moving to Easton Lane these people were deliberately altering their relationship to place and community. They may have allowed Winnall Down I and II to decompose by leaving timbers *in situ* to rot, or partially filled ditches to silt up. In turn, these places would have become a lived metaphor for the decomposition or fragmentation of histories, practices and social relationships that needed to be sterilised before reoccupation could occur.

## Household identities and relationships

Hill (forthcoming) has argued that we know very little about Iron Age household composition. I have already defined a household as an extended family who share a living space, but what actually would have been an extended Iron Age family and how would the members of such a group have organised themselves and their living arrangements? Key to our understanding is a consideration of the ambiguous terms family and household, in particular drawing from ethnographic discussions of domestic organisation.

Dorjahn (1977) examining the Temne, of Sierra Leone, defined a household as the people occupying the houses or huts that shared a common yard, which may or may not be enclosed from other yards. Yet this raises questions about how to define the boundaries of a household, especially as some members may move between dwelling units as a result of marriage, fosterage or seasonal cycles of dispersal and concentration. Others have argued that a household is a task-focused group, consisting of overlapping sets of people, who participate in various activities within a specific kind of space such as a dwelling (Wilk and Rajthe 1982; Bulmer 1960; Yanagisako 1979). An important part of household membership therefore seems to be participation in sets of tasks, particularly those usually labelled as 'domestic' such as food consumption and production, sexual reproduction and child rearing. Indeed, Bourdieu (1990) has argued that 'the household' is a symbolic construct that is defined through practice. In this sense, whereas the referent of the family is kinship, the referent of the household is both common residence and shared activities.

In many societies co-residence is often between members of the same family, but in others it can be a collection of both kin and non-kin. Bulmer (1960), examining the social organisation of the Kyaka people of New Guinea, describes a situation where groups of non-kin regularly participate in meal sharing, gardening and co-residence. In this situation the term household may be inadequate since it is implicitly associated with the completion of certain sets of domestic functions. Bulmer (*ibid.*) proposes that in these circumstances the term 'domestic group', in which people acknowledge authority in domestic matters, is the more salient social unit.

A household therefore consists of social actors differentiated by age, gender, roles and power whose agendas and interests need not always coincide. Yanagisako (1979: 167) has argued that biological concerns such as life expectancy have an impact on the composition of households. Yet there is also social control over household size and organisation, which are embedded in kinship customs such as marriage and adoption practices. Activities such as food preparation and craft specialisation also affect the way that household members allocate their time and divide up work. For instance, the acquisition, processing and cooking of food requires the acquisition of certain kinds of knowledge, skills, utensils and materials (Hendon 1996: 50). Food preparation may also require significant inputs of time that may reduce the amount of time that some household members have to spend on other tasks.

Membership of specific households may also determine the choice of particular craft activities, especially the access to the necessary training. Healen (1986) has suggested that skill is a significant factor in the organisation of obsidian tool production of Tula communities in Mexico. The less skilled work of grinding the cores to produce a striking platform occurs in and around houses. Conversely, striking blades, which requires much more skill, is concentrated in areas away from houses. In this sense, multiple members of a household are assigned specific tasks in the production process, which is primarily organised by skill, but also by age and gender.

So what can we say about Iron Age households? Households probably differed in size and composition between different parts of Wessex. At Winnall Down, Fasham (1985: 138–40) estimated a population of around 24 to 34 persons for the Early Iron Age enclosure (phase 3). This number was based upon an analysis of the available floor area (one person per 10m²) assuming that between four and six houses were standing at any one time. This range of values for the population during phase 3 is tentative at best, since there are many uncertainties relating to the life of a building and its function, but they provide an idea of the potential size of the domestic group. If we agree that multiple households are present at Winnall Down I during the Early Iron Age (see below for further discussion) then this suggests that each household consisted of around 8 to 12 members.

However, it is not easy to disentangle the age and gender composition of such a group. The skeletal remains of six adults, one male and five female, and 25 children were recovered from Winnall Down (Fasham 1985). This relatively small assemblage of human skeletal fragments and skeletons is clearly not representative of an entire population. Analysis of stable isotopes by Jay and Richards (2007: 187) also suggests that some of these individuals may have been buried away from the areas in which they spent a significant part of their lives, the implication being that these individuals had spent their childhood and adolescence elsewhere. Nevertheless, mortality profiles based on this limited assemblage (Bayley *et al.* 1985: 119) suggest high infant mortality and few adults surviving beyond 30 years of age. Hill (forthcoming) has argued that high adult mortality (around 30 years) might point to a large degree of child fosterage as one or both biological parents could have died before a person reached the age of 15.

A number of instances of oesteoarthritis were also observed, especially in the vertebrae, arms and shoulders of the female adults (*ibid.*: 120). This suggests repetitive use of the joints over many years degenerating the cartilage, and might point towards participation in repetitive tasks such as grinding corn, spinning and weaving, and pottery and textile manufacture. Indeed, burial B629, a female adult 17 to 25 years old, showed evidence of excessive attrition of the lower incisors and canines, which was suggested to be the result of an occupational habit such as chewing leather for softening (*ibid.*). The single adult male, an individual between 35 and 40 years of age, showed extensive oesteoarthritic lipping on the distal ends of the left ulna and radius, and healed fractures in the left wrist and elbow joint, which was probably the result of a severe trauma of the left arm (*ibid.*: 119). The absence of signs of oesteoarthritis in the back probably suggests prolonged participation in different activities to the female adults.

Taken together, the evidence suggests division of labour by sex and age. This has important implications for the ways in which Iron Age personhood was constituted through social practices. Routine activities can reinforce a core sense of identity, especially through the type, nature and settings of such action. Women were likely to have been responsible primarily for food processing and preparation, textile production, small animal care (dogs) and child rearing, close to the household dwelling. Men may have tended to be responsible primarily for larger animals (sheep, pigs, cattle), cultivation, and bureaucratic affairs, performed some distance from the household's living quarters. In this sense the different patterns and locations of activity engendered different constructions of identity. This generalising scheme should be approached with some caution however, since the particular tasks might have varied from one region to another, or even from one community to another. There would also have been some times when certain tasks, such as harvest, would have demanded the collective activity of all or several household members. Indeed, it is possible that women's engagement in the harvest, or other collective enterprises, would have been key to maintaining and negotiating their identities and enhancing the prestige of their household.

## Household organisation at Winnall Down I

Are we able to decipher household organisation from the architectural arrangement of the Early Iron Age enclosure Winnall Down I? The excellent preservation of structural remains has facilitated a detailed analysis of the Iron Age social and spatial organisation. However, the discussion has resulted in significantly different readings of the data, especially concerning the number of households present within the Early Iron Age enclosure. Sharples (pers. comm.) favours the estimates of the original excavator since he suggests that in the later phases of occupation there are at least three to four households present. Certainly, I advocate the presence of multiple households, especially since the size and dimensions of the circular structures, interpreted as ancillary structures by Hill (1995) and Parker Pearson (1996), are no different to those labelled 'residential' at other enclosures such as Little Somborne (Neal 1980) and Houghton Down (Cunliffe and Poole 2000).

An alternative is to consider the structural arrangements as the result of the activities of three households. Each household occupied a broadly similar area of the interior and consisted of two houses and a number of other post structures and pits (Figure 4.6). Within these new outlines, an analysis of the ceramic assemblage suggests similar distributions of fine and coarse wares in each area rather than a concentration of fine wares close to houses E and K as suggested by Parker Pearson (1996). The cardinal compass points were also important. The three living areas occupied space in the north, south and east of the enclosure. The west of the enclosure was marked by the entrance, but it was also crucially the location of the Late Bronze Age cluster of four houses, perhaps considered the space of an historic or ancestral household. It may also be significant that a line drawn from the enclosure entrance to the eastern ditch in between houses H and K produces a broadly asymmetrical mirror image. It is interesting to note that a similar asymmetrical pattern has been noted for the enclosure Winnall Down II.

If there were three households occupying the Early Iron Age enclosure then why were the depositional patterns of artefacts such as loom weights and animal bones not equally distributed between each household's living space? Fasham (1985: 129) suggests this is a result of several households specialising in particular agricultural or craft activities. Hill (1995) argues that the depositional patterns are the result of a single household. Could the reality lie somewhere in between? Although I have argued that three households occupied the internal space of the Early Iron Age enclosure that is not to say that they were necessarily complete productive units. In this sense, although Hill (1995: 85) argues that the depositional patterns formed a coherent whole, this may not have been the result of a single household, but rather the outcome of shared activities and pooled labour of several households. The surviving evidence for fences within the enclosure suggests that each household attempted to emphasise their spatial independence from each other. The similar distributions of fine and coarse ware pottery might suggest that this independence was also maintained through some social practices such as the preparation

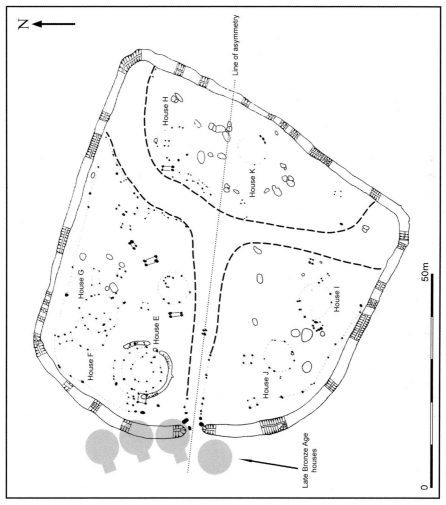

Figure 4.6: Three household arrangement of Winnall Down I (based on Fasham 1985: figure 84).

and consumption of food. However, for the performance of other activities, such as crop processing, textile production, and bone and wood working, pooled labour may have been required, or desired, for the different stages of processing and production. In these cases, the distinctiveness of each household would have become blurred as overlapping sets of people participated in co-operative tasks. In this sense, we should label these units co-residential groups so as to avoid making the false assumption that any of these households were the most important for the performance of domestic functions. Furthermore, we should recognise that because some domestic functions were for the most part carried out through reciprocal relationships between households as a group, then at times the whole enclosure formed the domestic unit. At certain times during the agricultural cycle, this domestic unit would have been extended to incorporate other enclosed settlements in the local neighbourhood group such as Winnall Down II.

Households were therefore bound together by networks of co-operation, close ties of kinship and defence of shared resources. How then should we understand the abandonment of both of the enclosures on Winnall Down at the end of the Early Iron Age? Hill (1995: 87) has argued that given the social importance of enclosure boundaries, the failure to replicate one when settlement moved westward implies a major change in the natural unit it defined, the household. I have already suggested that by moving the focus of settlement to Easton Lane changed the relationship people had with place and community. Should we assume that such settlement reorganisation also reflected changes in the nature of household composition and relationships? Certainly, the association between shifting settlement and change in ceramic style, with the introduction of undecorated saucepan pots, might suggest changes in social practices.

As already outlined (above) the new settlement at Easton Lane consisted of two clusters of structures separated by a curving ditch. The northern cluster was comprised of two sets of two circular structures arranged one in front of another. This was a continuation of the two house unit recognised within the Early Iron Age enclosure Winnall Down I. It is likely that a similar arrangement of structures existed to the south, but this was not fully excavated.

It is clear that there was no attempt to isolate the settlement components within the northern and southern halves of the settlement, although all of the circular structures were defined by penannular gullies. One possibility is that the settlement organisation reflected a desire to diminish the spatial independence and social distinctiveness of individual households. Household yards were no longer clearly separated from other household yards. This would have altered the nature of the locales in which the majority of domestic activities could have been performed. These different patterns and settings of action would have formed an important part of identity composition.

Household independence through social practices, such as food preparation and consumption, was not easily achieved since such activities were no longer clearly spatially isolated from similar activities of other households.

The layout and organisation of the Middle Iron Age settlement, on the site of the former Early Iron Age enclosure Winnall Down I, also emphasised the collective domestic group at the expense of individual households. Two sets of circular structures were arranged north to south in linear rows, one in front of another. Each house was defined by a penannular gully with an entrance orientated to the southeast. Sharples (1991: 97) has argued that regimented rows of houses may have been an attempt to break down the extended kinship ties of individual families and strengthen the importance of the community. The similarity of architecture certainly suggests a desire to blur social distinctiveness, perhaps emphasising communal control of place and key resources.

## Conclusion

This paper began by questioning how Iron Age communities might have maintained and negotiated a sense of space and place in a densely settled landscape. An examination of Late Bronze Age and Iron Age activity on and around Winnall Down has been offered. I have emphasised that enclosures should not just be regarded as independent homesteads, but were often part of much larger complexes of settlement. One of these complexes, comprised of a cluster of at least five enclosures and other evidence for settlement and activity, has been suggested to have existed to the east of the River Itchen on and around Winnall Down. I have argued that these settlements would have been bound together as a neighbourhood group through mutual obligations and co-operation, kinship ties, labour sharing and locality.

Particular importance has been given to trying to understand how Iron Age communities might have conceived of their place in the landscape. The biography of the landscape, developed through engaged praxis and existing Iron Age traditions and perceptions, has been considered as crucial for how community identity could have been created and maintained. The Iron Age communities on Winnall Down helped to create a sense of place by fitting the enclosures of Winnall Down I and II into the already existing field system pattern. This produced a place-relation between the community and the agricultural landscape and was a means of establishing a collective and corporate identity that referred to both people and place. Co-operative labour projects such as ditch digging would not only have been a way that networks of debt and obligation could have been generated, but also an embodied means of creating an attachment to place.

Finally the nature of the settlement on Winnall Down has also been discussed. Previous interpretations (Fasham 1985; Hill 1995; Parker Pearson 1996) have attempted to explain the settlement in terms of continuums of development, such as increasing socio-economic centralisation, or as a social model in which settlement space and landscape are structured in reference to cosmology and symbolism. This paper has suggested that we should consider the depositional patterns and structural arrangements of the Early Iron Age enclosure Winnall Down I as the result of the shared activities and pooled labour of at least three households. Changes in the organisation and layout of settlement in the Middle Iron Age were a result of a deliberate desire to blur the social distinctiveness of individual households.

## Acknowledgements

My thanks are extended to Niall Sharples for detailed comments on many of these ideas.

## Bibliography

Amit, V. (2002). Reconceptualising community. In V. Amit (ed.) *Realizing Community: concepts, social relationships and sentiments*: 1–20. London: Routledge.

Bayley, J., P. J. Fasham and F. V .H. Powell (1985). The human skeletal remains. In P. J. Fasham (ed.) *The Prehistoric Settlement at Winnall Down, Winchester*, 119–22. Gloucester: Hampshire Field Club and Archaeological Society, Monograph 2.

Bersu, G. (1940). Excavations at Little Woodbury, Wiltshire. *Proceedings of the Prehistoric Society* 6: 30–111.

Bourdieu, P. (1990). *In Other Words: essays towards a reflexive sociology*. Cambridge: Polity Press.

Bowden, M. and D. McOmish (1987). The required barrier. *Scottish Archaeological Review* 4: 76–84.

Bulmer, R. N. H. (1960). *Leadership and Social Structure Among the Kyaka People of the Western Highlands District of New Guinea*. Unpublished Ph.D. thesis.

Campbell, G. (2000). Charred plant remains. In B. Cunliffe and C. Poole. *The Danebury Environs Programme: the prehistory of a Wessex landscape: volume 2, part 3: Suddern Farm, Middle Wallop, Hampshire, 1991 & 1996*: 193–4. Oxford: English Heritage, Monograph 49.

Collis, J. (1978). *The Winchester Excavations, 1949–60, Volume 2*. Hertford: Winchester City Museum.

Collis, J. (1981). A theoretical study of hillforts. In G. Guilbert (ed.) *Hillfort Studies*: 66–76. Leicester: Leicester University Press.

Cunliffe, B. (1991). *Iron Age Communities in Britain*. London: Routledge.

Cunliffe, B. and C. Poole (2000). *The Danebury Environs Programme: the prehistory of a Wessex landscape: volume 2, part 6: Houghton Down, Stockbridge,Hampshire, 1994*. Oxford: English Heritage, Monograph 49.

Davies, S. M. (1981). Excavations at Old Down Farm, Andover. *Proceedings of the Hampshire Field Club and Archaeological Society* 37: 81–163.

Davis, O. P. (2008). *The Early Iron Age Enclosure at Winnall Down II, Hampshire: an interim report on the 2006 excavations*. Cardiff: Cardiff University Archaeology Series 28.

Davis, O. P. (in preparation). The pottery. In O. Davis (ed.) *A second Early Iron Age enclosure at Winnall Down*.

Dorjahn, V. R. (1977). Temne household size and composition: rural changes over time and rural-urban differences. *Ethnology* 16: 105–28.

Fasham, P. J. (1985). *The Prehistoric Settlement at Winnall Down, Winchester*. Gloucester: Hampshire Field Club and Archaeological Society, Monograph 2.

Fasham, P. J., D. E. Farwell and R. J. B. Whinney (1989). *The Archaeological Site at Easton Lane, Winchester*. Gloucester: Hampshire Field Club and Archaeological Society Monograph 6.

Fleming, A. (1985). Land tenure, productivity and field systems. In G. Barker and C. Gamble (eds.) *Beyond Domestication in Prehistoric Europe*: 129–46. London: Academic.

Fleming, A. (1989). Coaxial field systems in Later British Prehistory. In. H.A. Nordström and A. Knape (eds.) *Bronze Age studies: transactions of the British-Scandinavian colloquium in Stockholm, May 10–11 1985*: 151–62. Stockholm: Statens Historiska Museum.

Giles, M. (2007). Good fences make good neighbours? Exploring the ladder enclosures of Late Iron Age east Yorkshire. In C. C. Haselgrove and R. E. Pope (eds.) *The earlier Iron Age in Britain and the near continent*: 174–84. Oxford: Oxbow Books.

Hawkes, J. W. (1985). The pottery. In P. J. Fasham (ed.) *The Prehistoric Settlement at Winnall Down, Winchester*: 57–76. Gloucester: Hampshire Field Club and Archaeological Society Monograph 2.

Healen, D. M. (1986). Technological and non-technological aspects of an obsidian workshop excavated at Tula, Hidalgo. In B. L. Isaac (ed.) *Economic Aspects of Prehispanic Highland Mexico*: 133–52. Greenwich: Research in Economic Anthropology Supplement 2.

Hendon, J. A. (1996). Archaeological approaches to the organisation of domestic labour: household practice and domestic relations. *Annual Review of Anthropology* 25: 45–61.

Hill, J. D. (1993). Can we conceive of a different Europe in the past: a contrastive archaeology of later prehistoric settlement in southern England. *Journal of European Archaeology* 1: 57–76.

Hill, J. D. (1995). *Ritual and Rubbish in the Iron Age of Wessex*. Oxford: British Archaeological Reports, British Series 242.

Hill, J. D. (1996). Hillforts and the Iron Age of Wessex. In T. C. Champion and J. R. Collis (eds.) *The Iron Age in Britain and Ireland: recent trends*: 95–116. Sheffield: J.R. Collis Publications.

Hill, J. D. (forthcoming). *How did Middle and Late pre-Roman Iron Age societies work (if they did)*.

Hingley, R. (1984). The archaeology of settlement and the social significance of space. *Scottish Archaeological Review* 3: 22–27.

Hingley, R. (1990). Boundaries surrounding Iron Age and Romano-British settlements. *Scottish Archaeological Review* 7: 96–103.

Jay, M. and M. P. Richards (2007). British Iron Age diet: stable isotopes and other evidence. *Proceedings of the Prehistoric Society* 73: 169–90.

Moore, T. (2007). Perceiving communities: exchange, landscapes and social networks in the Later Iron Age of western Britain. *Oxford Journal of Archaeology* 26: 79–102.

Neal, D. S. (1980). Bronze Age, Iron Age, and Roman settlement sites at Little Somborne and Ashley, Hampshire. *Proceedings of the Hampshire Field Club and Archaeological Society* 36: 91–144.

Parker Pearson, M. (1996). Food, fertility and front doors in the first millennium BC. In T. C. Champion and J. R. Collis (eds.) *The Iron Age in Britain and Ireland: recent trends*: 117–132. Sheffield: J. R. Collis Publications.

Parker Pearson, M. and C. Richards (1994). Architecture and order: spatial representation and archaeology. In M. Parker Pearson and C. Richards (eds.) *Architecture and Order: approaches to social space*: 38–72. London: Routledge.

Sharples, N. (1991). *Maiden Castle: excavation and field survey 1985–6.* London: English Heritage, HBMCE Archaeological Report 19.

Sharples, N. (2007). Building communities and creating identities in the first millennium BC. In C. C. Haselgrove and R. E. Pope (eds.) *The Earlier Iron Age in Britain and the Near Continent*: 174–84. Oxford: Oxbow Books.

Wainwright, G. J. (1979). *Gussage All Saints: an Iron Age settlement in Dorset.* London: HMSO.

Wilk, R. R. and W. L. Rathje (1982). Household archaeology. In R. R. Wilk and W. L. Rathje (eds.) *Archaeology of the Household: building a prehistory of domestic life*: 617–39. American Behavioural Science 25.

Yanagisako, S. J. (1979). Family and household: the analysis of domestic groups. *Annual Review of Anthropology* 8: 161–205.

## CHAPTER 5

# INFORMATION HIGHWAYS – WESSEX
## LINEAR DITCHES AND THE TRANSMISSION
## OF COMMUNITY

### Andy Tullett

*(University of Leicester)*

## Abstract

Long linear earthworks, dating to the Late Bronze and Early Iron Age, are found running across most of the Wessex downlands. Current interpretations of these monuments focus on their role as boundaries, restricting movement and denoting either tenurial or territorial divisions. There is a steadily growing body of evidence that suggests many of these ditches are associated with trackways and other non-settlement related activities. The earthworks represent a shift to a transhumant, mixed agricultural regime so rather than restricting movement, they channelled and were symptomatic of more mobile elements within society.

The increased mobility of certain groups within society promoted regular contact between different communities, providing the opportunity for the creation of weak bridging ties between them. These bridging ties are essential to the flow of information and the spread of innovation and an increase in these at this time allowed the transmission of more news and ideas than in preceding periods. The construction of the linear earthworks and the agricultural regime that it represented therefore led to increased social interaction and the circulation of new ideas. The large midden deposits in the Vale of Pewsey with evidence for the congregation of large numbers of people and animals, along with evidence for early iron working are symptomatic of these social changes.

## Introduction

Linear earthworks are found across much of the Wessex downland and, after coaxial field systems, are the most extensive archaeological feature in the

Wessex area, with estimates that for Hampshire alone, 800km may have once existed (Bowen 1978: 119). Narratives created around these features have tended to dwell upon their role delimiting the landscape as tenurial or territorial boundaries (Bradley *et al.* 1994), the movement of land into private ownership (Cunliffe 2004) or a trend towards pastoralism (Bowen 1978). However, it was also recognised in the first half of the twentieth century that the Late Bronze Age/Early Iron Age linear earthworks that run across the Wessex downs provided potential routes across the wider landscape (Clay 1927; Hawkes 1939). Recent developer funded work across Wiltshire, whilst showing the highly variable nature of the earthworks, has highlighted their regular coincidence with a number of other features. Namely, these are the presence of trackways following the line of the ditches, the occurrence of post-holes perhaps indicating fence lines and non-settlement related pits, post-holes and hearths. The relationship of these features with some of the linear earthworks draws us back to the ideas raised by Clay (1927) and Hawkes (1939) to their role in channelling movement. This paper will review the evidence for movement through the landscape during the Late Bronze and Early Iron Age. It will look at the implications of journeys upon the individual and society in terms of communal ties, the passage of information and the uptake of innovations. It will then show how the large midden sites of the Vale of Pewsey were a product of the construction of the linear earthwork system both in terms of the transhumant regime that they represent and the growth of social contact and the ideas that were transmitted along them.

## Linear earthwork systems

Linear earthworks, also known as linear ditches, linear boundaries, boundary ditches and ranch boundaries, are divided on morphological grounds into two categories, spinal linears and subsidiary linears. The spinal linears are the longest, with Old Ditch West and the Old Nursery Ditch on Salisbury Plain running for 16km and 11km respectively (McOmish *et al.* 2002: 61). These often follow contours along false crests or more rarely watersheds and in some instances appear to divide areas containing coaxial field systems from higher rougher pasture (Field 2001: 60). Subsidiary linears are connected to spinal elements but rather than following contours usually plunge down into valleys (Bradley *et al.* 1994: 13). In the Wylye Valley, Wiltshire, subsidiary elements run down from Old Ditch West defining areas of land roughly 500m wide that enclose a range of ecological zones (McOmish *et al.* 2002: 64). Where they coincide with coaxial field systems, the linear earthworks are invariably older (Bowen 1978: 122; Field 2001: 60; McOmish *et al.* 2002: 53), although cases of Late Iron Age and Romano-British field systems overlying earlier linears have been noted (Ford 1982a, 1982b; Bradley *et al.* 1994: 123; Fulford *et al.* 2006: 43). In most instances this would mean that some of the earlier fields would be slighted and put out of arable production. Examples do exist where cultivation seems to have continued after the construction of the linear such as at Tidworth where asymmetrical lynchets either side of a linear suggest arable cultivation continued on one side with the linear cutting it off from an area of pasture (McOmish *et al.* 2002: 63). In some instances, linear earthworks focus on certain hilltops whereon early hilltop enclosures were constructed. In some cases, such as Quarley Hill, these were later upgraded to hillforts. It is considered that linears and early hilltop enclosures are broadly contemporary and mostly date from 1000–750 BC (Cunliffe 2004: 68). The paucity of internal structures within these early hilltop enclosures, along with their situation within the linear earthwork system, has led to suggestions that they were used for stock management, such as lambing, shearing or division of animals amongst owners (*ibid.*: 75). Together these point to the management of animals on an increasingly large scale towards the end of the Bronze Age. In the Earliest Iron Age, *c.* 850–750 BC, we see the first dark earth deposits being laid down at the large midden sites in the Vale of Pewsey (Needham 2007). Some, but not all of these sites, are found in conjunction with hilltop enclosures, specifically, All Cannings Cross and Stanton St. Bernard with Rybury, Martinsell hill with Martinsell and Westbury with Bratton Camp. These enclosures make excellent marshalling areas for the collection of animals on the downs in preparation for transfer into the valleys to the associated midden areas. The midden sites consist of huge dark humic deposits with a high density of ceramic, bone and artefact inclusions that cover several hectares. It is now becoming clear that the dark earth on these sites results from the regular corralling of animals in specific areas over long periods of time. It is hypothesised that the regular rhythms associated with holding animals for milking could produce such a deposit (Serjeantson 2007: 89) and the annual slaughter of large numbers of juvenile animals supports the hypothesis of dairy regimes being practiced at these sites, albeit on an annual rather than continual basis (Serjeantson *et al.* forthcoming). Overall the landscape data supports a supposition that animals were being managed in increasingly large numbers during this period.

Interpretations for the linear earthwork systems usually concentrate on their role as boundaries demarcating tenurial rights (Cunliffe 1991: 35; Bradley *et al.* 1994: 137; McOmish *et al.* 2002: 64) or their implication as a shift from arable to pastoral production (Arnold 1972: 39; Bowen 1978: 120; Brück 2007: 31). A connection between linear earthworks and trackways has been noted, particularly the first half of the twentieth century (Clay 1927; Stone 1934; Hawkes 1939), but also more recently (Bowen 1978: 122; McOmish *et al.* 2002: 65). C.F.C. Hawkes described the linear ditches at Quarley Hill most eloquently – 'a boundary when thought of transversely, a road when thought of lengthways' (1939: 147). However, work on linear earthworks has tended to focus on the way they restrict movement, either to prevent animals straying or in assertion of landholding, rather than explore how they channelled and even promoted movement.

In part, the pastoralist rationale for linear earthworks rests on their ability to provide a barrier that would prevent stock from straying from one side to the other. If they were simply a shallow ditch, it is much more likely that they acted as a territorial boundary. The movement of animals would require a means of control to drive them in the correct direction. This could be achieved either through the use of barriers, dogs or people on horseback. The remains of dogs are frequently recovered from settlements of this period although it is impossible to discern what function, if any, they served on the farm. Evidence for barriers has also been elusive. It has been maintained that the low banks that would have flanked the ditches would have been essential for the establishment of hedges (Pryor 1998: 87), but firmer evidence for hedges is harder to come by (Bowen 1978). Evidence for fences running along the earthworks, as well as associated trackways, has, however, been slowly accumulating. At Winterborne Dauntsey, post-holes were found to either side of a broad U-shaped ditch, three to five foot wide at the base, with a primary fill of compacted chalk dust and a few fragments of Early Iron Age pottery (Stone 1934: 451). The excavator's interpretation was that the chalk had been compacted through repeated trampling and that the ditch functioned as a channel for the movement of cattle with fences to prevent animals from straying (*ibid.*: 452). At Boscombe Down Sports Field, a row of post-holes over a distance of at least 75m, was found to parallel an Early Iron Age linear earthwork averaging 1m deep and 4m wide (Wessex Archaeology 1996).

Moving onto trackways, Clay (1927) suggested that ditches near the Early Iron Age settlements of Fifield Bavant and Swallowcliffe Down were used to move cattle in single file from neighbouring combs through areas of arable land. The compacted chalk deposit was also noted along a ditch baulk during Hawkes' excavation at Quarley Hill (Hawkes 1939: 153). More recently, the Wessex Linear Ditches Project uncovered a trackway with wheel ruts flanking a linear. The trackway was in part sealed beneath a small midden-spread containing Earliest Iron Age wares (Bradley *et al.* 1994: 50). At Britford, a trackway was found running alongside a Late Bronze Age linear that headed towards the Great Woodbury enclosure, and although no finds were recovered to date it, its similar alignment to the ditch suggested contemporaneity (Wessex Archaeology 1997). Also excavated alongside the linear were three shallow pits producing small amounts of Late Bronze Age and Earliest Iron Age ceramics (*ibid.*). This brings us to a further phenomenon of the linear earthworks, that of non-settlement related activity.

It is increasingly obvious that a range of non-settlement related activities took place alongside linear earthworks, though most excavations in the past have focused on the ditch and so failed to turn up evidence of this kind. A 1.57–hectare excavation, covering a 550m length of the Old Ditch near Breach Hill uncovered eight pits, four post- or stake- holes and three hearths (Birbeck 2006). Most of these features were undated due to lack of finds though one feature did produce a single sherd of Earliest Iron Age pottery. Indeed, the lack of finds generally associated with such features, along with the current focus on settlement archaeology has led to a general lack of attempts at explanation. At Quarley Hill, an occupation layer of charred matter was found next to one of the linears but underlying the later hillfort rampart (Hawkes 1939: 159). It is possible that this is contemporary with an earlier palisade enclosure although it may have started to accumulate prior to its construction. It may therefore suggest activity connected with the linears prior to the enclosure of the hilltop.

The coaxial field system would have placed constraints on the control and movement of animals and in particular the size of the flocks that were being managed. This would have been especially true for moving animals slowly from field to field. At the time the linear earthworks were created, it is apparent, that cultivation continued within some of the fields, whilst elsewhere some may have fallen out of arable use. The landscape through which the linear earthworks were dug, were a mix of rough, undemarcated downland, cultivated and abandoned fields, perhaps still marked by slowly thinning hedges or ramshackle fences. The result was that the linear earthworks opened up major thoroughfares through the landscape just through their creation. It is unlikely that the majority of the linear earthworks were created as routeways and this secondary function as pathways appears to be a fortuitous by-product of the way they unlocked clear passages.

Movement, albeit on a range of scales, is integral to daily life and agriculture can be broken down and viewed as a series of movements (Blaikie 1971: 4). There are many reasons for people to traverse the Wessex downs, including activities such as resource procurement, trade and war. However, the most likely reason for regular movement, concerns the movement of animals between areas of pasture, water, processing areas and areas of consumption. It is important here to note the important difference between pastoralism and transhumance. Pastoralists are highly mobile, with few if any permanent settlements, living off their animals as they move across the land. Transhumance however is a specialized form of mixed agriculture practised by sedentary communities (Krader 1959: 500; Jones 2005: 359). Communities that practice transhumance significantly differ from pastoralists in that they focus on arable production from permanent settlements with only a small proportion of the population involved with the movement of animals between seasonal pastures

(Johnson 1969: 18–19). Currently, there is no evidence to suggest that any communities in Wessex practiced a pastoral regime during the Late Bronze and Early Iron Age. Instead, the creation of the linear earthworks appears to represent a trend to a transhumant form of mixed agriculture.

Thus, I have shown that there is a small but growing body of evidence for the recurrence of certain archaeological features along linear earthworks in Wessex. Namely, these are the presence of boundaries, flanking trackways and other non-settlement contexts. I maintain that these are all important features that attest to the secondary use of some linear earthworks as roads and that their creation resulted in a concomitant rise in the mobility of communities at this time.

# Middens

A number of large midden deposits have been identified, over the last 30 years, in and around the Vale of Pewsey. So far, up to 11 large middens are known or proposed, with the best excavated evidence coming from All Cannings Cross (Cunnington 1923), Potterne (Lawson 2000) and East Chisenbury (McOmish 1996; Brown *et al.* forthcoming). The material culture recovered from the middens appears to reflect dispersed contacts across the region. So far, all of the published middens have produced Kimmeridge shale bracelets, and amber has been recovered from half of them (Brück 2007: 33). At Potterne, nearly 20 percent of the Earliest Iron Age phase ceramics were non-local, implying strong contacts with the Bristol Avon valley (Morris 2000). This suggests that the people visiting middens roamed extensively and were situated within a regional trade network, supporting the idea that sections of these communities were highly mobile.

Evidence from the middens appears to support the idea that these communities were practicing a transhumant regime. At All Cannings Cross, Maud Cunnington recovered 1360 hammerstones, mullers or pounders used for dressing querns, nine complete saddle querns stones and 'many' rubbers and fragments of more querns (1923). At Potterne, 115 fragments of saddle quern stones and 43 mullers, rubbers and hammerstones were recovered (Seager Smith 2000). Clearly, grain remained an important part of the diet, even though the animal bones from East Chisenbury alone are large enough to feed a full time population of up to 2000 (Serjeantson *et al.* forthcoming). The bones from East Chisenbury, Stanton St. Bernard and All Cannings Cross also indicate significant seasonality (Serjeantson *et al.* forthcoming; Tullett and Harrison forthcoming), implying influxes of large numbers of animals at certain times of the year. An estimate for the animal bones from East Chisenbury suggests that 3800 sheep/goats, 600 cattle and 450 pigs were slaughtered annually (Serjeantson *et al.* forthcoming). If we consider that this is one of up to 11 such sites it signals that huge numbers of animals must have been managed in order to support this rate of slaughter. These animals would require a large amount of land and labour to manage them and we must assume that they roamed over a large area. Among the concerns of herders, is the need to maintain the meat and milk yield of their animals, as well as the health of the following year's young, which is dictated by nutritional intake (Halstead 1996: 25). A prime policy used to maintain this is seasonal movement between rested pastures, so that lush vegetation is always available (*ibid.*). The construction of the linear earthworks therefore created the large areas of pasture required to raise such large numbers of animals and also provided the means for their movement between them.

The evidence from this period in Wessex suggests that the creation of the linear earthworks coincided with a trend towards transhumant mixed farming and by implication a concurrent increase in the scale and regularity of movement undertaken by people, especially those involved with the management of animals. I will now move on to look at the theory surrounding movement and journeys to assess some of the impact of this increased mobility suggested by the evidence.

# The sociology of travel

The pathway is usually viewed in functional terms, facilitating the movement of labour, goods and information between two places (Zedeño and Stoffle 2003: 60). Movement has an energy cost and a benefit to the participants in economic, social or mental terms. For these reasons the investigation of travel has previously been studied in terms of cost minimization versus opportunity maximization (e.g. von Thünen 1966; Chisolm 1962; Christaller 1966; Carlstein 1982; Paynter 1982). The flaw in these works is that humans rarely consider their actions or landscape in such simplistic mathematical terms. A whole range of social factors apply and even subordinate the purely economic (Stone 1991: 344). Recent archaeological work has been more sympathetic to these factors, helping to redress the balance (e.g. Tilley 1994; Zedeño and Stoffle 2003; Chadwick 2004a; Cummings and Johnston 2007). As a result we are becoming increasingly aware of the role of travel in the creation of knowledge and identity, the way it structures social interaction, its liminal nature, its implications for non-travellers, and its importance in the spread of innovation.

People grow up within the cultural confines of their community, wherein the core communal code and behavioural framework is considered the norm (Cohen 1982: 4). This code is rarely explicit and members of the community are usually unaware of it, as it is considered the proper way of doing things or conducting oneself (Cohen 1978: 454). This framework is used as a frame of reference for how to act, interpreting the actions of others and allowing them to understand the world around them (*ibid.*). When an individual comes into contact with a culture or community with differing values, this concept of normality is challenged, confronting them with novel experiences and forcing them to reassess their world view (Cohen 1982: 4–5). This reassessment is never confined to similarity or difference, but always involves a value judgement as to right or wrong, good or bad, us and them (Gupta and Ferguson 1997: 13). Travel precipitates these encounters with the new, thereby facilitating the generation of knowledge and the awareness of social identity.

Basso (1996) notes that for the Cibecue Apache of Arizona, features in the landscape are used to teach moral lessons on the conduct of behaviour and everyday life. The journey through their landscape is therefore also a journey of knowledge with features acting as mnemonics for important moral lessons. Although such journeys of discovery cannot be substantiated for the Late Bronze and Earliest Iron Age, the linear earthworks do appear to incorporate many earlier features such as settlements, and long and round barrows (McOmish *et al.* 2002: 65). Division of rights in the landscape is usually based upon observable features providing obvious markers. The incorporation of these structures into the course of the linears may therefore reflect pre-existing land rights or an agreement on division. However, for people travelling along the linear earthworks the occupants of the barrows or possibly even their original purpose could have passed out of living memory. The structures would therefore have provided excellent reference points, both culturally and geographically. They may have been woven into tales of mythology to teach morality, cultural identity and reinforce the community's embeddedness in the landscape.

The dislocation of the journey itself often provides the time and opportunity for introspection and self awareness (Curtis and Pajaczkowska 1994: 212). Movement is usually, though not always, pre-empted by the functional requirement to undertake an activity, though who takes the activity and where it takes place are determined by social factors. Activities may be drawn along social factors such as age, gender and status (Brück and Goodman 1999: 12; Chadwick 2004b: 202; Brück 2007: 32) leading to differential experience that may vary over the course of the year and a lifetime. Certain paths are associated with the activities that are undertaken at their destination or whilst being traversed (Zedeño and Stoffle 2003: 61). So, just as different people undertake different activities, different people take different paths and different journeys. The routes that people undertake sequentially order the places that they visit, the people that they meet, the activities they undertake and the experiences they accrue. The result is a highly variable set of experiences, knowledge and interaction that is core to individuality and identity. These aspects of identity however are not limited to the routes and the people that traverse them. Animals and material culture also take these journeys and attain their own distinct identities as a result. The identity of animals is often tied up with that of their rearers and the landscape of their origin (Gray 2002), whilst material culture carries associations of their purpose and makers. However, a new identity may accrue with their transactional history and thus the journey they have taken (Ingold 1986: 182), when they are taken out of context a new meaning may be attained that bears little resemblance to that assigned them by their creators (Hodder 1982: 202).

In a world without instruments for the measurement and monitoring of time, the passage of the day is punctuated by a routine of daily activities, just as the year is ordered by the demands of the agricultural calendar. During a journey, the individual is removed from the progression of their domestic routine and may acquire the feeling of being outside of time (Curtis and Pajaczkowska 1994: 199). Whilst it is now accepted by some, that paths form places of their own (Zedeño and Stoffle 2003: 59), for the traveller the experience is of being between places, origin and destination (Delanty 2003: 142). The result is that the traveller experiences the physicality of a place between places and outside of the normal strictures of time. These liminal aspects of travel may only be limited to the initial stages of the journey as a new set of routines becomes adopted and life on the road becomes a form of dwelling in itself. It is for these reasons that the existence of nomads is not, at least for them, to be considered as liminal. For nomads, their daily routines are based upon travel, and if home is to be defined as the place where one best knows themselves (Rapport and Dawson 1998a: 9), then their home is on the road and they never leave it (Rapport and Dawson 1998b: 22). For others, the liminality of the journey is not limited to those that take it. For more sedentary members of the communities, travellers away from home are in a liminal state. Until their return or news is received of their well-being, the travellers could be alive or dead. The members of the community at home are linked mentally by their memories of the travellers, but also more physically by the road by which they left. The path is therefore a mnemonic of their departure and a tenuous connection to their continued existence. Return brings closure and conclusion, but the journey lives on through the experiences, knowledge and objects acquired during it. The journey continues whilst its stories are retold, much as the historic journeys of Marco Polo, Livingstone, Speke and more recently Michael Palin live on with their constant retelling. Stories of the journey allow non-travellers to experience it for themselves, bringing faraway places home (Minh-ha 1994: 22), facilitating vicarious travel, experience, knowledge and interaction for the sedentary (Dawson and Johnson 2001: 320).

With movement goes pause. Periods of pause and rest punctuate the journey and lead to the creation of place. Pause may be connected to a physical need to recuperate energy or with a need to undertake certain activities. The regularity of pause in certain locations over time gives these places history and meaning (Zedeño and Stoffle 2003: 61) and is usually connected with the activities undertaken there. The traces of these periods of rest may be represented materially through residues of the activities undertaken. Principally these might include hearths and animal bones, but usually not ceramics as their fragility prohibits their use during journeys in favour of more durable organic wares. One result is that we would expect ceramics to be relatively sparse at sites representing periods of pause because of both the infrequency of occupation of the site, and the likelihood that few ceramics were brought there and even fewer broken. For this period we are largely dependent on ceramics for dating features and the lack of these in most of the features found alongside linear earthworks usually precludes us dating them with any certainty. However, the finds from Breach Hill (Birbeck 2006) and Britford (Wessex Archaeology 1997) suggests near contemporaneity with the linears and in turn an association with movement. At Quarley Hill, the pre-hillfort deposits (Hawkes 1939) are good evidence for periods of pause alongside elements of the Quarley linear system. Pauses taken on the hilltop during journeys suggests that the repetition of stays here was important in the creation of this site as a place and in turn made it suitable for the construction of the palisade enclosure and finally the hillfort. If the linear ditch builders had chosen a route across a different hill, leaving Quarley Hill unblemished, then that alternate route would have been taken, people would have paused on that hill and it seems unlikely that Quarley hillfort would have been constructed.

Travel also has a pivotal role in the spread of innovation. To understand the way that this works we need to look at the ideas of Mark Granovetter and especially his work on the strength of weak ties. Granovetter suggested that the strength of social bonds that bind individuals together into larger social groups, results from the amount of time spent together, the intensity, the intimacy and the reciprocity of the relationship (1973: 1361). These can then be broadly categorized as strong, weak, negligible and absent ties. Negligible ties reflect only a nodding relationship with recognition, but little or no interaction and/or knowledge of each other, whilst an absent tie is self evident. These categories tend to have little importance on social groups under normal circumstances and so will not be dealt with further in this paper. Strong ties reflect long periods of time spent together and hence a high degree of interaction with individuals sharing a significant amount of knowledge about each other with the desire to lend assistance in need. They are usually associated with close kin, neighbours and friends and tend to be confined within small social groups of strongly bonded individuals (Blau 1974: 623). By definition, strong ties involve a high degree of reciprocity, and hence these groups form the primary medium for assistance and insurance in times of trouble and hardship, providing a minimum level of economic security to its members (Granovetter 1983: 212). Weak ties result from less contact but still denote a degree of interaction and social knowledge of each other. These probably result from participation within structural social groups undertaking specific activities. Individuals with whom you share weak ties are likely to belong to other social groups to whom they are connected by strong ties. As such, weak ties provide an opportunity for bridging between different, small, strongly-bonded social groups, although it is important to note that not all weak ties will act as social bridges (Granovetter 1973: 1376). These social bridges integrate the individual and their core social group into the wider society and are important in the flow of information and innovation.

By definition, a strong tie involves common interests and a lot of time spent together, so people with whom an individual shares strong ties are also likely to share strong ties. Thus, if individual X has strong ties with Y and Z, Y and Z are likely to spend a lot of time together, if only in the company of X, and share common interests. The result is that even if Y and Z did not know each other prior to their relationship with X, a strong tie is still likely to develop (Granovetter 1973: 1362). People deliberately manipulate the membership of the groups within which they partake and this may mean that they take part in more activities with which friends are associated or deliberately include friends within activities that others are excluded from. The result is that the people that form one person's strong ties will regularly come into contact with each other. People are most likely to share new information with their strong ties, so news will quickly circulate around their small strongly bonded social groups usually in the form of gossip. Whilst this is good for maintaining the strong bonds of the group, they are only likely to receive information on the group itself unless it comes from an external source, typically through a weak bridging tie. Information coming through a weak tie is therefore less likely to have been heard before and be novel to the group (*ibid.*: 1366). As a result, a group with lots of strong ties, but few weak bridging ties, is likely to be isolated from new information and ideas, and unlikely to be able to pass them on when they themselves generate them (Granovetter 1983: 202). Thus, weak bridging ties are essential to the flow of information and innovation, as they allow access to new ideas and provide more social opportunities. Ideas diffused through weak bridging ties are likely to travel over greater social distances, reaching more people in less time than when passed through strong ties (Granovetter 1973: 1366).

Strong ties are not irrelevant to the spread of innovation though. Whilst new ideas are most likely to be passed on through weak bridging ties there is evidence to suggest that new information is more likely to be given credence when it comes through a strong tie and this applies equally to the uptake of innovations (Weimann 1980: 12 cited in Granovetter 1983). So for a community to avoid isolation, its members need to maintain a healthy mix of both strong and weak ties, most importantly weak bridging ties, between the social groups that constitute it and with social groups from other communities (Granovetter 1973: 1378). In turn, there must be a means for individuals to create these bridging ties and distinct ways or contexts in which they may be formed (Granovetter 1983: 229). That is, there must be lots of different points of interaction within and outside of the community. The movement of people around the landscape, albeit undertaking tasks and activities, provides opportunities for encounters with individuals from other social groups. As many activities that require interaction and movement are likely to be agriculturally based, the prospects for contact will be governed by the agricultural cycle. Thus certain individuals will routinely encounter each other on an infrequent but cyclical basis. Whilst this might preclude the development of strong ties between these individuals, it would present perfect opportunities for the formation of weak bridging ties. Journeys connected to the agricultural cycle, such as those undertaken by transhumant groups, would therefore be instrumental in the creation of weak bridging ties, generating fertile conditions for social diffusion.

After the creation of the linear earthworks, a greater focus on transhumant farming and a concomitant rise in movement it is perhaps no surprise that we see the development of the Pewsey middens. They constitute centres where hundreds of people seem to have gathered, albeit seasonally. They contain evidence for large amounts of craft work: quern stone production, shearing, spinning, weaving, cheese making, metalworking and hide processing. In terms of material, they contrast sharply with the paucity of earlier sites. They are emblematic of an intensification of social interaction and production and the fruition of an increasingly mobile society. The increase in the range of movement afforded by the linear earthwork systems provided the social conditions for the formation of the middens but as we are finding out it is just one factor within their creation. With the Pewsey middens, evidence is starting to suggest that they were participating in a dairy and pastoral regime leading to the accumulation of massive amounts of stabling waste (Serjeantson 2007; Tullett 2008). The middens imply that truly huge herds were maintained to support such large annual slaughter rates. These herds required hundreds of people to manage them as they traversed the downs and for these the midden sites may have acted as semi-seasonal home bases.

It is of interest that these deposits are concurrent with the adoption of iron. Iron working is known is this country as early as the tenth century BC at Hartshill Copse in Berkshire (Collard *et al.* 2006) but its uptake appears to have been slow. Although the lack of iron artefacts from this period may result from intensive recycling (Needham 2007), it is also possible that society was not structured in a way that allowed the diffusion of the 'idea' of iron and the technology to work it. The rise in the degree of mobility represented by the linear earthworks, would have allowed more weak bridging ties to have been created between small strongly bonded social groups. As already mentioned, Granovetter's work suggests that weak bridging ties are invaluable in the diffusion of information and the adoption of innovation. A variety of iron artefacts are routinely found at the middens, as is evidence for iron working. Sources of iron can be found near the Vale at Seend, Westbury and Bromham. Although no evidence for iron extraction from these sites has yet been dated to the Earliest Iron Age, Potterne lies close to Seend and a further midden site has recently been found at Westbury. A possible interesting link for future research may therefore be the role played by movement, intensification in society and the middens in the adoption and dissemination of iron and iron working technology.

## Conclusions

Linear earthworks appear to have been constructed across the Wessex downland during the Late Bronze and Early Iron Age for a variety of reasons and it is difficult to attribute a single function for all of them from their outset. It is fair to say that their construction was concomitant with a trend towards transhumance and more mobile communities. However, it is over simplistic to consider them purely as an indication of a new agricultural regime. The linear earthworks channelled the movement of people and animals dictating who the travellers would meet and when. They were the medium that brought people from different communities together at physical meetings and linked them mentally. It has been argued that the construction of the Roman road network in Italy facilitated an increase in interaction, a mixing of cultures, and social and economic interdependence leading to the creation of a sense of *Italia* (Laurence 2001: 67). Likewise, the increase in contact in Wessex made communities aware of their situation within a larger sub-regional assemblage and may have been the first hesitant step towards the tribal groupings observed during the Late Iron Age. An increase in mobility allows the flow of information and ideas as well as people and things. The creation of toll roads and canal networks in eighteenth century Britain is considered as a necessary precursor to the following industrial revolution (Pawson 1977: 4–7) and although of a much smaller magnitude, the increased mobility appears to herald the acceptance of iron working. Thus, the creation of the linear earthwork system, although originating from tenurial or territorial concerns and a shift in farming practice, can be seen to have had a huge impact through their secondary, and probably unintentional, use as paths of movement.

# Acknowledgements

I would like to thank Prof. Colin Haselgrove and Dr. L. McFadyen whose supervision has provided valuable insight during my PhD; Dr. Robert Johnston for his excellent comments on this paper; Prof. John Barrett and David McOmish for providing access to the Vale of Pewsey archives and to the Arts and Humanities Research Council who have funded my research.

# Bibliography

Arnold, C. J. (1972). The excavation of a prehistoric ranch boundary at Quarley hill, Hampshire. *Proceedings of the Hampshire Field Club and Archaeological Society* 29: 37–40.

Basso, K. H. (1996). Wisdom sits in places: notes on a Western Apache Landscape. In S. Feld and K. H. Basso (eds.) *Senses of Place*: 53–90. Santa Fe: School of American Research.

Birbeck, V. (2006). Excavations on the Old Ditch Linear Earthwork, Breach Hill, Tilshead. *Wiltshire Archaeological and Natural History Magazine* 99: 79–103.

Blaikie, P. M. (1971). Spatial organization of agriculture in some North Indian villages. Part 1. *Transactions of the Institute of British Geographers* 52: 1–40.

Blau, P. (1974). Parameters of social structure. *American Sociological Review* 39(5): 615–635.

Bowen, H. C. (1978). 'Celtic' fields and 'ranch' boundaries in Wessex. In S. Limbrey and J. G. Evans (eds.) *The Effect of Man on the Landscape: the lowland zone*: 115–123. London: Council for British Archaeology Research Report No. 21.

Bradley, R., R. Entwistle and F. Raymond (1994). *Prehistoric Land Divisions on Salisbury Plain: the work of the Wessex Linear Ditches Project*. London: English Heritage.

Brown, G. D., Field and D. McOmish (forthcoming). *The Late Bronze Age – Early Iron Age Site at East Chisenbury, Wiltshire*.

Brück, J. and M. Goodman (1999). Introduction: themes for a critical archaeology of prehistoric settlement. In J. Brück and M. Goodman (eds.) *Making Places in the Prehistoric World: themes in settlement archaeology*: 1–19. London: UCL Press.

Brück, J. (2007). The character of Late Bronze Age settlement in southern Britain. In C. C. Haselgrove and R. E. Pope (eds.) *The Earlier Iron Age in Britain and the Near Continent*: 24–38. Oxford: Oxbow Books.

Carlstein, T. (1982). *Time Resources, Society and Ecology Volume 1: preindustrial societies*. London: Allen and Unwin.

Chadwick, A. M. (2004a). *Stories from the Landscape: Archaeologies of Inhabitation*. Oxford: British Archaeological Reports, International Series 1238.

Chadwick, A. M. (2004b). Footprints in the sands of time. Archaeologies of inhabitation on Cranbourne Chase, Dorset. In A. M. Chadwick (ed.) *Stories from the Landscape: archaeologies of inhabitation*: 179–256. Oxford: British Archaeological Reports, International Series 1238.

Chisholm, M. (1962). *Rural Settlement and Land Use: an essay in location*. London: Hutchinson.

Christaller, W. (1966). *Central Places in Southern Germany* (translated by C. W. Baskin). Prentice-Hall: Englewood Cliffs, New Jersey.

Clay, R. C. C. (1927). Some prehistoric ways. *Antiquity* 1(1): 54–65.

Cohen, A. P. (1978). 'The same – but different': the allocation of identity in Whalsay, Shetland. *The Sociological Review* 26: 449–469

Cohen, A. P. (1982). Belonging: the experience of culture. In A. P. Cohen (ed.) *Belonging: identity and social organisation in British rural cultures*: 1–17. Manchester: Manchester University Press

Collard, M., T. Darvill and M. Watts (2006). Ironworking in the Bronze Age? Evidence from a 10th century BC settlement at Hartshill Copse, Upper Bucklebury, West Berkshire. *Proceedings of the Prehistoric Society* 72: 367–422.

Cummings, V. and R. Johnston (2007). *Prehistoric Journeys*. Oxford: Oxbow Books.

Cunliffe, B. (1991). *Iron Age Communities in Britain: an account of England, Scotland and Wales from the seventh century BC until the Roman conquest* (3rd Edition). London: Routledge.

Cunliffe, B. (2004). Wessex cowboys? *Oxford Journal of Archaeology* 23(1): 61–81.

Cunnington, M. (1923). *The Early Iron Age Inhabited Site at All Cannings Cross Farm, Wiltshire*. Devizes: George Simpson.

Curtis, B. and C. Pajaczkowska (1994). 'Getting there': travel, time and narrative. In G. Robertson, M. Mash, L. Tickner, J. Bird, B. Curtis and T. Putnam (eds.) *Travellers' Tales: narratives of home and displacement*: 199–215. London: Routledge.

Dawson, A. and M. Johnson (2001). Migration, exile and landscapes of the imagination. In B. Bender and M. Winer (eds.) *Contested Landscapes: movement, exile and place*: 319–332. Oxford: Berg.

Delanty, G. (2003). *Community*. London: Routledge

Field, D. (2001). Place and memory in Bronze Age Wessex. In J. Brück (ed.) *Bronze Age Landscapes: tradition and transformation*: 57–64. Oxford: Oxbow Books.

Ford, S. (1982a). Linear earthworks on the Berkshire Downs. *Berkshire Archaeological Journal* 71: 1–20.

Ford, S. (1982b). Fieldwork and excavation on the Berkshire Grims Ditch. *Oxoniesia* 47: 13–36.

Fulford, M. G., A. B. Powell, R. Entwistle and F. Raymond (2006). *Iron Age and Romano-British Settlements and Landscapes of Salisbury Plain*. Salisbury: Wessex Archaeology Report 20.

Granovetter, M. S. (1973). The strength of weak ties. *American Journal of Sociology* Volume 78(6): 1360–1380.

Granovetter, M. S. (1983). The strength of weak ties: a network theory revisited. *Sociological Theory* 1: 201–233.

Gray, J. (2002). Community as place-making: ram auctions in the Scottish borderland. In V. Amit (ed.) *Realizing Community: concepts, social relationships and sentiments*: 38–59. London: Routledge.

Gupta, A. and J. Ferguson (1997). Beyond 'culture': space, identity, and the politics of difference. In A. Gupta and J. Ferguson (eds.) *Culture, Power, Place: explorations in critical anthropology*. 33–52. Durham, North Carolina: Duke University Press.

Halstead, P. (1996). Pastoralism or household herding? Problems of scale and specialization in early Greek animal husbandry. *World Archaeology* 28(1): 20–42.

Hawkes, C. F. C. (1939). The excavations at Quarley Hill, 1938. *Papers and Proceedings of the Hampshire Field Club and Archaeological Society* 14(2): 136–194.

Hodder, I. (1982). *Symbols in Action: ethnoarchaeological studies of material culture*. Cambridge: Cambridge University Press.

Ingold, T. (1986). *The Appropriation of Nature: essays on human ecology and social relations*. Manchester: Manchester University Press.

Johnson, D. L. (1969). *The Nature of Nomadism: a comparative study of pastoral migrations in southwestern Asia and northern Africa*. Chicago: University Press.

Jones, S. (2005). Transhumance re-examined. *Journal of the Royal Anthropological Institute* 11(2): 357–359.

Krader, L. (1959). The ecology of nomadic pastoralism. *International Social Science Journal* 11: 499–510

Laurence, R. (2001). The creation of geography: an interpretation of Roman Britain. In C. Adams and R. Laurence (eds.) *Travel and Geography in the Roman Empire*: 67–94. London: Routledge.

Lawson, A. J. (ed.) (2000). *Potterne 1982–5: animal husbandry in later prehistoric Wiltshire*. Salisbury: Wessex Archaeological Report 17.

McOmish, D., D. Field and G. Brown (2002). *The Field Archaeology of the Salisbury Plain Training Area*. English Heritage: Swindon.

McOmish, D. (1996). East Chisenbury: ritual and rubbish at the British Bronze Age – Iron Age transition. *Antiquity* 70: 68–76.

Minh-ha, T. T. (1994). Other than myself/my other self. In G. Robertson, M. Mash, L. Tickner, J. Bird, B. Curtis and T. Putnam (eds.) *Travellers' Tales: narratives of home and displacement*: 9–26. London: Routledge.

Morris, E. L. (2000). Pottery – summary. In A. J. Lawson (ed.), *Potterne 1982–5: animal husbandry in later prehistoric Wiltshire*: 166–177. Wessex Archaeology Report No. 17.

Needham, S. (2007). 800 BC, the Great Divide. In C. C. Haselgrove and R. E. Pope (eds.) *The Earlier Iron Age in Britain and the Near Continent*: 39–63. Oxford: Oxbow Books.

Paynter, R. (1982). *Models of Spatial Inequality: settlement patterns in historical archaeology*. New York: Academic Press.

Pryor, F. (1998). *Farmers in Prehistoric Britain*. Stroud: Tempus.

Rapport, N. and A. Dawson (1998a). The topic and the book. In N. Rapport and A. Dawson (eds.) *Migrants of Identity: perceptions of home in a world of movement*: 3–17. Oxford: Berg.

Rapport, N. and A. Dawson (1998b). Home and movement: a polemic. In N. Rapport and A. Dawson (eds.) *Migrants of Identity: perceptions of home in a world of movement*: 19–38. Oxford: Berg.

Seager Smith, R. (2000). Worked stone. In A. J. Lawson (ed.) *Potterne 1982–5: animal husbandry in later prehistoric Wiltshire*: 213–219. Wessex Archaeology Report No. 17.

Serjeantson, D. (2007). Intensification of animal husbandry in the Late Bronze Age? In C. C. Haselgrove and R. E. Pope (eds.) *The Earlier Iron Age in Britain and the Near Continent*: 80–93. Oxford: Oxbow Books.

Serjeantson, D., J. Bagust and C. Jenkins (forthcoming). Animal bone. In G. Brown, D. Field and D. McOmish. *The Late Bronze Age – Early Iron Age site at East Chisenbury, Wiltshire*.

Stone, G. D. (1991). Agricultural territories in a dispersed settlement system. *Current Anthropology* 32(3): 343–353.

Stone, J. F. S. (1934). Three 'Peterborough' dwelling pits and a doubly stockaded Early Iron Age ditch at Winterbourne Dauntsey. *Wiltshire Archaeological and Natural History Magazine* 46: 445–453.

Tilley, C. (1994). *A Phenomenology of Landscape: places, paths and monuments*. Oxford: Berg.

Tullett, A. S. and C. Harrison (forthcoming). The Pewsey Middens – centres of feasting or symbols of community?

Tullett, A. S. (2008). Black earth, bone and bits of old pot. In O. Davis, N. Sharples and K. Waddington (eds.) *Changing perspectives on the first millennium BC*: 11–20. Oxford: Oxbow Books.

von Thünen, J. H. (1966 (originally published 1826)). *Von Thünen's isolated state*. (translated by C. M. Wartenburg), edited by P. Hall. London: Pergamon Press.

Weimann, G. (1980). *Conversation Networks as Communication Networks*. Abstract of PhD dissertation, University of Haifa, Israel.

Wessex Archaeology (1996). *Boscombe Sports Field, Boscombe Down, Wiltshire. Excavation in 1995*. Assessment report. Doc. Ref. 36875.1.

Wessex Archaeology (1997). *Land off Odstock Road, Britford, Salisbury*. Archaeological Excavation. Doc. Ref. 36932.

Zedeño, M. N. and R. W. Stoffle (2003). Tracking the role of pathways in the evolution of a human landscape: the St. Croix riverway in ethnohistorical perspective. In M. Rockman and J. Steele (eds.) *Colonization of Unfamiliar Landscapes: the archaeology of adaptation*: 59–80. London: Routledge.

## CHAPTER 6

# IT'S A SMALL WORLD... CLOSER CONTACTS IN THE EARLY THIRD CENTURY BC

*Greta Anthoons*

*(Bangor University)*

## Abstract

In the fifth and early fourth centuries BC, there were two culturally predominant regions in northern Gaul, the Middle Rhine-Moselle in Germany and the Aisne-Marne in France. They had a strong influence on the material culture of their neighbours, and there is evidence of a mutual exchange of ideas and technologies between the two regions. Both had high concentrations of chariot burials and other rich burials, often with grave goods of Mediterranean origin. However, in the second half of the fourth century BC, their hay days appear to have come to an end.

By 300 BC, the cards seem to be reshuffled. Chariot burials now appear in many different regions in northern Gaul, and even in Britain. They are less numerous and generally less rich, but they all seem to serve the purpose of establishing new centres of power and prestige, or alternatively reflect the struggle of an existing ruling class to preserve its power.

Other phenomena are characteristic for this period. The early third century BC is a time of innovation and standardisation. Novelties, many but not all in the field of weaponry, are quickly spread over a large distance. Contacts are no longer confined to a limited number of neighbouring regions, but reach as far as eastern Europe. The world has become a smaller place and internationalisation is the keyword.

The picture that emerges is one of more complex long distance networks, involving a larger number of actors. Via these networks the old concept of the chariot burial is spread and adopted, and innovations in art and technology disseminate at a rapid pace.

This paper will also seek to find an explanation for this evolution from a network with relatively few actors to the more complex system that can be discerned in the early third century BC.

# Introduction

In an earlier paper, *The origins of the Arras Culture: migration or elite networks?* (Anthoons 2007), funerary features typical for East Yorkshire in the Iron Age, like chariot burials and square ditched enclosures, were compared to those of various regions in Northern Gaul, in order to determine which alternative would offer the best explanation for the rise of the Arras Culture: small-scale elite migration or adoption of foreign burial rites by the local elite through contacts with their peers on the Continent. The comparison demonstrated that the various features cannot be connected with one specific area on the Continent, but are rather a compilation of elements from different regions, including a number of local British components, leading to the conclusion that it is probably more plausible for elite networks to have been at the basis of the change in burial rites in East Yorkshire. When discussing Iron Age elite networks, one must be aware that these are not stable, institutionalised or everlasting, but rather ephemeral, volatile and subject to internal and external factors. The present paper aims to illustrate how, based on the archaeological record, it is possible to capture changes in the functioning of these networks.

We know that towards the end of the fourth century BC, East Yorkshire was part of the Gaulish network. In northern Gaul itself, however, important changes took place around this time. In the fifth and earlier fourth centuries BC, there were two culturally predominant regions: the Aisne-Marne and the Middle Rhine-Moselle areas. However, in the course of the fourth century BC, these core areas seem to lose their cultural influence on their neighbours; they are no longer the only actors on the scene. Instead, several new regions now show signs of prosperity, displayed in rich burials and new artistic styles. To establish or maintain their power and prestige, the elite in these new regions reverts to using the chariot burial; this is the most ostentatious type of burial known from the former core areas, but now out of fashion. Mutual contacts are not limited to northern Gaul, but reach far into eastern Europe. At the same time, many innovations are spread very quickly across most of temperate Europe, to the extent that their place of origin can often not even be securely determined.

This paper will first focus on the situation in northern Gaul in the fifth and fourth centuries BC and will then discuss in greater detail the changes that took place at the end of the fourth century BC. It will argue that these changes reflect a restructuring of the existing networks. Finally, a few possible explanations will be presented to clarify the evolution in the network system.

# Northern Gaul in the fifth and fourth centuries BC

During the Early La Tène period, two regions, both near major rivers, are generally considered as the core areas of the La Tène culture in northern Gaul : the Middle Rhine-Moselle region in Germany and the Aisne-Marne region (in the past often imprecisely referred to as 'Champagne') in France. This acknowledgement is initially based on the high concentration of rich burials (with artefacts including chariots, weapons, fine jewellery, Mediterranean imports and precious materials), which make these regions stand out from their neighbours. Diepeveen-Jansen studied these with the aim to 'identify the concepts which are linked to elite identities in these societies' (2001:15) and proposed that both regions be considered as cultural unities that can be split up into a number of micro-regions (2001: 74–6, 145–6). However, the importance of these regions surpasses the sole presence of rich burials. When focussing on certain aspects of material culture, the sphere of influence of the Aisne-Marne and the Middle Rhine-Moselle regions extends far beyond their geographical boundaries. The best illustration of this is the so-called 'Marnian pottery', which is spread over large parts of northern Gaul, including Belgium and the southern Netherlands, and occurs in burial and settlement contexts alike. Marnian pottery is particularly fine pottery, characterised by its carinated shapes; it is often painted or slipped. The most extensive range of forms is attested in the Aisne-Marne region itself, including the most graceful tulip-shaped vessels, which do not occur further west and north (Hurtrelle *et al.* 1990: 220–1).

It is not always clear to which extent the Marnian pottery found in the various regions of northern Gaul is either imported or effectively belongs to the same tradition, or is simply of Marnian inspiration. On the basis of the pottery, Hurtrelle *et al.* (1990: 217–44) have even argued for extending the Aisne-Marne region to cover most of northern Gaul, a concept firmly dismissed by Leman-Delerive and Warmenbol (2006: 105) who state that the argument of differing burial rites weighs heavier than the analogy in ceramics.

The predominant formal burial rite in the Aisne-Marne region at this time is inhumation, as opposed to most other regions in northern Gaul, where cremation is preponderant or where no archaeologically visible type of burial has as yet been discovered. However, inhumation burials with Marnian-influenced pottery are occasionally found in places where they were least expected, like, for example, in the Dutch Rhine delta: a single inhumation burial dated to the late fifth or the early fourth century BC was unearthed in Someren (Noord-Brabant), while in Nijmegen-Lent and in Geldermalsen (Gelderland) small cemeteries with a mixture of inhumation and cremation were excavated. Some of the grave goods from Geldermalsen (a bronze and an iron torc, Marnian-influenced pottery and the rim of an imported vessel), as well as the use of inhumation in a region were cremation is the standard formal burial rite, are generally considered as proof of cultural links with the Aisne-Marne region (Van den Broeke 1999; Gerritsen 2003: 135).

In the same way, the influence of Middle Rhine-Moselle material culture and ritual can be discerned in zones far away from the core area, like, for example, in the burials of Wijshagen en Eigenbilzen (Belgian province of Limburg), which were exceptional for the area, with their metal vessels and *phalerae* (Van Impe 1998).

The region where the influence of the Aisne-Marne and the Middle Rhine-Moselle areas is clearest is that of the Belgian Ardennes, with a northern and a southern group, separated by an empty zone some 12km wide. In the southern group, most funerary data are from the period 450–390 BC; after an apparent gap of almost a century, a number of cemeteries were reused in the third and the beginning of the second century BC. The cemeteries of the (far less investigated) northern group were only in use for a short time and do not seem to include burials of the later period. Typical for both groups are the low, round barrows (*tombelles*), without ditched enclosures. Chariot burials are restricted to the southern group (Cahen-Delhaye 1998a; 1998b).

The traditional viewpoint is that the northern group represented immigrants from the Middle Rhine-Moselle, given the tight resemblance of ceramic and metal grave goods, while the cemeteries in the south were created by immigrants from the Aisne-Marne, again based on a close affinity in material culture (see e.g. Cahen-Delhaye 1991). However, it is obvious that the situation is not that clear-cut: the southern group presents characteristics of both areas, especially in the field of ritual. Chariot burials, for example, are typical for both core areas, while round barrows without ditched enclosures are a phenomenon of the Middle Rhine-Moselle region only: in the Aisne-Marne, there are no visible remains of barrows, whereas round and square ditched enclosures are fairly widespread. In this respect, the southern group has more in common with the Middle Rhine-Moselle. In other respects, (for example grave pit and general burial arrangement), the burials are much closer to what is customary in the Aisne-Marne. Typical for the Belgian Ardennes is that grave goods are generally less rich than in the core areas.

There is also evidence of cultural and material exchanges between the two core areas as such. Some of the earliest (LT A1) two-wheel vehicle burials in the Aisne-Marne were found in the south of Champagne and northern Burgundy (Aube and Yonne departments). As discussed by Verger (1995: 278–81), the vehicles were not all built in the local tradition, but were rather close to Rhineland chariots: the axle caps, the rod to reinforce the axle and the single and double ring headed pins (*Ösenstifte*) for the suspension system are lacking in contemporary chariot burials in the Aisne-Marne, but are typical for the Middle Rhine-Moselle. A local feature, however, were the iron linchpins with hollow, straight shanks. It is, therefore, unlikely that these were imported vehicles. Perhaps they were assembled by a wheelwright of Rhineland origin, who installed himself in the area, but the most plausible scenario is probably that of a local wheelwright who was strongly influenced by the Rhineland model, because he received (part of) his training in the Middle Rhine-Moselle region. In fact, the combination of local elements and external innovations is a clear illustration of the 'master-apprentice' model described by Karl (2005).

Apart from the exchange of technology, there are also similarities at the ritual level. One of these is the absence of horse harness, which distinguishes the area from that of the remainder of the Aisne-Marne, but brings it clearly in line with the Middle Rhine–Moselle. Another element in common are the wooden chambers (Verger 1995: 286–88).

A few decades later, at the transition from LT A1 to A2, and further north, the chariot burial of Somme-Bionne (Marne department) forms another illustration of a partial adoption of foreign burial models, which becomes visible in the grave goods. Instead of a dagger (until then the standard type of weapon), the deceased was buried with a sword. Other grave goods – most of them unknown in the Aisne-Marne but typical for the Rhineland – were a golden ring, a drinking horn, an Attic vase, a bronze jug, a decorated belt and a bronze scabbard. Some of these (golden ring, Attic vase, drinking horn) are not seen again in the Aisne-Marne, but others remain customary for a while after (Verger 1994: 654–6).

The Aisne-Marne and Middle Rhine-Moselle areas are not only considered as core areas because of their chariot burials and other rich burials, but also because of the impact they had on neighbouring and more distant regions. Their pottery was abundantly copied and their burial rites occasionally imitated, but the finest and most extensive range of pottery is only attested in the core areas, and burials outside these areas remain, at best, good copies, however exceptional they may be in their local context.

However, the existence of core and periphery areas in Northern Gaul in this period does not mean that the periphery regions had a less complex social structure. Gerritsen (2003: 3) rightly criticises that 'the designation of the West Hallstatt region and later the Marne-Moselle region, as core areas (themselves peripheries in the Mediterranean world economy), automatically implied that the areas further to the north were more peripheral, and consequently less complex and dynamic'. The elite of these regions may not have felt the need for pompous burial rites, or they may have preferred to invest their resources elsewhere. Alternatively, they may simply not have had the means: it is one thing to own a vehicle, but it is another to bury it. As more information becomes available from settlement contexts, it will be interesting to see if and how this could complement or adjust the core-periphery model of northern Gaul described above.

## Northern Gaul around 300 BC

At the end of the fourth century BC, the Aisne-Marne and the Middle Rhine-Moselle areas are no longer the main or only actors. Other areas now come to the fore. They have contacts all across Europe, and adopt the prestigious burial rites of the former core areas. Chariot burials and other rich burials appear in many different regions around this time: Paris, Normandy, the *Groupe de la Haine* (Belgian province of Hainaut), the second phase of the Belgian Ardennes and East Yorkshire. As opposed to the earlier period, the chariot burials are not very numerous; the highest number was found in East Yorkshire (about 20). They are also generally less rich than those of the fifth and fourth centuries BC.

The Paris area is, to a certain extent, comparable to East Yorkshire, in that there is an apparent gap in the funerary record in the period immediately preceding the establishment of a series of inhumation cemeteries. Some of these are large, but most burial sites are small and typically include a few relatively rich burials: one or two chariot burials and a few burials with (often beautifully decorated) weapons. Many objects, including several vehicle parts and pieces of horse harness, are decorated in Plastic Style.

Traditionally, the sudden appearance of cemeteries and chariot burials is believed to represent the arrival of newcomers. These newcomers are no longer seen as part of a large scale migration, but rather as small groups or even individuals (Ginoux and Poux 2002: 229). These small groups are also responsible for the introduction of the Plastic Style. According to Ginoux (2002: 22–3), there is no indication of a local artistic development: when the Plastic Style arrives in the Paris region, it has already reached its mature form. The development of the style can be observed elsewhere, in Danubian workshops, where significant progress was made in perfecting copper alloys needed to create volumetric shapes. Other technological assets, like the lost wax technique for casting bronze, originated from Moravia and Slovakia.

Marion (2007: 106), on the other hand, states that the sudden appearance of chariot burials in the Paris region reflects the need of the local aristocracy to affirm its territorial sovereignty in a spectacular way, suggesting that its power still required strengthening or legitimating. In this respect, Marion refers to Caesar's statement that the territory of the Parisii was established by separation of a part of the territory previously controlled by the Senones. He cites Caesar, who writes the following in *De Bello Gallico* (VI.3): '*(...) concilium Lutetiam Parisiorum transfert. Confines erant hi Senonibus civitatemque patrum memoria coniunxerant (...)'*. This could be translated as: '(…) he transfers the council to Lutetia of the Parisii. These were adjacent to the Senones, and had united their state to them during the memory of their fathers (…)', (my translation). This immediately raises the question of the exact meaning of *patrum memoria*. If this is to be taken literally, the unity of the Parisii and the Senones cannot go back further than about 50 years, whereas the time span between the chariot burials and the Gallic Wars is about 250 years. If, however, 'fathers' stands for 'ancestors', such a longer time span might be feasible.

There are, however, other issues regarding the exact meaning of the passage in Caesar, for which Marion refers to Duval (1961: 92). As Duval points out, the quotation suggests that both peoples were not originally united, but at a certain time the Parisii (at their own initiative) linked up with the Senones, maybe to better face a certain threat; once the threat was over, the fusion fell apart.

Marion (2007: 106) claims that, from an archaeological point of view, the period of the appearance of chariot burials is the best illustration of the Paris area emerging as an independent region, although he also warns of the dangers of matching material changes with political realities.

In the other new "centres", the reason for the introduction of chariot burials may have been similar. As a certain degree of mobility should not be uncritically dismissed, chariot burials may mark the arrival of a new elite that is alien to the area, but it may equally well accompany the emergence of a new local elite, or it may illustrate the struggle of the existing ruling classes to affirm their position, as a result of changes in power relations, with for example the rise of new lineages.

This last possibility would conform to the data available for the southern group of the Belgian Ardennes. After the period 450–390 BC discussed above, there is an apparent gap in the funerary data of almost a century. As from the early third century BC, new barrows are constructed in existing cemeteries and burials are interred in existing barrows. Two chariot burials belong to this second phase, one of which is dated to the earlier part of the third century BC, while the other is probably from the early second century BC. Although a change can be perceived in the type and typology of the grave goods, mortuary practices were not affected by the 'interruption' (Cahen-Delhaye 1997: 22–3, 64, 87; Cahen-Delhaye 1998a: 17; Cahen-Delhaye *et al.* 1989).

Generally, only the barrows have been investigated and rarely the surface around or in between. As a result, relatively few flat graves have been excavated (for some references see Cahen-Delhaye 1998b: 60, note 5). The numerical potential of flat graves is unknown. If this potential is relatively high, it may conceal the missing link between the fifth and the third centuries BC. Perhaps the barrows should be seen as ancestor cult places, where, in a first stage, secondary burials were given a place in the barrow, but later generations settled for a flat grave near the ancestors' barrows. Perhaps some of these flat graves contained chariot burials, what would explain why the tradition 'reappears' unaltered in the third and second century BC. The reason why in the third century BC new barrows were added and secondary burials were incorporated in existing barrows, may perhaps be found in the need of certain kin groups to confirm their position in the ancestral landscape.

Another region with chariot burials going back to around 300 BC, is that of the *Groupe de la Haine* (Mariën 1961). Unfortunately, most material originates from old, very poorly documented excavations, so that all information on context was lost. The best known example is that of Leval-Trahegnies, *La Courte*, with its linchpins and terret rings in Plastic Style.

In 2006, the first complete chariot burial was found in Normandy, in Orval, *Les Pleines* (Manche department). According to the preliminary publications (Lepaumier, Chanson and Giazzon 2007a; Lepaumier, Chanson and Giazzon 2007b), this chariot burial can be dated to the early third century BC. The heads of the linchpins are decorated in Plastic Style and the bronze horse bits have coral inlay. Grave goods include a sword and spearhead, as well as a golden ring. The burial contained the heads of two horses (only jaws and teeth preserved), one complete with its harness.

As the number of chariot burials of this period occurring in any one region is not very high, there may be other regions with (as yet undiscovered) chariot burials contemporary to those discussed above. Chariot burials were obvious tokens of status and prestige, and must have served a certain purpose. Furthermore, it is remarkable how fast the phenomenon spreads over a relatively large area.

## Internationalisation

The Belgian Ardennes offer a good illustration of the developments that took place in northern Gaul towards the end of the fourth century BC, by comparing the level of interaction with neighbouring and more distant regions. During the first phase of occupation (450–390 BC), the Belgian Ardennes had a very close and exclusive relationship with the two core areas, the Middle Rhine-Moselle and the Aisne-Marne. As from the third century BC, however, the people of the Belgian Ardennes broadened their contacts and widened their views. Although the former core areas still play a certain role, they are clearly no longer the only source of inspiration; there are now interactions with a multitude of others regions, in Northern France (Oise, Somme, Val-d'Oise), but also as far away as central Europe (Cahen-Delhaye 1997: 87–89). The early third century chariot burial of Neufchâteau-Le-Sart even included a piece of jewellery consisting of beads that were probably produced in an oriental workshop (Cosyns and Hurt 2007; Gratuze and Cosyns 2007).

This internationalisation is typical for a large part of temperate Europe and goes hand in hand with several technological innovations, for example in the field of chariot building. The evolution to flat tyres, without nails to secure the tyre to the felloe, clearly proves that considerable progress had been made in mastering the technique of shrinking the tyre onto the felloe by contraction (Anthoons 2007). Furthermore, there are a few novelties in the field of weaponry that become characteristic for LT C, but make their first appearance at the end of LT B2 (early third century BC). One innovation is the introduction of a new suspension system for swords, replacing the old leather belts by metal chain belts, while another concerns the reappearance of metal fittings (umbo, spine and rim) on shields (Rapin 1999: 49, 54–58).

A further illustration of this internationalisation is the rapid spread of art styles, like the Plastic Style, mentioned above, and the Sword Style. Based on historical sources, this is often interpreted within a context of migration and/or expansion, as for example by Megaw and Megaw (1996: 123) who claim that the presence of 'near-identical artefacts in this period right across the Celtic world, from Romania to England can be explained by the wanderings of these marauding Celts'. There may, however, have been other processes at work, as will be further discussed below.

# Evolution of elite networks between the fifth and the third centuries BC

As demonstrated above, between the fifth and the third centuries BC important changes took place in the interregional and long distance contacts in Northern Gaul. The situation of the fifth and fourth centuries BC is schematically shown in Figure 6.1. There are two core areas, along with several peripheral areas. The interaction takes place between the core areas themselves and between the core and the periphery areas.

Information between the core and the periphery areas may have spread in different ways. In the case of the inhumation burials of the Dutch Rhine delta (geographically distant from the Aisne-Marne), for example, the practice of inhumation and the presence of Marnian (influenced) grave goods may be the result of information cascading through a number of vulnerable nodes, forming a 'percolating vulnerable cluster' (Collar 2007: 152); this process could be either rapid or slow. Alternatively, the network distance between the Dutch Rhine delta and the Aisne-Marne region may have been short: it may have represented a so-called 'weak tie', a random contact. Weak ties are extremely important in the rapid diffusion of information. Between strong ties (family,

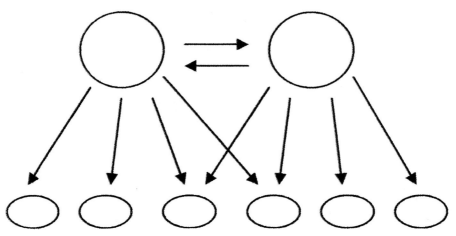

Figure 6.1: Schematic presentation of interaction during the fifth and fourth centuries BC.

friends), news does not spread very far, whereas through communication with a loose acquaintance, news escapes the boundaries of one's own social group. In this way, weak ties can act as social bridges (Buchanan 2002: 34–47; Granovetter 1973, 1983). In modern networks 'weak ties' usually refer to social rather than geographical distance, but the term does not seem out of place in the current context either. Strong and weak ties together make up the 'small-world' network (Collar 2007: 151).

Towards the beginning of the third century BC, there are several centres, with no clear core area and with interaction between the various centres (schematised in Figure 6.2). What can be perceived here is an evolution from a relatively simple core-periphery structure, with two predominant actors, influencing neighbouring regions, both at a ritual and a material level, to more complex long distance networks, with many actors of equal preponderance and multiple streams of interaction. Along these networks, new technologies and ideologies travel fast, and contacts are no longer confined to a limited number of neighbouring regions, but reach as far as eastern Europe or even beyond.

The change reflects a kind of 'phase transition', which occurs when by adding a few interconnecting links between existing isolated clusters, a network undergoes a leap from one state to another (Collar 2007: 150). In the fifth and early fourth centuries BC, there are a number of regional clusters (like for example the Belgian Ardennes) which are only connected with the core areas, but not between themselves, and are as such rather isolated. In the early third century BC, however, the various regional clusters are connected into a 'giant component', which allows for communication across the whole network. In order for the network to achieve this new state, only a limited number of interconnecting links need to be created between the isolated

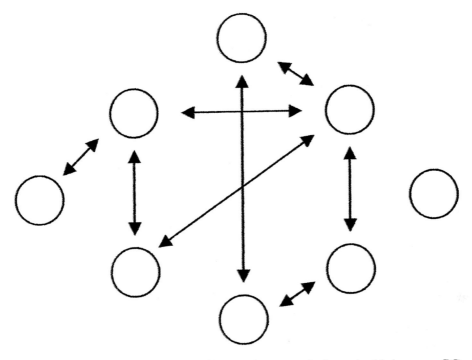

Figure 6.2: Schematic presentation of interaction towards the early third century BC.

clusters. What triggered this change in network structure, in other words, how were these new links created, and why did it happen at this point in time?

## Cultural-historical hypothesis

In the early third century BC burial sites of the Paris region, weapons occur on a regular basis and in the Île-de-France as a whole, an increase in weapons burials can be discerned compared to the preceding phase (Marion 2004: 212).

The men buried with weapons may have been genuine warriors or were only presented as a warrior, but in any event, weapons were high social status symbols and warfare may have been considered an integrated part of society. If this was the case, it is hard to retrieve the percentage of males involved in war activities; in normal circumstances, warfare was probably local and occasional in nature, and not a full-time occupation. However, Gaulish mercenaries have repeatedly been reported by classical authors; hence it is not inconceivable that if an occasion arose causing a substantial increase in the demand for mercenaries, part of the male population became professional warriors for a shorter or longer period of time.

Such an occasion may have presented itself when, in the aftermath of the death of Alexander the Great in 323 BC, a war for succession was fought between his successors, the so-called Diadochs, during several decades. As a matter of fact, Wells (2001: 80) notes that Celtic mercenaries are mentioned increasingly in the early third century BC in this respect. It is not always clear from the classical accounts where particular contingents of mercenaries came from (Wells 1999: 47), but some of them may have been recruited in Gaul. The increase in mercenaries, in turn, must have boosted the production of weapons, implying that more craftsmen were required to meet the rising demand. Simultaneously, the continuous and rapid evolution of weaponry in a wider international context suggests that at least some of these craftsmen were highly specialised.

As pointed out by Marion (2004: 350; 2007: 112), technological innovations, initially focused on reducing the number of man-hours required for the production of food, were a logical consequence of the drop in work forces available in the agricultural sector; in the course of the third century BC, the pressure on food production was to lead to more efficient ways of exploiting the land and to more efficient tools, like, for example, the rotary quern.

War and fighting together is considered 'the most powerful force of social cohesion between men' (Van de Noort 2006: 282) and forms, therefore, an important mechanism in the creation of social networks. Once their mission was accomplished, many mercenaries must have returned to their respective homes (see Wells 1999: 46–7, 54; 2001: 80–1) and it is not unreasonable to assume that the bonds forged during their time as a mercenary resulted in more frequent and more intense contacts between their regions of origin. It is even plausible that mercenaries were recruited via these networks. This would explain why larger bands would often comprise members from different regions and peoples, as, for example, in the case of the Gaesatae (Tomaschitz 2002: 84–85). These were mercenaries from Transalpine Gaul, who were known for fighting naked. They were hired by the Boii and the Insubres in Cisalpine Gaul to fight against the Romans. In spite of their reputation as elite warriors, they were defeated by the Romans in the battles of Telamon (225 BC) and Clastidium (222 BC).

## Alternative theory

Another possibility is that the increasing complexity of elite networks in northern Gaul came about without any interference from the Mediterranean, but rather as the result of a process inherent to the system. In an initial phase, the relationship between the centre and periphery is one of asymmetrical reciprocity. However, as stated above, networks are not stable: certain parts of the network may fall in disuse when previously strong ties are loosened, while new relationships are created by the various mechanisms that can be envisaged to underpin Iron Age elite networks, like political marriages, fosterage, exchange of hostages and clientship.

Within the framework of the evolution described above, fosterage in particular may have played an important role. There is no direct evidence that fosterage was practised in Gaul at this time. For the later Iron Age, Caesar's observation in *De Bello Gallico* (VI.18) that Gauls do not allow their sons to approach them openly until they have grown to an age when they can bear the burden of military service, is often interpreted as an indication for the existence of fosterage (see for instance Karl 2005: 256). Parkes (2003: 751, 754) notes that such parental avoidance exactly matches Kovalevsky's observations of paternal avoidance during fosterage among the Ossetes.

Assuming that fosterage as an educational practice existed in Gaul as early as the fifth and fourth centuries BC, it should be considered which type of fosterage would best account for the streams of influence that can be perceived in the archaeological record. This would not be kinship fosterage, but rather alliance fosterage, or allegiance fosterage, as described by Parkes (2006: 359 note 2), who distinguishes between patronal (child-raising by status superiors) or cliental (child-raising by status inferiors) allegiance fosterage. It is very hard to judge which type of allegiance fosterage would best accord with the core-periphery model depicted above. At first sight, patronal allegiance fosterage seems the more logical option, but this would imply extrapolating the core-periphery model to the political level, with a concentration of "patrons" in the core areas and of "clients" in the periphery zones, which is obviously incorrect. The situation is certainly more complex and will require further study, which falls outside the scope of this paper.

In any event, the core areas may have attracted many foster children from the nobility in peripheral zones, thus creating a situation where children from different regions grew up in the same families. It is known that in societies where fosterage was customary, the bond between foster-brothers was very strong and lasted for life, as for example in medieval Ireland (Kelly 2003: 90). It is not unreasonable to assume that this situation gradually created new and more complex networks, bringing about multiple opportunities for other mechanisms like political marriages. This may gradually have given rise to changes in local power relations in the periphery zones. The phenomenon of chariot burials, almost completely fallen into disuse in the core areas, was picked up as a prominent status marker, that was considered appropriate to affirm newly acquired political positions.

Ultimately, this will have engendered the rise of several new centres in the former periphery zones. The relationship between these centres, and between the new centres and the former core areas, is one of symmetrical reciprocity.

# The Arras Culture of Eastern Yorkshire

Chariot burials were introduced in East Yorkshire around the same time as in the "new centres" discussed above. This becomes particularly clear when examining the vehicles. In the evolution of the iron wheel tyres, the Yorkshire vehicles are at the same stage as those from around Paris, while both are later than the Aisne-Marne vehicles (Anthoons 2007: 144–145). Also the five terret system – always considered as one of the basic differences between East Yorkshire and the Continent, where four terrets are the rule in the Aisne-Marne – has been attested a few times in Paris, as for example in Plessis-Gassot (Ginoux 2003: 46; personal observation) and Roissy (Lejars 2005: 77, fig. 4). The typically dismantled vehicles of the Yorkshire Wolds even find a possible parallel in a chariot burial from Bouqueval (Guadagnin 1984: 44–53). Both in East Yorkshire and in the Paris region, the typical burial rite is inhumation, but the position of the body is different: extended on the back in Paris, the usual position on the Continent during the Iron Age, and flexed, crouched or contracted in East Yorkshire, an old Bronze Age tradition still used in Britain at this time.

Another feature of the Arras Culture is the square barrows, with their typical joined ditched enclosures. Good parallels for these can be found in the Aisne-Marne region, on the cemeteries of Ménil-Annelles and Ville-sur-Retourne (Stead, Flouest and Rigby 2006); both of these sites, postdate the chariot burial period in the region, but are contemporary with the cemeteries of the Arras Culture. In the Paris area, square enclosures are rare, and joined square enclosures are absent altogether. It seems, therefore, that the burial rites practised by the population of East Yorkshire cannot be linked to one particular area in Northern Gaul, but are composed of elements adopted from various regions, and are also anchored in local British traditions.

It is unclear to what extent East Yorkshire took part in the spirit of innovation, standardisation and internationalisation outlined above. Worth noting with regard to weaponry and fighting, is that there are several indications that swords were carried on the back, rather than slung on the right side, with the sword handle at the waist, as is the case on the Continent and in southern Britain (Stead 2006: 61–3, plate 9). This suggests that the involvement of East Yorkshire in the Gaulish networks is more likely to be found on the religious and spiritual level, rather than in the ranks of an elite that is frequently engaged in warfare.

# Conclusion

The early third century BC is a time of many changes, not only at the level of material culture, with rapid innovations, especially in weaponry, but also in the field of funerary practices, with the establishment of new cemeteries and the spread of the chariot burial phenomenon across several regions in northern Gaul and even into Britain. Contacts are no longer restricted to close neighbours but reach further and are more diverse in nature. These changes reflect an evolution to more complex elite networks.

This evolution could be the result of an increased demand for mercenaries, originating from several regions in Gaul and possibly from Britain, creating a highly mobile elite, thus taking existing embryonic, simple networks to a more complex level. Alternatively, the evolution to more complex networks could represent an internal process, inherent to the network system itself, where an initial core-periphery model developed into a model with several centres at equal footing, via the mechanisms that underpin elite networks, like political marriages, fosterage, clientship and the like. As a matter of fact, both hypotheses may have played a role in the changes that can be observed in the early third century BC.

Finally, the analogous developments in funerary practices in East Yorkshire demonstrate that this region was part of the northern-Gaulish network which reached beyond the borders of Gaul into central Europe.

# Bibliography

Anthoons, G. (2007). The origins of the Arras Culture: migration or elite networks? In R. Karl and J. Leskovar (eds), *Interpretierte Eisenzeiten. Fallstudien, Methoden, Theorie. Tagungsbeiträge der 2. Linzer Gespräche zur interpretativen Eisenzeitarchäologie (Studien zur Kulturgeschichte von Oberösterreich, Folge 19)*: 141–52. Linz: Oberösterreichisen Landesmuseum.

Buchanan, M. (2002). *Nexus: Small Worlds and the Groundbreaking Science of Networks*. London: W. W. Norton.

Brown, F., C. Howard-Davis, M. Brennand, A. Boyle, T. Evans, S. O'Connor, A. Spence, R. Heawood and A. Lupton (2007). *The Archaeology of the A1 (M). Darrington to Dishforth DBFO Road Scheme (Lancaster Imprints, 11)*. Lancaster: Oxford Archaeology North.

Cahen-Delhaye, A. (1991). Les sépultures de La Tène. In H. Remy, *Archéologie en Ardenne. De la Préhistoire au XVIIIᵉ siècle. Exposition au Centre Touristique et Culturel de Vresse-sur-Semois*: 65–80. Bruxelles: Crédit Communal.

Cahen-Delhaye, A. (1997). *Nécropole de La Tène à Neufchâteau-le-Sart (Monographie d'Archéologie Nationale, 10)*. Bruxelles: Musées Royaux d'Art et d'Histoire.

Cahen-Delhaye, A. (1998a). Les rites funéraires laténiens en Ardenne belge. In G. Leman-Delerive (ed.), *Les Celtes. Rites funéraires en Gaule du Nord entre le VIᵉ et le Iᵉʳ siècle avant Jésus-Christ (Etudes et Documents. Fouilles, 4)*: 15–30. Namur: Direction de l'Archéologie, Ministère de la Région Wallonne.

Cahen-Delhaye, A. (1998b). Rites funéraires au sud de l'Ardenne belge. *Revue Archéologique de Picardie* 1(2): 59–70.

Cahen-Delhaye, A., V. Hurt and H. Gratia (1989). Une tombelle celtique exceptionnelle à Sberchamps. Rapport préliminaire des fouilles de 1989. *Archéo.-Situla* 4: 21–30.

Collar, A. (2007). Network Theory and Religious Innovation, *Mediterranean Historical Review* 22(1): 149–162.

Cosyns, P. and V. Hurt (2007). Les perles en verre de Neufchâteau-le-Sart. *Arduinna* 62: 1–5.

Diepeveen-Jansen, M. (2001). *People, Ideas and Goods. New Perspectives on 'Celtic Barbarians' in Western and Central Europe (500–250 BC) (Amsterdam Archaeological Studies, 7)*. Amsterdam: Amsterdam University Press.

Duval, P. M. (1961). *Paris antique. Des origines au troisième siècle*. Paris: Hermann.

Gerritsen, F. (2003). *Local identities. Landscape and Community in the Late Prehistoric Meuse-Demer-Scheldt Region (Amsterdam Archaeological Studies, 9)*. Amsterdam: Amsterdam University Press.

Ginoux, N. (2002). Les productions iconographiques. In A. Bulard, V. Delattre and J.M. Séguier (eds.) *Les Celtes en Île-de-France. Dossiers d'Archéologie* 273: 20–23.

Ginoux, N. (2003). L'excellence guerrière et l'ornementation des armes aux IV$^e$ et III$^e$ s. av. J.-C. Découvertes récentes. *Etudes Celtiques*, 33–67.

Ginoux, N. and M. Poux (2002). Les Parisii, entre Gaule Belgique et Gaule Celtique: peuplement et territoire. In D. Garcia and F. Verdin (eds.) *Territoires celtiques : espaces ethniques et territoires des agglomérations protohistoriques d'Europe occidentale. XXIV$^e$ colloque international de l'AFEAF, Martigues, 2000*: 226–43. Paris: Errance.

Granovetter, M. S. (1973). The strength of weak ties. *American Journal of Sociology* 78(6): 1360–80.

Granovetter, M. S. (1983). The strength of weak ties: a network theory revisited, *Sociological Theory* 1: 201–33.

Gratuze, B. and P. Cosyns (2007). Les perles en verre de Neufchâteau-le-Sart. *Arduinna* 63: 1–7.

Hurtrelle, J., E. Monchy, F. Roger, P. Rossignol, and A. Villes (1990), Les débuts du second âge du fer dans le Nord de la France, *Les Dossiers de Gauheria 1*.

Karl, R. (2005). Master and apprentice, knight and squire: education in the 'Celtic' Iron Age. *Oxford Journal of Archaeology 24 (3)*, 255–71.

Kelly, F. (2003). *A Guide to Early Irish Law (Early Irish Law Series, 3)*, Dublin: Dublin Institute for Advanced Studies.

Lejars, Th. (2005). Le cimetière celtique de La Fosse Cotheret, à Roissy (Val-d'Oise) et les usages funéraires aristocratiques dans le nord du Bassin parisien à l'aube du III$^e$ siècle avant J.-C.. In O. Buchsenschutz, A. Bulard and Th. Lejars, *L'âge du Fer en Île-de-France. XXVIe colloque de l'Association Française pour l' tude de l'Âge du Fer, Paris et Saint-Denis 2002 (26$^e$ supplément à la Revue archéologique du Centre de la France)*: 73–83.Tours: FERACF, Paris: INRAP.

Leman-Delerive, G. and E. Warmenbol (2006). Le Ve siècle dans le Nord-Ouest de la France et de la Belgique actuelle. In V. Kruta, G. Leman-Delerive and E. Warmenbol (eds) *Celtes: Belges, Boïens, Rèmes, Volques…*, Catalogue exposition: 90–106. Musée Royal de Mariemont.

Lepaumier, H., K. Chanson, and D. Giazzon (2007a). La tombe à char d'Orval. Présentation préliminaire. *Bulletin de l'Association Française pour l'étude de l'Âge du Fer* 25: 68–70.

Lepaumier, H., K. Chanson, and D. Giazzon (2007b). La tombe à char d'Orval. *Archéopages* 19: 14–15.

Marion, S. (2004). *Recherches sur l'âge du Fer en Ile-de-France. Entre Hallstatt final et La Tène finale. Analyse des sites fouillés. Chronologie et sociéte*. Oxford: British Archaeological Reports International Series, S1231.

Marion, S. (2007). Les IV$^e$ et III$^e$ avant notre ère en Île-de-France. In C. Mennessier-Jouannet, A.-M. Adam and P.-Y. Milcent, *La Gaule dans son contexte Européen aux IV$^e$ et III$^e$ s. av. n.è.. Actes du XXVII$^e$ colloque international de l'Association Française pour l' tude de l'Âge du Fer (Clermont-Ferrand, 29 mai-1er juin 2003). Thème spécialisé (Monographies d'Archéologie Méditerranéenne)*: Lattes: édition de l'Association pour le Développement de l'Archéologie en Languedoc-Roussillon.

Mariën, M. E. (1961). *La période de la Tène en Belgique. Le Groupe de la Haine (Monographies d'Archéologie Nationale, 2)*. Bruxelles: Musées Royaux d'Art et d'Histoire.

Megaw, V. and R. Megaw (1996). *Celtic Art. From its beginnings to the Book of Kells*. London: Thames and Hudson.

Parkes, P. (2003). Fostering fealty. A comparative analysis of tributary allegiances of adoptive kinship. *Comparative Studies in Society and History* 45: 741–82.

Parkes, P. (2006). Celtic fosterage: adoptive kinship and clientage in northwest Europe. *Comparative Studies in Society and History* 48 (2): 359–95.

Rapin, A. (1999). L'armement celtique en Europe: chronologie de son évolution technologique du Vᵉ au Iᵉ s. av. J.-C.. *Gladius* 19: 33–67.

Stead, I. M. (1979). *The Arras Culture*. York: The Yorkshire Philosophical Society.

Stead, I. M. (2006). *British Iron Age Swords and Scabbards*. London: British Museum Press.

Stead, I. M., J.-L. Flouest, and V. Rigby (2006). *Iron Age and Roman Burials in Champagne*. Oxford: Oxbow Books.

Tomaschitz, K. (2002). *Die Wanderungen der Kelten in der antiken literarischen Überlieferung. (Mitteilungen der Prähistorischen Kommission Band 47)*. Wien: Verlag der Österreichischen Akademie der Wissenschaften.

Van den Broeke, P. (1999). Een uitzonderlijk grafveld uit de ijzertijd in Nijmegen-Lent, *Ulpia Noviomagus* 7.

Van Impe, L. (1998). Nécropoles et tombelles aristocratiques dans le Limbourg belge: Wijshagen et Eigenbilzen. In G. Leman-Delerive, *Les Celtes. Rites funéraires en Gaule du Nord entre le VIe et le Ier siècle avant Jésus-Christ (Etudes et Documents. Fouilles. 4)*: 41–57. Namur: Direction de l'Archéologie.

Van de Noort, R. (2006). Argonauts of the North Sea – a Social Maritime Archaeology for the 2nd Millennium BC, *Proceedings of the Prehistoric Society* 72: 267–87.

Verger, S. (1994). *Les tombes a char de La Tène ancienne en Champagne et les rites funéraires aristocratiques en Gaule de l'est au Vᵉ siècle avant J.-C.* Unpublished PhD thesis, Université de Bourgogne, Dijon.

Verger, S. (1995). Les premières tombes à char laténiennes de Champagne. In A. Villes and A. Bataille-Melkon (eds.) *Fastes des Celtes entre Champagne et Bourgogne aux VIIᵉ-IIIᵉ siècles avant notre ère. Actes du colloque de l'AFEAF tenu à Troyes en 1995 (Mémoires de la Société Archéologique Champenoise, 15, Supplément au Bulletin n°4)* : 271–294.

Wells, P. S. (1999). *The Barbarians Speak. How the Conquered Peoples Shaped Roman Europe*. Princeton: Princeton University Press.

Wells, P. S. (2001). *Beyond Celts, Germans and Scythians*. London: Duckworth.

were deliberately placed within specific sites gone with pressure of adeuate

# RITUAL, HOARDS AND HELMETS: A LATE IRON AGE SHRINE AT HALLATON, EAST LEICESTERSHIRE

*Vicki Score and Jennifer Browning*

(University of Leicester Archaeological Services)

## Abstract

Although shrines are a recognised feature of the Late Iron Age in southern Britain, their discovery is often due only to their existence beneath later, more visible Romano-British temples and little is known of ritual sites further north. This paper outlines some of the findings from the extensive programme of excavation and research undertaken by University of Leicester Archaeological Services on a Late Iron Age shrine from Hallaton, East Leicestershire. Although the site shares a number of similarities with shrines further south, the lack of any associated temple structure suggests that this may be a different type of open air ritual site.

At the East Leicestershire site, over 5000 coins and items of metalwork were deliberately placed within specific zones, along with deposits of selected types of animals, with evidence pointing towards feasting activities. The presence of large numbers of coins in discrete hoards deposited over a short period of time (perhaps no more than 20–30 years), has enabled detailed numismatic study. This analysis suggests a society consisting of a number of small co-existing groups each simultaneously producing coinage, rather than the traditional model of a regional *Corieltavi* tribe with a linear chronological succession of coins produced by a succession of rulers. This paper suggests that this site represents an open air meeting place without a formal building, in which smaller groups assembled to perform ritual acts. It also suggests that similar finds of coins and metalwork in Britain previously interpreted as single hoards could potentially be part of similar open air ritual sites. This makes Hallaton a key site for the understanding and re-interpretation of other such sites, where excavation has been minimal.

# Introduction

The release in 2003 of information regarding hoards of gold and silver coins and artefacts and a Roman cavalry helmet from a field in Leicestershire captured the imagination of the press, the public and archaeologists alike. The real value of these finds however, is that they were recovered using controlled excavation techniques. Unlike many previous discoveries of Late Iron Age metalwork and coinage in the landscape, much has been learnt about the specific context of this find and close co-operation between the finder, land owners, the local community, amateur and professional archaeologists and national bodies have meant that the site was excavated without significant damage from illicit metal detecting. The discovery has important implications for analysing the complex social dynamics of the population before and during the Roman Conquest. It may also provide a model for understanding other deposits of metalwork and coins that are common in Late Iron Age Europe.

The site is a native shrine located on a hilltop in Hallaton, some 10km north-east of Market Harborough. Although the earliest depositions date the site to the late first century BC, the main phase of activity belongs to *c*. AD 30–60, a period of considerable social and cultural change in southern Britain encompassing the Roman Conquest in AD 43. Finds include one of the largest groups of Iron Age and Republican/Early Imperial Roman coins found in Britain, along with a number of silver objects including an extremely rare, decorated iron and silver Roman helmet, as well as evidence for animal sacrifice and possibly feasting. The finds were acquired by Leicestershire County Council with the help of the Heritage Lottery Fund and are on public display at Market Harborough Museum.

# The discovery of the shrine

The site was discovered in 2000 during fieldwalking and subsequent metal detecting by the local fieldwork group. During this initial work, more than 200 Iron Age and Roman coins were recovered from the ploughsoil of a field lying on the brow of a small hill, with extensive views across the Welland Valley. Evaluations by University of Leicester Archaeological Services (ULAS) were undertaken in response to a potential threat from illicit metal detecting and ploughing; this led to several seasons of excavation. Investigations have so far concentrated on the main area of the site and fieldwalking, geophysical survey and limited excavation have also been carried out to understand the wider context of the deposits.

The earliest evidence for activity on the site comes in the form of a number of gold staters found scattered in the ploughsoil just to the east of the shrine

(Figure 7.1). The coins are *Gallo-Belgic* and early British (mainly Southern QC quarters) dating to the second half of the first century BC, and may represent an early hoard or votive offering disturbed by the later deposition of animals (Leins 2007). Other potential early features include a badly truncated circular gully close to the later entranceway to the shrine; this appears stratigraphically earlier than the animal bone deposits and may have been an early ritual focus.

The shrine is demarcated by a narrow ditch with an entranceway, approximately one third of the way down the eastern side (Figure 7.1). The ditch ends with a rounded terminal to the north, possibly representing a second entrance although its continuation, if it exists, lies beyond the excavation trench. To the south, the ditch also appears to continue beyond the excavations but its full extent is unclear as it was not detected during geophysical survey.

Although the lack of stratigraphy makes the site difficult to phase, three main groups of deposits appear to have been made during the first half of the first century AD. These occur within specific zones of the site and are each associated with the placing of different combinations of materials. The first group consists of animal bones, silver metalwork and coins within the boundary ditch, the second group comprises animal bone deposits east of the entranceway, while the third deposit includes coin hoards in the entranceway along with the Roman helmet and associated coins. The close spatial association of the groups suggests that although the deposits may have taken place at different times, they were all part of one main phase perhaps lasting no more than a few decades.

## The entranceway

The entrance was approximately 6m wide and the gap was divided in two by a shallow elongated pit positioned at an angle. The angle was emphasised by kinks in the terminals, with the southern terminal turning to the north-west and the northern terminal turning to the south-east. The arrangement suggests a controlled portal, perhaps similar to a turnstile; 'in' to the south and an 'out' to the north (Figure 7.1). Traces of fine pebble metalling were found around the southern terminal suggesting a possibly contemporary trackway.

The central pit had at least two phases. The upper fill of the pit contained the partial skeleton of an adult dog lying on its side with front legs drawn back beneath the body and head and neck pushed back at an unnatural angle (Figure 7.2). The skeleton appears to have been originally deposited intact but had been disturbed by ploughing and the insertion of a land drain and the hind legs were therefore not recovered. The recovery of parts of a second skull, along with neck vertebrae, in the lower fill of the pit was indicative of an

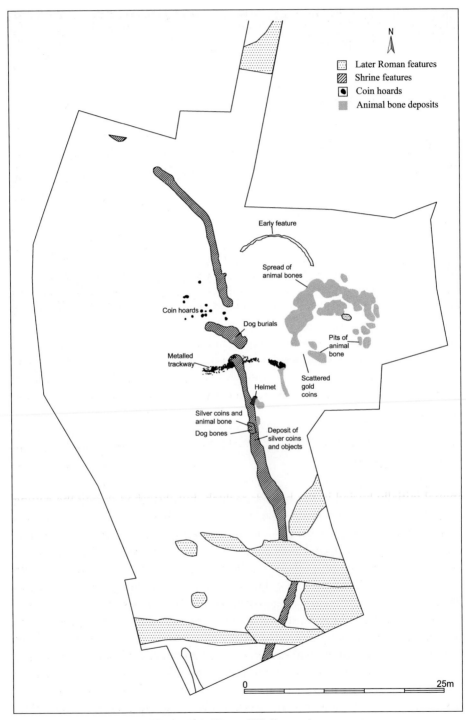

Figure 7.1: Plan of Hallaton site.

Figure 7.2: Dog burial in the entranceway.

earlier dog burial, possibly disturbed during remodelling of the entranceway feature. A third group of dog bones, comprising elements from the fore and hind feet, was also found in the base of the enclosure ditch just south of the entranceway (Figure 7.1).

The placing of the dogs in the entranceway may be seen in the light of practices widely encountered in Iron Age contexts. It is not possible to state with certainty that the second or third dogs were originally complete, although this seems likely. The third group of dog bones may belong to an animal initially buried in the boundary ditch, but disturbed during the cutting of a later pit. This sequence might suggest that either the burial was unmarked and was therefore unobserved when the new pit was excavated or conversely that the pit was excavated in that location precisely because of the presence of the dog, whose bones would become partially incorporated into the new deposit. The association of the burial of the latest (and most complete) dog with the remodelling of the shrine implies a spiritual dimension. Deposition of the animals at different times may suggest that the spiritual protection and significance afforded by the burial of the first animal may have required renewal when the shrine was altered. Burial of dog bones within boundary ditches has a precedent in several hillforts in southern Britain (Smith 2006: 71). The prevalence of dogs in ritual deposits at settlements lies in contrast to their infrequency within domestic assemblages (Wait 1985: 132; Fulford 2001: 215), although Smith (2006: 8) notes that they are rare in constructed Iron Age sacred space. A number of dog burials described as 'special deposits' were observed at Danebury (Grant 1984) and there are many examples of dogs in ritual pits in both Britain and Europe (Green 1992: 112).

## Sacred boundaries

At some point during the life of the shrine, further deposits were made in the boundary ditch immediately south of the entranceway. In the very base of the ditch, two round glass beads were recovered along with 35 Iron Age coins. Fragments of gold, silver and copper alloy were also found in the surrounding soil. Placed vertically against the eastern side of the ditch was a semicircular silver ingot (approximately 189mm x 98mm wide, 9mm thick) still retaining a small sprue from casting. Just above this in the centre of the ditch a triangular silver ingot and silver bowl had been positioned vertically on their edges. The items had been placed together with the rounded edge of the bowl pressed up against the flat edge of the ingot (Figure 7.3). The ingot (approximately 115mm x 113mm) is the typical shape of British Middle and Late Iron

Figure 7.3: Placed silver artefacts within the boundary ditch.

Age crucibles and at least two coins are visible on the upper surface suggesting it had been created by the melting down of coins (Hill 2008). The silver bowl (approximately 100mm diameter) has a cut in the side probably inflicted during the digging of a land drain trench immediately above it (Figure 7.3).

Just to the north, in the upper fill of this section of the ditch, another circular silver object had been placed face down with 76 Iron Age coins scattered above it. The decorated item had holes around the outer rim for fastening, possibly to armour or harness. The object had been badly damaged in antiquity but new holes had been made so that it could still be attached. Deposits of pig and dog bones and coins also appear to have been made in the boundary ditch immediately to the north of the group of silver artefacts. Unfortunately they had been disturbed by a later pit dug into the top of the backfilled ditch making it impossible to further define patterns of deposition in this area.

The deposits within the ditch appear to have occurred at the beginning of the main phase of activity, suggesting a date during the first half of the first century AD, which can possibly even be refined to the AD 30s, based on the amount of uninscribed Iron Age coinage present (Leins 2007). The items buried in the boundary ditch include coins as well as silver objects, various fragments of gold, silver and copper alloy, glass beads and animal bones. This range of materials is very different from the later separate deposits outside the entrance of specific artefact types (animal bone, coins and the helmet). The early metalwork includes some unusual items. The silver ingot and crucible base suggest metalworking – melted coins are actually visible within the crucible base), and the silver decorated mount had clearly been badly damaged and was modified to be re-used. Also in this collection is the silver bowl which has no known parallels and the two round glass beads with their fittings. All of these objects had been positioned within a short section of the ditch with each carefully placed upright on one edge and scattered with a selection of coins. It seems unlikely that the crucible, ingot and a few other drops of silver and gold represent coin manufacture on the site; despite the excellent condition of many of the coins, no other evidence was found during excavations or fieldwalking for their manufacture. However, excavations along the east side of the riverbank at Leicester have uncovered a number of flan tray fragments, suggesting mid-first-century AD manufacturing of coin blanks (Clay and Mellor 1985: 69; Buckley *et al.* 2007), so the coins need not have travelled very far.

The boundary ditch and entranceway appear to be foci during all phases of deposition. While it is not currently known whether the ditch enclosed the entire hill top, it is clear that this was a visible boundary that defined a specific area. It may have been an open ditch during earlier phases of activity but was later backfilled and possibly palisaded. The importance of the boundary is shown by the deposition within it of metalwork, coins, and animal bones, together with the later placing of the helmet and its associated coins in a pit overlying its eastern edge. Boundaries are often associated with specific rituals (Smith and Brookes 2001: 6), and are one of the most common locations for depositions of coins in the later Iron Age, particularly those defining areas associated with high status or religious practices (Curteis 2005: 208, 224). In this case the boundary ditch and entranceway may have been used to control access to the sanctuary, although exactly who was allowed to enter is unknown.

## Ritual consumption

The main area of animal bone deposition lies just east of the entranceway (Figure 7.1), comprising a large spread of fragmented bones over an area of approximately 10m x 5m. Excavation of the upper layer revealed a number of pits packed with partially articulated bones lying beneath the spread. Several separate pits were noted to the south of this group. Other features containing animal bones include a short gully and a pit between the main deposits and the boundary ditch, as well as the previously mentioned bones from the boundary ditch itself. The assemblage showed strong evidence for selectivity in terms of both species and age structure. Nearly all of the bones came from pigs, the recovered sample represented at least 82 animals and these were overwhelmingly immature, aged between six months and a year at death. The age of the animals, coupled with probable time of birth, suggested that most were slaughtered during the winter of their first year.

All parts of the body are represented to some extent, suggesting that the pigs may have been whole when brought onto site. However, the proportion of elements represented in each pit suggests that they were not buried complete and unbutchered. Anatomical parts common in one pit were often scarce in an adjacent feature, implying that the carcasses were divided and dispersed. Although, clear patterns of anatomical representation did not emerge, the careful placement of other types of finds at the site argues that deposition was not arbitrary. A striking characteristic of the assemblage is the under-representation of the right lower forelimb, an absence occurring with such regularity that it must denote symbolic significance, resulting in differential treatment. Hill's study of whole or partial skeletons (Associated Bone Groups or ABG's) revealed that it was not unusual for fore or hind limbs to be absent, with no evident preference for side (Hill 1995: 59), for example, the skeleton of a two-year old sow, minus the right forefoot, was recovered from a pit at Winnall Down (Maltby 1985: 25) within a feature later reinterpreted as ritual (Hill 1995: 70). The ultimate repository for these missing elements is currently unknown and it is by no means certain that they were removed from the site. As a number of pits remain unexcavated, future work may shed light on this. The sheer quantity of pig bones suggests that deposition took place in the context of large gatherings and, despite a relative scarcity of butchery marks, seem likely to relate to ritualised feasting. A copper alloy Celtic tankard handle also found in this area may provide some support for a feasting hypothesis.

Evidence for selection, in terms of species, age and body part, are normally key criteria of animal bone assemblages characterised as ritual. The offering of animals or animal parts appears to have been widespread, occurring in different contexts, including graves, sanctuaries and settlements, where votive offerings tend to take the form of structured deposits in pits (King 2005: 363). Although the animals concerned are frequently domestic species (Green 1992: 97) they are usually found in differing proportions to the domestic sphere, often with an emphasis on horses and dogs but under-representation of sheep (Green 1992: 102). Pigs appear to have been the ritual animals of choice at several sacred places, such as High Pasture Cave (Drew 2005) and, Chanctonbury Ring (Rudling 2008: 115) where the remains of 84 pigs, mostly represented by skulls and teeth were recovered. The choice of species may have been partially practical; pigs tend to have larger litters than sheep or goats, enabling a surplus of meat to be produced more easily, but they may also have been selected for symbolic reasons. Wait observes that pork was 'the meat of champions and particularly favoured by... the warrior nobility' (1985: 152) and in Celtic myth pigs are often associated with feasting, war and the underworld (Green 1992: 18). It was suggested that the high percentage of pig bones at the Romano-Celtic temple at Hayling Island could indicate a cultural link with Gaul, where temples often have an abundance of pig (King 2005: 341). Within British Iron Age sanctuaries, the chosen species varied, presumably influenced by the specific nature of the associated cult and perhaps, local husbandry regimes. One common factor seems to have been the preference for juvenile animals, which is clearly shown at comparable sites. At Hayling Island, the main peaks of slaughter were between 7–14 months and particularly 14–21 months (King 2005: 338). Similarly the pigs slaughtered at Uley were generally subadults or juvenile (Levitan 1993: 261), and young animals were also common in the Iron Age phases at Wanborough (Williams 2008: 89).

## Buried treasure – helmets and coin hoards

Thirteen separate coin hoards containing more than 2000 coins were excavated in the northern section of the entranceway. Most of the hoards are likely to have lost the upper part of their deposit from ploughing; however they still had group integrity with several hoards retaining the shape of a possible textile or leather container (Figure 7.4). All of the hoards were broadly similar in terms of composition suggesting that they were deposited at a similar time and from the same circulation pool. A coin of Claudius gives a *terminus post quem* of *c.* AD 41/42 suggesting the most likely date for the deposition of these groups was in the AD 40s – 50s, although as the coin was unworn, and no later coins were found, an end date of *c.* AD 41–42 for the deposition

Figure 7.4: Excavated coin hoard retaining the shape of a container. (Photo courtesy of the Trustees of the British Museum)

of the groups is possible (Leins 2007). Although later Roman coins were found these are all likely to belong to later features outside the shrine.

The quantity and quality of the Iron Age coins is exceptional. Most of these belong to the series minted in the East Midlands in the first centuries BC and AD, which is generally attributed to the *Corieltavi*. Overall, the metalwork and coins in the ditch and the coin groups appear to have been deposited within a relatively short period of time, perhaps no more than 20–30 years (Leins 2007).

Common approaches to the identification of Iron Age coinage in the Midlands classify coin types into a linear production sequence, related to successive rulers. However, this idea of a linear succession of tribal leaders relies on the assumption that similar coinages imply a unified social and political group, influenced by modern ideas of kingship and social groupings, rather than archaeological or numismatic evidence (Leins 2007). The coins from the East Leicestershire site, however, indicate that all the main types of coinage were produced simultaneously over no more than one or two decades. That this is the case is further supported by similar denominations and weight standards as well as shared craftsmanship and technologies represented in the series (Leins 2007). The narrow date range for the coins from the site, spanning perhaps as little as a generation, therefore suggests an alternative social model to the traditional 'tribal' theory, instead pointing towards the co-existence of several coin-producing groups within the region. All of the known main coinages were present in the hoards – if the different types represent individual communities, the deposits also suggest that the shrine was a place where these different communities were coming together.

South of the entranceway, a pit had been dug into the eastern edge of the boundary ditch, cutting through an earlier pit containing animal bones. The later pit contained over a thousand coins and a concentration of iron fragments, identified as part of a Roman cavalry helmet. The helmet had been placed upside down in the pit with the coins deposited over the top. Several fragments of pig bone, including a fairly intact maxilla and a rib, were found interleaved with the helmet cheek pieces. These are likely to have been disturbed from the bone deposits in the earlier pit but may have been recognised as significant and been deliberately incorporated and buried with the helmet. The distal portion of a human humerus was also recovered and found to conjoin with a shaft fragment from the adjacent boundary ditch. It may have been broken and displaced by the excavation of the pit through the ditch and, as with the displaced pig bones, the re-interment of the human bone within the pit, suggests an acknowledgement of its significance.

Due to its fragile nature the helmet was lifted as a single block and transported to the British Museum for excavation and conservation. Although still awaiting full excavation a substantially complete helmet skull or bowl, at least six loose cheek pieces and other fragments of metalwork have been revealed. So far, all of the identifiable components are consistent in design, manufacture and embellishment with certain early imperial Roman helmet types believed to have been intended for cavalrymen or mounted officers (Hockey and James 2008). The cheek pieces are decorated with images including a mounted Roman with arm outstretched, crowned by the goddess Victory, with a barbarian beneath; such imagery might suggest the depiction of a member of the Imperial family (Figure 7.5). Although Roman cavalry helmets have been found in Britain, the closest parallels for the East Leicestershire deposit comprise two finds from the river bed of the Waal at Nijmegen, Holland (Robinson 1975: 99). Interestingly the second helmet at Nijmegen was found with some beads and rings, and an extra pair of cheek pieces. Few of the known helmets are closely dated, but such types appear to be current in the first half of the first century AD. The Leicestershire helmet components may have been no more than two or three decades old when buried.

Figure 7.5: The partially excavated Roman Cavalry Helmet
(Photo courtesy of the Trustees of the British Museum)

# Gods and beliefs – reasons for deposition

The motivation behind the activities and offerings identified at East Leicestershire are difficult to comprehend. Although the shrine was probably in use over several generations, the deposition of both the metalwork and the animal bones appears to represent activity over a relatively short period on a regular basis. The animal bone evidence suggests that the pigs were killed over the winter season; perhaps indicating an annual event, although other less perceptible rituals may well have taken place during other times. The main depositions appear to have started early in the first century AD and probably continued after the Roman invasion in AD 43, ceasing shortly afterwards. Artefacts and later coins (including brooches, jewellery and a possible bronze sceptre handle similar to those found at Wanborough (O'Connell and Bird 1994)) suggest ritual activity continued into the first and second centuries AD, although any such activity appears to have been concentrated outside of the shrine. Certainly activity on the shrine itself appears to have ceased during the later first century AD, although the later Roman settlement avoids the area of ritual focus, suggesting that there was a lingering awareness of the sacred area. Geophysical survey has identified several roundhouses to the north indicating an Iron Age settlement but its date and relationship to the shrine remains unknown.

That the people practicing rituals here had links with the Romans is made clear by the presence of a cavalry helmet buried on the site. Exactly how the helmet came to be on a native British shrine on a hilltop in rural Leicestershire around the time of the Roman invasion is one of the most puzzling questions raised by the site. In contrast to La Tène Gaul, where helmets are frequently found in ritual contexts, often rivers (Roymans 1996: 30–31), helmets do not seem to have been a feature of indigenous pre-Roman Iron Age armaments and warfare in Britain (Hockey and James 2008). Helmets were alien artefacts in earlier first-century Britain, although they would have been seen on Caesar's troops in 55–54 BC, and encountered by British mercenaries and travellers in Gaul. It is possible that a helmet may have reached East Leicestershire from Roman auxiliaries conceivably already stationed in the 'friendly kingdoms' of the south before the Claudian invasion of AD 43 (Creighton 2006: 61–3). Alternatively it could have belonged to a Briton who served in the Roman army as an auxiliary cavalryman on the continent. However, it could also represent a direct Roman diplomatic gift to a prominent, potentially friendly individual. A similar suggestion was put forward for the Winchester jewellery, which was believed to be a gift from a Roman patron (Hobbs 2003: 63), although jewellery does not have the military connotations associated with a helmet.

The use of coins in ritual deposits during the Late Iron Age in Britain and the continent is well known. Coin deposits in Britain in later Iron Age hoards were dominated by gold, with silver (and copper alloy) appearing to become more important with the appearance of the Romans (Creighton 2005: 69). The high value of silver and gold coins means they were unlikely to have an economic monetary use and may have been used as a way of storing wealth and showing status while at the same time, having a ritual significance. Early British coinage appears to have been gifted during social and political interactions between leading groups, rather than simply for economic transactions (Haselgrove 2005: 25; Creighton 2005). In a study of the feature types in which Iron Age coins occur in the South Midlands, Curteis suggested that rather than casual losses, coins were preferentially deposited in ditches, pits and alluvium to enhance the ritual significance given to these types of features (Curteis 2005). The large quantity of coins at the Leicestershire shrine, together with the presence of ingots made from melted coins could represent the accumulated wealth of several communities, while at the same time providing a ritual focus. This may be similar to other hoard sites where a storage function has been argued, such as at Snettisham where rich deposits are interpreted as a storage place for communal wealth rather than a sacred space with offerings to the gods (Hobbs 2003: 140; Haselgrove 2005). There is no reason why an area used as a ritual place might not also be utilised for storing the wealth of a community.

## A new type of ritual site?

The excavated evidence suggests this was an open air hilltop location where different social groups might gather together to perform ritual activities, which included the deposition of coin hoards and offerings of animals. It is becoming clear that open air shrines and/or ceremonial meeting places, at which large quantities of coins and other precious metal objects were 'sacrificed' or deposited for safe keeping by the gods, were an important feature of later Iron Age landscapes in Britain and the near Continent (Haselgrove and Wigg-Wolf 2005). However, this is the first time in Britain that a well preserved site of this kind, with clearly differentiated deposits, has been excavated relatively intact. Unfortunately, the others are either poorly recorded antiquarian finds or were severely damaged by illegal metal detecting before proper investigation could occur, most notoriously at Wanborough (O'Connell and Bird 1994). Comparing the East Leicestershire shrine with other ritual places throughout Britain is therefore difficult as it does not seem to conform to known examples. Previous knowledge of the use of shrines within Britain is largely confined to a number of structures in the south, usually found as a result of being overlain by later Romano-Celtic temples or containing structures. As such, it may be that the Hallaton shrine represents a new form of site that simply has not been recognised elsewhere. However, the site does contain elements that are paralleled on other known shrine sites, particularly in terms of specific practices of deposition. The deposition of coins and metal artefacts is common on Late Iron Age shrine sites such as at Harlow (France and Gobel 1985; Haselgrove 1989), Hayling Island (King and Soffe 2001) and Uley (Woodward and Leach 1993). The selective animal deposits, usually from juveniles, are also paralleled at these shrines: Harlow, mostly sheep; Hayling Island, sheep/goat and pig; and Uley, sheep/goat (King 2005). Another possible British parallel is the early pre-temple phase at Wanborough, which contained a large number of Iron Age and Early Roman coins deposited around the mid first century AD, without an associated structure (O'Connell and Bird 1994: 16). Unfortunately much of the stratigraphy where the coins were found had been destroyed, making assumptions about the nature of the deposits difficult. Further excavations identified a curving trackway linking a number of Late Iron Age features, tentatively suggested as ritual, to the site of the later temples (Williams 2007: 163). There is also evidence for deposits of animal bone and possible feasting as well as large numbers of coins (O'Connell and Bird 1994). Williams (2007) suggests that there may have been a grove of trees or an open area within a woodland acting as a pre-temple focus.

Shrine sites on the continent are often richer in terms of finds and have also been more extensively excavated than those in Britain. A number of 'open air cult sites' without more formally constructed shrines/temples are known. The site at Hoogeloon, Holland comprised a ditch and low banked enclosure with evidence for trees and posts as ritual foci within it, dating to the first half of the first century AD (Derks 1998). At Ribemont-sur-Ancre, France, pre-conquest activity included a Late Iron Age enclosure ditch, with a coin hoard and the deposition of individual coins and torc fragments (Brunaux 1988; Wellington 2003). At Gournay-sur-Aronde an enclosure ditch with an eastern entrance surrounded a series of central shrines and pits. Selective animal deposits and broken weapons were placed in particular zones in the ditch, including horse skeletons and cattle skulls deposited in the entranceway. Gournay-sur-Aronde provides quite distinct evidence for both chthonic sacrifice (where the deposits were for the gods alone) with parts of cattle and horses deposited in zones within the ditch, as well as feasting, predominantly on pig and sheep. The site was originally an open air structure, with a shelter erected over the site in the third – second century BC and followed by a square temple in the first century BC (Brunaux 1988 Wellington 2003). Similarly, at Mirabeau (Brunaux 1988) an early sanctuary enclosure was superseded by later Gallo-Roman temples. However, unlike the East Leicestershire site these large sanctuaries had earlier origins, contained ritual structures and were often linked with substantial settlements. Gournay and Ribemont also contained large quantities of human bone.

# Conclusions

The Leicestershire site appears to present an alternative model to the traditional southern British Late Iron Age shrine; open air and characterised by large quantities of coins and metalwork and selective animal bone deposits. The numismatic evidence indicates the possible existence of several near-contemporary *Corieltavi* coin issues and suggests that the site served as a meeting place for a number of different social groups, perhaps utilised for particular festivals at certain times of the year.

Rather than being unique, it seems more likely that the East Leicestershire shrine may represent a type of rural shrine that has simply never been previously recognised in Britain. In this case there may be more similarities with hoard sites rather than known shrines. Hoards are rarely extensively excavated and may well have associated features similar to those at Hallaton that remain undiscovered due to an emphasis on the metalwork. Hoards such as those from Snettisham (Stead 1998; Hobbs 2003) and the Winchester jewellery hoard (Hobbs 2003; Hill *et al.* 2004) are often interpreted as being buried as a store of wealth with a view to retrieval, but it is possible that they may be unrecognised ritual deposits belonging to shrines in natural locations.

The East Leicestershire site may therefore help to provide a new interpretation for many of the numerous metalwork and coin hoards found in Late Iron Age Britain. Fieldwork has uncovered the largest archaeologically-excavated Iron Age coin hoard in the country to date, and the evidence for ritual activity challenges current thinking about shrines. Not only does it suggest that some known Late Iron Age shrines may have begun life as open air ritual sites, it also raises the possibility that such sites may not have been uncommon in the British landscape. Without this programme of excavation, the find would have undoubtedly been recorded as a dispersed hoard and many of the other associated features, such as the substantial animal bone deposits, would have remained unidentified. As very few hoard sites have been extensively excavated, it may well be that some of them deserve reconsideration in the light of the East Leicestershire discoveries.

# Acknowledgements

The authors owe a debt of gratitude to many people who have been involved in this project. The fieldwork and research would not have been possible if not for the involvement of the local Fieldwork Group and their friends and families. In particular their silence has meant that over the four years of the initial project, the site was untroubled by illegal metal detecting.

Invaluable help and advice was provided by the British Museum, particularly from J. D. Hill, Jonathan Williams, Ian Leins and Marilyn Hockey. Further advice during post-excavation was provided by the School of Archaeology and Ancient History at the University of Leicester, particularly Colin Haselgrove, Simon James and Jeremy Taylor. We would also like to thank Jeremy Taylor, Lynden Cooper, Patrick Clay and an anonymous reviewer for their helpful comments on drafts of this paper. The project was funded from numerous sources, notably English Heritage, the Townley project at the British Museum and the BBC for the fieldwork. The post-excavation and publication was funded jointly by English Heritage, the Society of Antiquaries and University of Leicester Archaeological Services.

# Bibliography

Brunaux, J. L. (1988). *The Celtic Gauls: gods, rites and sanctuaries.* (translated by Daphne Nash). London: Seaby.

Buckley, R. T. Higgins, J. Coward, A. Gnanaratnam and R. Kipling (2007). Recent excavations in Roman Leicester. *ARA The Bulletin of the Association for Roman Archaeology* 18: 47–53.

Clay, P. and J. E. Mellor (1985). *Excavations in Bath Lane, Leicester.* Leicester: Leicestershire Museums Arts and Records Service, Archaeological Report 10.

Creighton, J. (2005). Gold, ritual and kingship. In C. C. Haselgrove and D. Wigg-Wolf (eds.) *Iron Age Coinage and Ritual Practices*: 69–84. Mainz: Studien zu Fundmünzen der Antike 20.

Creighton, J. (2006). *Britannia: The creation of the Roman province.* London: Routledge.

Curteis, M. (2005). Ritual coin deposition on Iron Age settlements in the south Midlands. In C. C. Haselgrove and D. Wigg-Wolf (eds.) *Iron Age Coinage and Ritual Practices*: 207–226. Mainz: Studien zu Fundmünzen der Antike 20.

Derks, T. (1998). *Gods, Temples, and Ritual Practice: the transformation of religious ideas and values in Roman Gaul.* Amsterdam: Amsterdam University Press.

Drew, C. (2005). *Specialist Report 2005 – Mammal bone assemblage (interpretation & comparison with other assemblages). Refuse or ritual? – the mammal bones from High Pasture Cave, Skye.* http://www.high-pasturecave.org/index.php/the_work/article/specialist_report_2005_mammal_bone_assemblage_interpretation_comparison_wit [Date accessed: July 2008].

France, N. E. and B. M. Gobel, (1985). *The Romano-British Temple at Harlow.* (West Essex Archaeological Group). Gloucester: Alan Sutton.

Fulford, M. (2001). Links with the past: pervasive 'ritual' behaviour in Roman Britain. *Britannia* 32: 199–218.

Grant, A. (1984). Animal husbandry. In B. Cunliffe (ed.) *Danebury: an Iron Age hillfort in Hampshire. Vol. 2: the excavations 1969–1978*: 102–119. York: CBA Research Report 52.

Grant, A. (2002). Food, status and social hierarchy. In P. Miracle and N. Milner (eds.) *Consuming passions and patterns of consumption*: 17–23. Cambridge: McDonald Institute.

Green, M. (1992). *Animals in Celtic Life and Myth.* London: Routledge.

Grimm, J. (2007). A dog's life: animal bone from a Romano-British ritual shaft at Springhead, Kent (UK). In N. Benecke (ed.) *Beiträge zur Archäozoologie und Prähistorischen Anthropologie* Band VI: 54–75. Langenweißbach.

Haselgrove, C. (1989). Iron Age coin deposition at Harlow temple, Essex. *Oxford Journal of Archaeology* 8(1): 73–88.

Haselgrove, C. (2005). A trio of temples: a reassessment of Iron Age coin deposition at Hayling Island, Harlow and Wanborough. In C. C. Haselgrove and D. Wigg-Wolf (eds.) *Iron Age Coinage and Ritual Practices*: 381–418. Mainz: Studien zu Fundmünzen der Antike 20.

Haselgrove, C. C. and D. Wigg-Wolf (eds.) (2005) *Iron Age Coinage and Ritual Practices*. Mainz: Studien zu Fundmünzen der Antike 20.

Hill, J. D., A. J. Spence, S. La Niece and S. Worrell (2004). The Winchester Hoard: a find of unique Iron Age gold jewellery from southern England. *The Antiquaries Journal* 84: 1–22.

Hill, J. D. (1995). *Ritual and Rubbish in the Iron Age of Wessex*. Oxford: British Archaeological Reports, British Series 242.

Hill J. D. (2008). The small finds. In V. Score (ed.) *Rituals, Hoards and Helmets: a Conquest Period shrine in east Leicestershire*. Unpublished University of Leicester Archaeological Services (ULAS) Report.

Hobbs, R. (2003). *Treasure: finding our past*. London: British Museum Press.

Hockey, M and S. James (2008). The Roman helmet: a preliminary note. In V. Score (ed.) *Rituals, Hoards and Helmets: a Conquest Period shrine in east Leicestershire*. Unpublished University of Leicester Archaeological Services (ULAS) Report.

King, A. (2005). Animal remains from temples in Roman Britain. *Britannia* 36: 329–369.

King, A. and G. Soffe (2001). Internal organisation and deposition at the Iron Age temple on Hayling Island (Hampshire). In J. R. Collis (ed.) *Society and Settlement in Iron Age Europe* : 111–124. Sheffield: Sheffield Archaeology Monograph 11.

Leins, I. (2007). Coins in context: coinage and votive deposition in Iron Age south-east Leicestershire. *British Numismatic Journal* 77: 22–47.

Levitan, B. (1993). Vertebrae remains. In A. Woodward and P. Leach (eds.) *The Uley Shrines: excavation of a ritual complex on West Hill, Uley, Gloucestershire 1977–9*: 257–301. London: English Heritage Archaeology Report 17.

Maltby, J. M. (1985). Animal husbandry. In P. J. Fasham (ed.) *The Prehistoric Settlement at Winnall Down, Winchester*: 97–125. Hampshire Field Club and Archaeological Society: Monograph 2.

O'Connell, M. G. and J. Bird (1994). The Roman temple at Wanborough, Excavation 1985–1986. *Surrey Archaeological Collections* 82: 1–168.

Robinson, H. R. (1975). *The Armour of Imperial Rome*. London: Arms & Armour Press.

Roymans, N. (1996). The sword or the plough. Regional dynamics in the Romanisation of Belgic Gaul and the Rhineland Area. In N. Roymans (ed.) *From the Sword to the Plough. Three studies on the earliest Romanisation of Northern Gaul*: 9–126. Amsterdam: Amsterdam University Press.

Rudling, D. (2008). Roman period temples, shrines and religion in Sussex. In D. Rudling (ed.) *Ritual Landscapes of Roman South-East Britain*: 95–138. Oxford: Heritage/Oxbow Books.

Smith, A. T. and A. Brookes (2001). *Holy Ground: theoretical issues relating to the landscape and material culture of ritual space*. Oxford: British Archaeological Reports, International Series 956.

Smith, K., (2006). *Guides, Guards and Gifts to the Gods: domesticated dogs in the art and archaeology of Iron Age and Roman Britain*. Oxford: British Archaeological Reports, British Series 422.

Stead, I. M. (1998). *The Salisbury Hoard*. Gloucestershire: Tempus Publishing.

Wait, G. A. (1985). *Ritual and Religion in Iron Age Britain*. Oxford: British Archaeological Reports, British Series 149.

Wellington, I. (2003) *Gifts to the Gods? Votive deposition in north-eastern France from 250 BC to the Age of Augustus: a numismatic perspective*. Unpublished PhD thesis. Department of Archaeology, University of Durham.

Williams, D. (2007). Green Lane Wanborough: excavations at the Roman religious site 1999. *Surrey Archaeological Collections* 93: 1149–265.

Williams, D. (2008). The Wanborough temple site. In D. Rudling (ed.) *Ritual Landscapes of Roman South-East Britain.* Oxford: Heritage/Oxbow Books.

Woodward, A. and P. Leach (1993). *The Uley Shrine: excavation of a ritual complex on West Hill, Uley, Gloucestershire. 1977–9.* London: English Heritage Archaeology Report 17.

## CHAPTER 8

# DEATH, DESTRUCTION AND THE END OF AN ERA: THE END OF THE IRON AGE AT CADBURY CASTLE, SOMERSET

*Sue Jones and Clare Randall*

(*Bournemouth University*)

## Abstract

A deposit of largely disarticulated human remains in the south-west gateway of Cadbury Castle hillfort, Somerset excavated in the late 1960's, has been explained as the aftermath a massacre of the hillfort defenders by Roman forces in or shortly after AD 43. However, information obtained from original studies of the bone was cursory and little used in the interpretation of the 'massacre deposits'. Re-examination of the material has enabled a re-consideration of this interpretation. Analysis revealed patterns in the location of skeletal of elements and age groups, and different treatment of remains depending on the age, and possibly sex, of individuals. Information from fragmentation and burning indicates episodic deposition, curation and accumulation over a period of time. The nature of the deposit has parallels with treatment of human, and to some extent animal remains, on the rest of the hillfort from the Middle Iron Age onward, and may relate to the first century AD putative shrine within the hillfort. Ongoing reassessment of the hillfort animal bone indicates highly selective deposition occurring throughout the Iron Age, and becoming increasingly associated with metalwork and other objects toward the end of the period. Evidence from the South Cadbury Environs Project has revealed a re-orientation of land use at the end of the Iron Age, intensification of deposition in pits and in boundary locations, and involvement of human remains and animal bone. A dislocation in settlement in the mid first century AD had been assumed to be directly related to the events of AD 43; disruption, change and social upheaval may have had deeper roots.

# Introduction

This article takes its somewhat lurid title from the rather idiosyncratic naming of contexts that occurred during the excavations of Cadbury Castle hillfort, South Cadbury, Somerset, by Leslie Alcock in the late 1960s. 'Death and destruction' was the name given to a particularly burnt and apparently gruesome deposit of silts and human remains discovered in the south-west gate of the hillfort, which comprise part of what came to be known as the 'Massacre Deposits'. This designation has followed discussion of this material ever since, despite misgivings expressed in the publication of the material (Woodward and Hill 2000), and has dominated consideration of the final Iron Age occupation of the hillfort. Now, however, it is possible to reconsider what this deposit may signify in the light of work on other material from the hillfort, the ongoing survey of the surrounding landscape by the South Cadbury Environs Project, and, most importantly, a detailed re-examination of the human remains themselves.

# Background

Cadbury Castle is a multi-period site in south-eastern Somerset. The Iron Age hillfort covers seven hectares. It was excavated in a series of trenches by Leslie Alcock between 1966–70 and 1973. Preliminary publications were followed by one covering the early medieval archaeology (Alcock 1995) and an apparently definitive volume on the late prehistoric archaeology (Barrett *et al.* 2000). This unfortunately did not deal with all periods and left much of the material archive unstudied, including the majority of the animal bone. The examination of the human remains was in some respects cursory, passing through the hands of a number of specialists, and was not fully integrated into interpretation. It is this faunal and human skeletal material which has been reconsidered.

The South Cadbury Environs Project (SCEP) commenced in the early 1990s, prompted by the preparations for publication of the hillfort excavations, and continues to date. The project area covers 64 sq km centred on the hillfort, sampled by way of six localities on differing geologies and topographies. An extensive programme of geophysical survey, test pitting and excavation has enabled the construction of phased maps of the landscape, and the exploration of a number of specific locales (Tabor 2008). SCEP has identified a number of Middle and Late Iron Age boundaries, field systems and settlement evidence both close to and further away from the hillfort. This has included enclosures and houses as well as more enigmatic but extensive unenclosed scatters of pits and other features (Randall 2006). Many of the excavated examples have produced a range of material that is contemporary with several phases of use of the hillfort and can be directly compared with the hillfort assemblages. Recording and analysis of the animal bone from the hillfort and SCEP sites are being carried out as part of a wider PhD project looking at animal exploitation in the south-west of Britain in prehistory (Randall in preparation). The human remains from the hillfort have been re-examined as part of a separate study (Jones 2008), with those from the SCEP sites considered using the same methods (Randall and Jones in prep).

## Shrines, calves, pits and landscape

One of the features for which Cadbury Castle is best known is the putative shrine, Building N5. This was located in the central part of the hillfort (Figure 8.1), to the west of a series of Middle – Late Iron Age rubbish layers. The ceramic evidence seemed to place the building in the mid first century AD. The building faced the east, along a line of probably earlier animal burials (Figure 8.2), which in turn appear to relate to the rubbish deposits. The location and rectangular layout of the building, having an inner room and porch, were seen as supporting its designation as a shrine (Barrett *et al.* 2000b: 172–3). This could however be regarded as somewhat tentative. Nevertheless, recent re-examination of the animal bone revealed a collection of disarticulated human remains that had not been previously noted. This represented a number of individuals including younger juveniles, subadults and adults. In addition, the archive indicates that a number of metal objects, including tools and weapon fragments came from the building. Not only may the human remains and metalwork bolster this building's claim to represent a ritual focus, but they provide other linkages that will be discussed further below.

The group of cattle associated bone groups (ABGs), aligned on the axis of the 'shrine', was included in the examination of a small proportion of the animal bone assemblage that was carried out in advance of publication (Hamilton-Dyer and Maltby 2000). It was confirmed that there were a large number of calves, as well as some adult cattle. Additionally many calf bones came from the rubbish layers, and were also present in a large proportion of the selection of pits examined, distributed across a wider area. Radiocarbon dates obtained from two of the articulated individuals provided determinations of cal 390 BC–AD 60 and cal 360 BC–AD 20. An estimate of at least 30 calves was made from these deposits, with none of the material showing any sign of butchery or gnawing by dogs, and many of the individuals were newborns or very young animals. The presence of a large amount of disturbed material might imply a repeated habit of deposition in this part of the hillfort, although it was not possible to ascertain the period over which the calves were

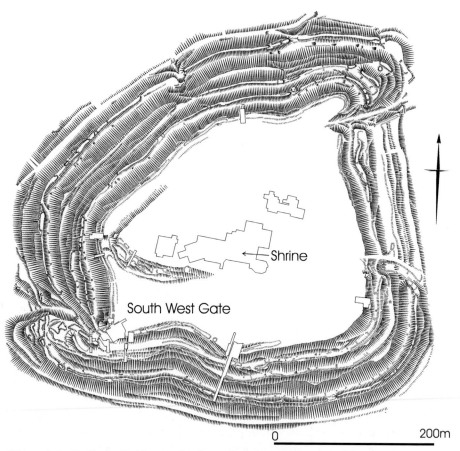

Figure 8.1: Cadbury Castle plan, indicating the location of the south west gate and shrine. (After RCHME plan Figure 7, Barrett *et al.* 2000: 16).

deposited. Explanations of the deposits as natural mortalities as a result of the area having been used for calving appear inadequate due to the number of individuals in a relatively restricted area (Hamilton-Dyer and Maltby 2000: 279, 281–2; Barrett *et al.* 2000b: 172). This seems to suggest a particular concentration on the utilisation and/or deposition of young animals, particularly cattle, throughout the Middle and into the later Iron Age. Work in progress on the rest of the animal bones seems to support this apparent emphasis. Alcock noted that the animal burials lay to the south of a concentration of metalwork finds, which mainly occurred in the rubbish layers (1973). This took on additional importance in consideration of the location of these deposits near the shrine.

Behind the ramparts on the southern side of the hillfort, the contents of a single Middle Iron Age pit, SC/D 817, stand out from most of the Middle

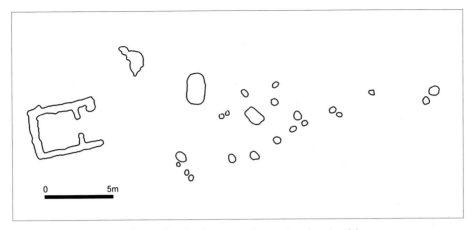

Figure 8.2: Cadbury Castle shrine and associated animal bone groups.
(After Figure 84 Barrett *et al.* 2000: 170).

Iron Age animal bones considered to date. This was a particularly large cylin-drical pit with several fills. The upper fill, probably slumped into the body of the pit, contained in excess of 8,000 animal bones. For such a large assem-blage from a single feature, it contained a very limited range of species. A high proportion was identifiable with a very low loose-teeth count, and low degrees of fragmentation. All areas of the body were well represented. The expected and actual incidence of elements implies that whole or largely whole skeletons of sheep and goats, cattle, pigs and dogs were incorporated into the deposit. Some of the cattle vertebrae were definitely in articulation when deposited. Dogs were the least well represented species, and may have had different treatment with the notable complete absence of skulls, cervical verte-brae, pelvis and hind limb bones, whilst there are additional pig limb bones, possibly representing joints of meat. There was an extremely low degree of gnawing, implying rapid covering of the remains, and few burnt fragments, which might be interpreted as a lack of cooking. There are a small number of cuts on the sheep bone, the majority being transverse cuts on astragali but lit-tle evidence of fresh helical or longitudinal breaks. Carcases were not por-tioned, but they may have been skinned.

Over 80 percent of the animals were sheep/goat, a high proportion, espe-cially when compared to assemblages from other sites of the same period sur-rounding the hillfort. Although a number of goats were identified, the majority of animals were sheep. This is intriguing given the complete lack of evidence for goats from other sites in the environs and may have particular significance for this deposit. Cattle and pig were almost equally represented, with a small amount of dog. The patterns indicated in the ageing data are quite marked. The vast majority of sheep/goat were young juvenile animals (< 6 months).

Two additional much smaller groups represent sub-adults of one year to 18 months and young adults (2–4 years) with a single older individual (4–6 years). This may imply a seasonal cull, possibly occurring in summer. As such, it is unlikely that this would relate to autumnal flock management or winter losses. All of the pig mandibles fall at the younger end of the juvenile range. Both adult and juvenile dogs are represented. The ageing data for the cattle indicated the presence of at least one old adult but the majority were calves with a number of juveniles of around one month represented.

Pit SC/D 817, stands out for the sheer volume of material that it contains, and if the interpretation is correct, and the animals were largely articulated on deposition, this is so far unique. An Early Iron Age pit at Winnall Down (2431) contained a high proportion of sheep/goat compared to cattle, and these predominantly comprised bones from young animals (Maltby 1985: 97–8), but it contained only 298 fragments. Whilst the Winnall Down pit shares similarities in the composition, Cadbury Castle pit SC/D 817 is of a different order of magnitude. It seems evident that the majority of this deposit derived from a single incidence of slaughter or consumption. There was a marked focus on young animals and this must be seen in relation to the calf burials, some of which at least may be contemporary, and the associated 'shrine'. At the very least, this seems to confirm a long standing activity involving the deposition of juvenile animals, representing a considerable commitment of resources.

The pits within the hillfort need to be considered in the light of those which occur beyond its bounds. The South Cadbury Environs Project has identified a number of locations in the landscape surrounding the hillfort where large numbers of pits were dug and filled with a variety of objects from the Middle Iron Age through to the end of the Late Iron Age. One site at Sigwells, Charleton Horethorne, which overlooks the hillfort and lies along a prominent ridge to the south, may comprise up to 5,000 pits. The contents have been shown to be patterned, with articulated animals, dumps of bone, pottery and a variety of other materials, human remains, metalwork and deliberately included a variety of contrasting soils and stone. Some pits were evidently open for long periods of time, silts accumulating slowly and allowing for accumulations of the bones of small vertebrates. In addition, some had internal features such as posts, one cut into the base of the pit, and all of them marking the location of articulated animals. It has been postulated that the selection of objects, timescale and evident visibility related to complex activities that went beyond rubbish disposal. With regards to activities on the hillfort, the scale of these sites may challenge the assumption that pits within the hillfort related to the control of resources and production as there is a degree of contemporaneity. They are clearly beyond its immediate purview and are unenclosed. It was also noted that the number of pits, volume of selected materials and complexity increased through the Late Iron Age, in particular in the inclusion of metal objects (Randall 2006). The apparent reduction of settlement activity within the hillfort (Barrett *et al.* 2000b: 169), seems to be counterbalanced by an increase in, and complexity of, activity beyond its banks.

The floruit of these pit clusters seems to coincide with the growth, use and abandonment of a number of field systems including those through the South Cadbury Valley and across the Sigwells ridge to the south. These appear to have come into being during the Middle Iron Age, and continued in use for a couple of centuries before silting up. However, once they were almost filled, but evidently still visible, they attracted a range of selected deposits, that have led to the conclusion that this was part of a deliberate closing down of the landscape in the middle of the first century AD (Tabor 2004: 92–3;Tabor forthcoming). The assumption, based partly on the original interpretation of the 'massacre', was that this directly related to the Roman invasion. However, it is clear that the field systems had fallen into a degree of disrepair and possible disuse before the arrival of the Romans. Activity on the hillfort and in the surrounding fields appears to have been declining at the point when most pits were being dug in the wider landscape and deposits were being made within them, and in the remnants of the old field ditches. The focus of the landscape had shifted from the hillfort itself into the wider environs.

# Massacre?

In describing what he found in the South West Gateway of Cadbury Castle, Leslie Alcock wrote:

> "*Scattered along a twenty metre passage were parts of at least twenty-eight human bodies of both sexes, ranging in age from about four to thirty-five. These human remains were curiously disjointed, a complete left limb, a trunk with the right forearm and so on. Associated with these remains were about 150 brooches, iron weapons, shield bosses and a repousse bronze plaque with a Romano-Celtic head on.*"

Relating to an assault by Roman forces, these were interpreted as *in situ* remains of massacre victims left to rot and:

> "*were... pulled to pieces by wolves and other wild beasts*" *(1972: 106).*

Discussion of the exact dating, whether it related to events in AD 43, 47 or the Boudiccan revolt (Alcock 1972: 170–2; Manning 1976), has been dependent on the interpretation of the deposit as a massacre. The radiocarbon dates however provide a date range of several hundred years which makes it problematic to associate the deposit with any particular campaign (Campbell *et al.* 1979: 32), or any single short-term depositional event.

The massacre theory was constructed from a number of observations made from the archaeological data including:

- The human remains did not show a demographic profile reflecting deaths caused by natural attrition;
- Some articulated remains were found in the gateway passageways;
- Weapons, both Roman and native were found in the deposit;
- Evidence of burnt timber was identified in the gateway and guard chamber;
- A small number of human remains showed evidence of trauma (Woodward and Hill 2000: 114–5).

The information provided in the publication of the hillfort excavations is how-ever contradictory on some points and the human remains themselves were not subjected to an examination that included consideration of taphonomic factors. Whilst Woodward and Hill offered a variety of interpretations (2000: 111), inferences about the deposit were not drawn from the remains them-selves, and the overarching interpretation remained that of a massacre follow-ing a battle. It was felt that the application of a variety of techniques could be beneficial in providing a more nuanced interpretation, and a re-examination of the material was carried out.

Adapting zooarchaeological principles to this disarticulated assemblage, a system of recording non-repeatable zones was utilised. This was modified from Knüsel and Outram (2004) to take into account breakage and burning patterns in this very fragmented assemblage (Jones 2008). Each fragment was identified and examined, recorded onto a relational database with pathology, trauma, burning, and other taphonomic factors noted for each fragment. Where possible, morphological and metrical analyses were used to estimate sex and age, using fusion data and relative degenerative change. Given that the original analysis and publication had not included human remains from a variety of locations and periods in other parts of the hillfort, these were included in the study to provide context for the deposit. It was clear that there had been a long history of deposition of partial, complete and disarticulated human remains elsewhere on the hillfort. Within the 'massacre' deposit itself, the data were grouped and considered in the series of stratigraphical units devised by Woodward (2000: 96–7). This consists of four abutting groups of contexts spread along the gate passageway (Figure 8.3), with a rubble sealing layer overlying the outer groups.

Re-examination of the remains produced a total of 6,006 human bone frag-ments from the hillfort, with a revised count for the 'massacre deposits' of 4,256. The original published total was somewhat less than 2,000, as the most

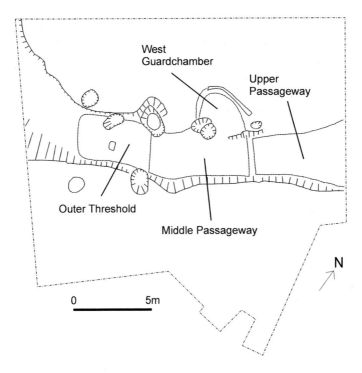

Figure 8.3: Cadbury Castle south-west gate showing the location of units within the 'massacre deposits'. (After Figure 49, Barrett *et al.* 2000: 96).

fragmented and burnt bones were not quantified. Consideration of the demographic profile had previously revealed that the range of ages present indicated a catastrophic event. However, although the mortality profile largely exemplifies the expected profile of a living population, the taphonomic evidence shows that this deposit cannot be related to a single event or contemporary population. The remains accumulated over a period of time. It should also be noted that no individuals under the age of one year occurred in the deposit, although these occurred regularly in other areas of the hillfort. There was minimal representation of old adult individuals aged above 50 years.

In addition, the location of remains of individuals in particular age ranges and particular elements and groups of elements was seen to be patterned (Figure 8.4). For example more remains belonging to individuals under the age of *c.* twelve years occurred in the outer threshold, with increasing age represented in the stratigraphical units leading into the hillfort interior. The inner threshold had a higher proportion of adults in their thirties. Also, there was an under-representation of particular elements. There is a lack of loose teeth that should have been evident had the remains decomposed *in situ*. There was a total absence of adult pelvic girdles. Collections of hand and foot bones in the

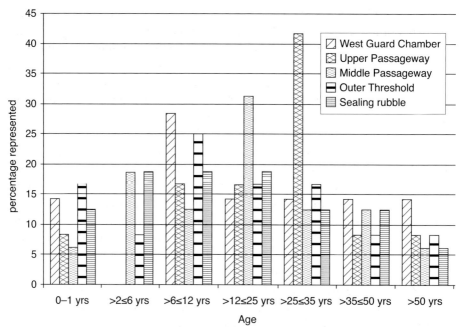

Figure 8.4: The distribution of skeletal material by age group within the south west gate.

middle passageway, thoracic elements in the outer threshold and an overriding proportion of skull fragments across the whole gateway, indicates that selective deposition and post-mortem manipulation of bones was taking place. Where it was possible to make an estimation of the likely sex represented, the skull fragments in the gate appeared exclusively male, whilst all the limb bones appeared to lie within the female range.

The almost total lack of animal gnawing not only fails to support the hypothesis of a pile of rotting bodies left in the open, but also cannot explain the missing elements. Many individual contexts included the remains of several clearly different individuals. For example, one context containing mainly foot bones had at least five individuals represented by left fifth metatarsals. Most deposits contained either skull fragments or long bones but these rarely occurred together, in both the burnt and unburnt material. The articulated limbs that were originally noted were in fact a very small element of the entire deposit. However, their juxtaposition with brooches may indicate that they had been wrapped.

The evidence of burnt timber in the gateway and west guard chamber suggested to Alcock (1972: 105) that the gate had been burned down by attackers and the remains left to silt up. However, the location of burnt human remains only correlates with burnt timbers in the west guard chamber. The lack of calcined bone around the outer threshold (which Woodward described as an area of intense burning (2000)) and the greater number of burnt remains in the upper passageway (not identified as an area that suffered burning) suggests that these bones were not burnt *in situ* along with the gate. There was evidence of selection within the burnt material itself, and heterogeneous concretions on some bones seem to indicate transport from other areas of the site. Small amounts of animal bone and pottery from these deposits seem to indicate the silts contained domestic refuse. Moreover, analysis of the fracture patterns resulting from burning (Thompson 2003: 106; Pope and Smith 2004; Baker 2004) indicate that some bone was fleshed and some unfleshed at the time it was burnt, but was incorporated in the same deposits. This can only indicate that the individuals concerned did not all die at the same time.

The presence of weapons and armour both native and Roman in the gateway have been viewed as a testimony of contact with the Roman army (Alcock 1972: 105). A hoard of weapons in the west guard chamber was interpreted as arms gathered up after the battle whilst many brooches scattered through the passageway were regarded as dropped stock-in-trade from someone fleeing the hillfort; a deposit of keys and latchlifters were similarly dropped in flight (Woodward 2000: 114). However, further consideration of this material indicates a number of problems. The metalwork represented did not merely consist of weapons and jewellery, but encompassed tools, scrap bronze and unidentifiable ferrous objects. Other objects included worked bone and spindle whorls. This is similar in many respects to the suite of objects from elsewhere in the Iron Age deposits on the hillfort, and to a lesser degree other neighbouring sites. The number of metal objects that can be identified as of exclusively Roman origin is limited. A hoard of weapons previously regarded as being an *in situ* store in the west guard chamber are not described as melted or burnt, despite this having been an area of intense burning, with burnt timbers extant, but rather, a number of them are corroded (Olivier 2000: 138), implying exposure to the elements.

Few brooches were burnt, even in other areas of apparently intense burning. It is also notable that many weapons were bent and broken, whilst other metal objects such as bronze strips and foil were folded. Other objects such as shields are only represented by small fragments. If these had been rapidly abandoned, one might have expected greater completeness. It should therefore be considered that folded and broken weaponry and other items do not represent battle damage, but relates more to a longstanding history of ritualised destruction of weapons that is evident in many late prehistoric locations in southern Britain (Brück 1995: 125–7; Bradley 1990; Woodward *et al.* 1980). In Roman Gallia Belgica, Roman military equipment was found in post-conquest native votive deposits (Fontijn 2005: 151) and possibly a similar situation might be indicated here.

Originally only nine examples of traumatic injury were noted in the 'Massacre Deposits' (Woodward and Hill 2000; Forbes 2000: 117–21), from which the inference of violence was taken. On re-examination it became clear that there were at least sixty cases of sharp weapon trauma including cuts, chops and puncture marks. Blunt trauma was also indicated by bevel-edged skull fractures. Peri-mortem and post-mortem fracturing of long bones were identified by helical fractures with both smooth and slightly roughened edges, which indicated that the breaks had occurred before the bone had entirely dried out. Locations of some cuts seem to indicate that they relate to post-mortem treatment and manipulation of the body, as well as injuries that occurred before and around the time of death. This is significant as there has been a lack of evidence for this type of practice from elsewhere (Madgwick 2008: 107).

Evidence for decapitation was found on two individuals, and may indicate that some of the heads, which were particularly well represented along the area of the threshold of the gate, may have been deliberately removed and possibly displayed. It is notable that there is a concentration of examples of peri-mortem trauma in the upper passageway area, in contrast to the outer threshold where breaks seem to have occurred to bone once it had dried out. The range and variety of insults to bone do not appear to be consistent with the type of injury, or post-mortem treatment, one would expect to see simply as the result of a battle.

It is apparent that the deposits appear to be the result of a complex sequence of events and may relate to a variety of activities. The complex stratigraphy itself indicates that the entire deposit cannot be regarded as a single contemporaneous incident. Clear patterns can be ascertained within the deposits, with preferred locations for material from individuals of different ages, different parts of the body, and particular treatment of remains. The over-arching conclusion is that this deposit cannot be the result of a single event, with bone and other material possibly being curated over time before final deposition. The exact date of the deposit is therefore open for further debate, and the spread of radiocarbon dates more explicable if the deposit reflects long-term practices.

In the absence of the simple explanation of the deposits as the result of a single event, two broad areas need to be considered in approaching the issue of what this material actually represents: funerary treatment and deposition and the possibility of ritualised use of human body parts, possibly incorporating a sacrificial element. The human remains from the 'massacre deposits' must not be considered in isolation from those contemporary examples recovered from the hillfort and the surrounding environs. Disarticulated human bone is a frequent inclusion in a range of contexts across the hillfort in all periods; some of the later Iron Age material occurs in relation to metalwork and other objects, such as in the 'shrine', whilst evidence for sharp weapon trauma has been identified in a number of cases in material elsewhere in the hillfort.

Disarticulated human remains have also been recovered in smaller quantities from Milsom's Corner and Homeground, two contemporary settlement sites on the flanks of the hillfort, and from various contexts at Sigwells on the ridge to the south. In addition, there are two known articulated burials from the hillfort, one of a young man buried in the final phase Iron Age rampart, and interpreted by Alcock as a foundation burial (1972: 102–3). Re-examination of the remains revealed a number of conditions that may have affected his mobility in life (Jones 2008), and can perhaps be viewed in the context of ideas of sacrifice (Green 2002: 157–60). The other individual from the hillfort, has a less certain provenance having been recovered in 1942 during the digging of a potato clamp, but represents an elderly female, whose bones were associated with Middle Iron Age pottery. The few articulated burials located by the SCEP have all been older males or neonates.

Within the hillfort, there is evidence that the bodies of different age groups may have been afforded different processing treatment. Perinates were commonly deposited in a number of locations around the hillfort interior from the Early Iron Age onwards, but do not occur in the gateway deposits. Juveniles in the 'massacre' deposits do not appear to have been subjected to burning to the same degree as adults. There are, however, reasons to believe that this is not merely the result of relative survivability of the juvenile bone. Young adults and adolescents in particular seem to have been located within the gate area itself. Given that many of the cutmarks noted may relate to deliberate disarticulation of bodies, and some articulated body portions may have been wrapped, we appear to be seeing the result of a long term habit of complex treatment of bodies, curation and circulation of elements, and the final drawing together of that material into a deliberate deposit. Collections of some elements such as metapodials may have been deliberately curated, and incorporated into the final deposit as a method of incorporating relatives into a body of ancestors. Both fresh and dried bones were burnt, and as such, the act of burning may relate to a final action of processing, at a particular time, of curated individuals prior to incorporation in the deposit.

Whilst the point of division between funerary ritual and other ritualised activity utilising human remains is problematic, there are elements of this deposit that may reflect activities that move beyond the disposal of bodies. There appears to have been a concern with the curation and deposition of heads, with evidence of beheading, some cuts possibly relating to scalping and faces smashed. Some of the violent injuries sustained ante- and peri-mortem may relate to specific acts of killing for incorporation in the deposit. It also may well relate to combat, but that in itself may have been ritualised or have marked out individuals as suitable for incorporation. Some long bones display charring around the broken edges and may relate to a number of cases where helical breaks have similarity to the manner in which many animal bones on the site have been broken for marrow extraction. This may be an elaboration of the funerary treatment, or have taken on further meaning. Likewise, the tentative identification of skulls at the gate threshold as generally male and the limb bones possibly female, may have both funerary and/or broader meaning.

The nature of the metalwork deposited with the human remains incorporating weapons, some of which appear to have been deliberately placed beyond use, has resonance with many other deposits that have been recognised as ritual contexts. There are similarities with Ribemont-sur-Ancre, France, where around 200 nearly complete weapons were found bent and corroded with many disarticulated and partially-articulated human remains at a ritual complex (Craig *et al.* 2005: 173). These large deposits may reflect practices relating to the collection of spoils of battle, and display in hallowed places referred to by Caesar (*De Bello Gallico* VI 17). Some evidence from the non-metric traits in the 'Massacre' population hints at a heterogeneous group, raising the question of whether these individuals were drawn from a wide area, possibly captured and transported.

The general juxtaposition of deposits of these types of material with shrines and special places may relate to the structure of the gate itself. Not only may there be considerable significance in the location of the deposit in the route-way through the hillfort boundary, but the role of so-called guard chambers at hillforts would bear re-examination (*cf.* Bowden 2006). Perhaps this enclosed space should not automatically be defined as a guard chamber, rather it may have fulfilled a role as a shrine, or a place for votive offerings associated with the mortuary remains within its locale. An earlier phase chamber did not open into the passage but into the interior and was associated with more than one perinatal burial. A bronze repousse face plaque and a horse skull (unusual in relation to the rest of the animal bone assemblage recorded to date) from the middle passageway may have originated from the chamber and do not necessarily relate to gate furniture, but may actually represent shrine furnishings.

Although different in scale, it must be stressed that the suite of items included in the deposit echoes other smaller collections of items from all over the hill dating to the later part of the Iron Age, where the remains of children in particular were incorporated. In this context it must also be considered in the light of the putative shrine structure in the central part of the hillfort, especially as this study has found that disarticulated human remains were related to that mid first century AD building in association with metal objects including weapons. This building brings together the habit of deposition of infant humans and juvenile animals that had been regularly practiced from the Middle Iron Age onward, with the practice of deposition of human remains from older individuals with metalwork. The deposits from the gate do not relate to a massacre, despite the evidence of violence, but probably relates to a series of complex ritualised and funerary practices with their origins deep in the Iron Age, but marked out by their scale.

An unusual burial discovered during SCEP excavations in a field called The Moor at South Cadbury, directly to the east of the north eastern gateway of the hillfort may be of interest in informing discussion of practices involving human remains in the mid first century AD. The skeletal remains were found in a cist in the intersection of two Late Iron Age silted ditches. Adjacent sections of the ditch contained several cattle skulls and an earlier dump of pots largely broken *in situ* (Tabor and Randall in prep). The individual was folded into the cist torso downward with the lower body doubled over on top, backwards, bent at the lower spine. It was immediately apparent that this fully articulated individual was missing the lower legs from the knee, the lower right arm at the elbow and the left hand. This had occurred prior to deposition, and the body appeared to have been tightly bound. The manner in which the body had been folded up backwards could only have been achieved at a point at which considerable decomposition had already occurred.

Detailed osteological study (Jones 2008) has indicated a number of inci-dences of trauma, both ante and peri-mortem. This male individual, probably over 50 years old at death, had a history of healed fractures and sharp weapon trauma to the skull. This distinguished him from other individuals of the period found in other parts of the SCEP area (*cf.* Randall in prep). However, most interestingly, fine cuts and marks apparently from a knife tip within the joint capsules of the right elbow (distal humerus), and the distal articulation of the left wrist (radius), at the points where the rest of the limb was missing. Additional fine cuts on the lateral end of the right clavicle may indicate an attempt to remove the right arm at the shoulder. In addition, a number of other peri-mortem injuries had occurred. A small puncture wound occurred to the left side of the pelvis (ilium) and a cut to the left eye orbit (zygomatic). The indications are that this individual was retained for some time after death and processed to remove particular areas of the body before disposal. In the light of the findings of the study of the 'massacre deposits', it must be considered that this may be an individual part way through a similar process that resulted in the eventual production of the types of disarticulated material seen in these other deposits, with some limbs removed and deposited in disparate locations. The location of this particular individual, may relate to boundary marking and closure, an activity that is suggested by the earlier deposits of animal bone and pottery.

## Change, people and landscape

A primary intention of this paper is to demonstrate the necessity of pulling together a number of strands in seeking interpretation of a particular group of deposits. The key finding here is that the deposits of human remains and other objects in the south-west gateway of the hillfort are not the result of a massacre by Roman forces. In seeking to understand what the deposits actually represent, we must use the information that is internal to that deposit in the light of that which is external to it. There is a necessity to consider the animal remains, as the burial of cows and calves had played a crucial role in the identification of a possible ritual building. The currently ongoing study has confirmed a wider interest in depositing young cattle, but also other very particular deposits of young sheep and pigs. This habit is firmly rooted in the Middle Iron Age. The human remains that date from that period have a great tendency to represent infants and very young individuals. In the Late Iron Age there appears to be a change to include more metal items in deposits, fewer juvenile animals (although the habit may have continued in the area adjacent to the shrine), and more fragmentary human remains of older individuals. Although the scale of the gateway deposits of human remains is far greater, it bears all the same characteristics of these practices.

This change needs to be considered in the light of other treatments of human remains that we know of from the hillfort and wider landscape. All of the dated articulated burials that are known in the area have been assigned to the very end of the Iron Age. Additionally each of them seems to occur in very particular circumstances. The individual in the rampart on the hillfort, has been seen as placed to mark the boundary (Alcock 1972: 103). An older male from Eastcombe Farm, a few hundred metres from the eastern side of the hillfort, was inserted into a slight bank beside the Middle-Late Iron Age field system (Randall 2004), and could be regarded as fulfilling the same function. The male from Sigwells was the only adult articulated burial recovered from a pit in an area of the wider scatter that had been enclosed in the later Iron Age, and was directly opposite the elaborated entrance (Randall 2004; 2006). This appears to confirm that burial of the whole body was still a minority treatment at the end of the Iron Age, reserved for special circumstances. The individual from The Moor, described above, was also inserted in the intersection of ditches, and this individual seems to give us detailed evidence of how the body may have been treated, and how disarticulated human bone came to be frequently deposited in a range of locations. Rather than merely exposing bodies, remains appear to have been more deliberately processed.

The alterations in the organisation, control and use of the landscape also contributes to our understanding of how the gateway deposits came into being. It is apparent that changes in land use were well underway before the end of the Iron Age, with a decline in maintenance of field ditches and an apparent reduction in settlement within the hillfort. There was, however, an increase in marking the landscape, making deposits, and referring back to the past by marking disappearing boundaries and exploiting areas with views back over the hill. It is not therefore a great leap to postulate that the hillfort's role and social meaning had changed in the Late Iron Age. The gateway deposits and shrine, both relating to the mid first century AD, may mark this change in use most dramatically, and the occurrence of similar materials within both of these locations, links the practices involved in the formation of the deposits. Whilst some degree of sacrificial activity associated with the south west gate cannot be discounted, it seems possible that the gateway deposits may represent the culmination of a long term funerary habit in which human remains were deliberately divided and curated. The deposit itself may have come into being as a final closure deposit, sealing the hillfort enclosure. This final action may have related to a social dislocation resulting from the arrival of Roman forces, but it is entirely indigenous in character and the culmination of centuries of activity.

## Conclusion

Re-examination of a well known deposit, using a variety of current techniques, and considering it more thoroughly in its context has provided us with a far more textured understanding of the end of the Iron Age occupation and use of Cadbury Castle hillfort. It is clear that whilst there is a degree of continuity in the practices that people carried out, there were alterations in the focus of that activity, and the intensity of it. This must relate to a reorientation of social organisation and may betray a group of people feeling some form of pressure long before the Romans arrived. Where there is evidence for violence and display of body parts, this may indicate a level of conflict that had already broken out or relate to a variety of social practice. This is one sequence of events for which we cannot continue to blame the Roman army.

## Acknowledgements

We would like to thank Ellie Hambleton and Mark Maltby for their comments and advice. Steve Minnitt, Somerset Museums Service has been generous with his time in allowing access to the collections during building work at Taunton Museum.

# Bibliography

Alcock, L. (1972). *'By South Cadbury is that Camelot...' Excavations at Cadbury Castle 1966–1970*. London: Book Club Associates.

Alcock, L. (1995). *Cadbury Castle, Somerset: the Early Medieval Archaeology*. Cardiff: University of Wales Press.

Baker, A. J. (2004). *A Taphonomic Analysis of Human Remains from the Fox Hollow Farm Serial Homicide Site*. Unpublished PhD Thesis: University of Indianapolis.

Barrett, J. C., J. M. Downes, P. W. M. Freeman and C. R. Musson (2000). The excavated areas. In J. Barrett, PWM Freeman and A Woodward (eds.) *Cadbury Castle, Somerset: the later prehistoric and early historic archaeology*: 153–178 London : English Heritage.

Barrett, J. C., P. W. M. Freeman and A. Woodward (2000). *Cadbury Castle, Somerset: the Later Prehistoric and Early Historic Archaeology*. London: English Heritage.

Bowden, M. (2006). Guard chambers *Proceedings of the Prehistoric Society* 72: 423–436.

Bradley, R. (1990). *A Passage of Arms: an archaeological analysis of prehistoric hoards and votive deposits*. Oxford: Oxbow Books.

Brück, J. (1995). A place for the dead – the role of human remains in Late Bronze Age Britain. *Proceedings of the Prehistoric Society*: 61: 245–277.

Campbell, J. A., M. S. Baxter, and L. Alcock (1979). Radiocarbon dates for the Cadbury Massacre. *Antiquity* 43: 31–8.

Craig, C. R., C. J. Knüsel and G. C. Carr (2005). Fragmentation, mutilation and dismemberment: an interpretation of human remains on Iron Age sites In M. Parker Pearson and I. J. N. Thorpe (eds.) *Warfare, Violence and Slavery in Prehistory*: 165–180. Oxford: British Archaeological Reports, International Series 1374.

Fontijn, D. (2005). Giving up weapons. In M. Parker Pearson and I. J. N. Thorpe (eds.) *Warfare, Violence and Slavery in Prehistory*: 145–54. Oxford: British Archaeological Reports, International Series 1374.

Forbes, S. (2000). The human skeletal material. In J. Barrett, P. W. M. Freeman and A. Woodward (eds.) *Cadbury Castle, Somerset: the later prehistoric and early historic archaeology*: 117–121. London : English Heritage.

Green, M. A. (2002). *Dying for the Gods: human sacrifice in Iron Age and Roman Europe*. Stroud: Tempus.

Hamilton-Dyer, S. and M. Maltby (2000). The animal bones from a sample of Iron Age contexts. In J. Barrett, P. W. M. Freeman and A. Woodward (eds.) *Cadbury Castle, Somerset: the later prehistoric and early historic archaeology*: 278–291. London: English Heritage.

Jones, S. (2008). *'Slain at the Gate': a reassessment of the 'massacre' deposits from Cadbury Castle, Somerset* Unpublished MSc. dissertation: Bournemouth University.

Knüsel, C. J. and A. Outram (2004). Fragmentation: the zonation method applied to fragmented human remains from archaeological and forensic contexts *Environmental Archaeology* 9: 85–98.

Madgwick, R. (2008). Patterns in the modification of animal and human bones in Iron Age Wessex: revisiting the excarnation debate. In O. Davis, N. Sharples and K. Waddington (eds.) *Changing Perspectives on the First Millennium BC*: 99–118. Oxford: Oxbow Books.

Maltby, J. M. (1985). The animal bones In P. Fasham (ed.) *The Prehistoric Settlement at Winnall Down, Winchester*: 97–112 (Hampshire Field Club Monograph 2), Gloucester: Alan Sutton.

Manning, W. H. (1976). The conquest of the West Country. In K. Branigan and P. Fowler (eds.) In *The Roman West Country: classical culture and Celtic society*: 15–41. Newton Abbot.

Olivier, A. (2000). The brooches. In J. Barrett, P. W. M. Freeman and A. Woodward (eds.) *Cadbury Castle, Somerset: the later prehistoric and early historic archaeology*: 132–143. London: English Heritage.

Pope, E. J. and O. C. Smith (2004). Identification of traumatic injury in burned cranial bone an experimental approach. *Journal of Forensic Science* 49: 431–440.

Randall, C. E. (2004). *Burials from Sigwells Farm and Eastcombe Farm, near Cadbury Castle, Somerset: placing two Iron Age burials in biocultural and social context.* Unpublished BSc dissertation: Bournemouth University.

Randall, C. E. (2006). *More ritual rubbish: a study of animal bone deposition during the Iron Age at Sigwells, Charlton Horethorne.* Unpublished MSc dissertation: Bournemouth University.

Randall, C. E. (2010) Recycling 'Ritual and Rubbish' : a study of deposition in Iron Age pits at Sigwells, Somerset. In J. Morris and M. Maltby (eds.) *Integrating Social and Environmental Archaeologies: Reconsidering Deposition* Oxford: British Archaeological Reports, International Series 2077.

Randall, C. E. (2010). *Livestock and landscape: exploring animal exploitation in later prehistory in the South West of Britain.* Unpublished PhD Thesis: Bournemouth University

Randall, C. E. and S. Jones (in preparation). The human remains. In R. Tabor and C. E. Randall (eds.) *The South Cadbury Environs Project Volume 1: the landscape survey.* Oxford: Oxford University Press.

Tabor, R. (ed.) (2004). *South Cadbury Environs Project interim fieldwork report 2002–2003.* Bristol: Centre for the Historic Environment University of Bristol.

Tabor, R. (2008). *Cadbury Castle: the hillfort and landscapes.* Stroud: History Press.

Tabor, R. and C. E. Randall (eds.) (in preparation). *The South Cadbury Environs Project Volume 1: the landscape survey.* Oxford: Oxford University Press.

Thompson, T. J. U. (2003). *An Experimental Study of the Effects of Burning on the Hard Tissues of the Human Body and its Implications for Anthropology and Forensic Science.* Unpublished PhD thesis: University of Sheffield.

Woodward, A. (2000). The massacre level: a contextual analysis. In J. Barrett, P.W.M. Freeman and A. Woodward (eds.) *Cadbury Castle, Somerset: the later prehistoric and early historic archaeology*: 105–113. London: English Heritage.

Woodward, A. and J. D. Hill (2000). Synthesis. In J. Barrett, P. W. M. Freeman and A. Woodward (eds.) *Cadbury Castle, Somerset: the later prehistoric and early historic archaeology*: 114–5. London : English Heritage.

## CHAPTER 9

# A Call to Arms: reinvestigating Warfare and Violence in the Iron Age of Britain

## Sarah S. King

*(University of Bradford)*

## Abstract

This paper addresses the study of warfare in prehistory and suggests future directions for identifying and understanding warfare in the Iron Age of Britain. In recent years, violence, and particularly warfare, has been recognized as endemic in almost all societies. Warfare is a socially constructed phenomenon and studies of warfare in the past must therefore integrate evidence for violence within a larger social context. This paper advocates a methodology based on the analysis of human remains, which provide clear evidence for intentional violence between individuals. When analyzed at a population-level scale and compared with archaeological mortuary data, evidence for violence is given meaning and context. Regional and temporal trends might be recognized allowing for greater interpretation and understanding. The case study of Wetwang in East Yorkshire will be discussed as a potential site for this kind of analysis.

## Introduction

The subject of warfare in prehistory has gained prominence recently with a growing body of work addressing the evidence for violent interactions in the past. While researchers have made great strides in explaining the origins and occurrences of violence, the focus is frequently small-scale. In order to move beyond these limitations, there must be a broader approach to the evidence. This paper calls for the use of population-level studies of human skeletal remains in order to see larger patterns in the evidence and facilitate higher-level interpretations regarding interpersonal violence and warfare. Human remains are unique in that they have the potential to provide unequivocal evidence for violent interactions, as they retain markers of trauma and injury. Used in tandem with other evidence for mortuary behaviour, evidence from skeletal populations will help place violence within a social context.

The platform for this study is the Iron Age of East Yorkshire and central southern Britain, which provides a good area for research due to the complexity of the mortuary behaviour. There is also a rich debate in the literature regarding the nature of the many hillforts and weapons, whether they are evidence for ritual or defence. When joined with mortuary data such as burial context, grave goods, and taphonomic processes, the social/cultural contexts of warfare during this period can be studied. This provides a richer view of Iron Age peoples and how they negotiated violence and warfare as part of a suite of social choices.

One of the most important distinctions to make is that interpersonal violence does not equal warfare. Though this may be an obvious statement, it is a vital point to clarify especially when dealing with archaeological remains where the evidence can only provide brief isolated glimpses of the whole story. For the purpose of this study, warfare is defined as per Ferguson (1984: 5). War is "an organized purposeful group action, directed against another group that may or may not be organized for a similar action, involving the actual or potential application of lethal force." To refer to archaeological evidence that does not fit the above definition, the term violence or violent interactions will be used. Violence is defined as the exercise of physical force so as to inflict injury on, or cause damage to, persons or property (Oxford English Dictionary). Violence, for the purpose of this study therefore, is the presence of interpersonally inflicted traumatic injuries in a skeletal population, whereas warfare is a higher-level interpretation of the patterns of injuries in the skeletal population, coupled with social context from burial evidence.

# Warfare

Evidence for violent interactions in prehistory has been recognized since the beginning of archaeology as a discipline. It is only in the last twenty years, however, that the in-depth study of prehistoric warfare has developed. Previous misconceptions about "primitive" warfare, or lack of treatment of it, caused a gap in prehistoric research. Scholars are catching up and literature on the subject has grown with the recognition that warfare and violent interaction is an important part of most modern as well as prehistoric groups (Keeley 1996).

The lack of research on prehistoric warfare was, in part, because many researchers did not believe it existed in any significant way prior to the advent of state-level civilizations. In small-scale societies, warfare was seen as ineffectual and ritualized (*contra* Keeley 1996; Walker 2001: 574). The myth of the peaceful past was compelling enough that cases of violence in the archaeological record were regarded as aberrant or rare. Archaeology is the pursuit of the human past, for history and origins. One does not want to find disturbing practices, which may reflect badly on current members of a given group. Images of a peaceful past are more palatable and fit preconceptions of social decline in the modern world and, for a long time, evidence of large-scale violence was disregarded (Parker Pearson 2005: 19).

In 1996, Lawrence Keeley attempted to combat these misconceptions with his book *War Before Civilization: The Myth of the Peaceful Savage*, in which he used three cross-cultural surveys of modern tribal and state societies around the world to identify differences in the patterns of warfare. The surveys consistently showed that warfare was endemic to all societies, irrespective of size or complexity. Of the groups surveyed, only thirteen percent were classified as not habitually participating in violent conflict (Keeley 1996: 28). Despite the lack of current, organized violent conflict, however, many of these societies were not strangers to violence and were active in conducting warfare before becoming isolated or governed by outside groups. Further, the concept of a completely peaceful group is misleading because often those who refrain from warfare do not necessarily refrain from violent conflict altogether (*ibid.*; Parker Pearson 2005: 21). The !Kung San of the Kalahari were seen as harmless, peaceful people, yet their murder rate from 1920–1955 was four times higher than that of the United States for the same period (Lee 1979: 398; Keeley 1996: 29).

It is not only the number of violent interactions that makes warfare a significant part of social interaction, but the effect of warfare on populations as a whole. In small-scale societies warfare between groups often includes the entire adult male population of the group. Larger societies do not mobilize every adult male, but active soldiers tend to represent circa 25 percent of the adult males in the society (Keeley 1996: 34). When injuries and casualties occur, the results can be damaging, especially in small or tribal societies. With the male population greatly reduced, the rest of the group suffers and, in the case of many tribal societies, results in its absorption into a new group for survival (*ibid.;* Bishop and Knüsel 2005: 212).

Since the explosion of violence studies from the mid 1990s, it is clear that there are still research gaps within the field. The most glaring issue in the current body of violence studies is the particularistic approach that has dominated the literature. This focus on individual incidents of interpersonal violence has left a theoretical vacuum. Despite much use of the word warfare, the tendency to focus on isolated events actually makes the identification of warfare, which must be built from the available evidence of violence, very difficult. Physicians played a dominant role in the early years of palaeopathology; in the past archaeologists have followed their lead and tended to focus on case-by-case interpretations of prehistoric violence, doing little to study population-wide occurrences (*contra* Walker 1997; 2001). This leads to a concentration on violent incidents and an under-reporting of actual violence rates. When there is no synthesis of the information, the advantages of time depth and distance are muted and the context for diachronic trends is lost. Not only is there a need for a population perspective, but also a social perspective of violent interactions. Violence, although nearly universal, is still a cultural construct and has to be addressed in those terms.

One of the problems involved in studying prehistoric warfare is the lack of a common definition of the term, which leads to confusion. Kelly (2000: 3–5) uses the most exclusive definition because he seeks to differentiate warfare from feuding and other forms of organized violence. He defines war as a premeditated collective armed conflict, which is carried out using weapons with deadly intention. The killing of an enemy is anticipated in advance and socially sanctioned by the community. The key feature of war is the social substitutability of the victim. The killing of any member of the enemy group is considered an injury to the whole. The drawback to this exclusivity is that it can lead to a false idea of peace. Kelly argues that in the Palaeolithic, warfare was rare enough to be nearly non-existent (*ibid.*). That does not mean, however, that the Palaeolithic was peaceful. Keeley demonstrated that even warless societies had high levels of violence (Keeley 1996: 29). Walker (1997) demonstrated that historically there are recognizable patterns of interpersonal violence that are guided by cultural ideologies. This has important implications when it comes to the study of violent interactions in the past. If some aspects of violence are culturally constructed, then why are others not? What we see as warfare may not be interpreted as warfare in other societies, and acts that we refer to as murder or feuding could constitute warfare in a tribal society. That is why this study uses Ferguson's definition mentioned above, which is inclusive, allowing for the discussion of many different types of violent interactions which may not be distinguishable archaeologically (Ferguson 1984). The important requirement is that warfare according to Ferguson is corporate and socially sanctioned (*ibid.*).

Even when using a broad definition, the term warfare may not be the best word to use in understanding the processes taking place. Sometimes the most one can say is that there were 'violent interactions' which covers warfare, capital punishment, murder, and other human interactions that result in physical injury or death. In prehistory, unlike the ethnographic and historical past, the evidence cannot always tell us whether the violent markers we see are a result of what would be considered warfare, or another action like ritualized violent contests (Brothwell 1999: 25). Thus, it is important to closely examine the evidence for violence and to distinguish warfare from other forms of violent interactions.

## The Iron Age

Classical authors like Caesar (*c.* 100–44 BC) and Poseidonius (*c.* 135–50 BC) illustrated the warlike attitude of the Iron Age peoples of Western Europe (Tierney 1960). Caesar's *The Gallic Wars* is the most complete literary reference we have on the late Iron Age peoples of Gaul and Britain. Much of what we know, or assume we know, about the style of warfare in the British Iron Age comes from this reference. He states, 'All Gauls are eager for political change and, because of their fickleness, are soon roused to war.' (Caesar, *The Gallic Wars*, 3.10) Caesar was not an impartial observer and the way he describes the Gauls may not necessarily reflect reality.

The British Iron Age does not constitute a unified entity. It is characterized by many different types of material culture, settlement type and, especially, burial type. This regionality is an important theme in the literature and has been discussed in great detail by many authors (notably Cunliffe 1993; 2004; McOmish 2001). Often these differences in the archaeological record are thought to be associated with tribal groupings, subsistence and economic differences, or with trade connections. The difficulty in these interpretations is that a lack of excavation and archaeological evidence from many areas of Britain obscure interpretations. The differences may therefore be more perceived than real and reflect only diversity in deposition (McOmish 2001: 79).

There are no large cemeteries except for East Yorkshire. In the rest of the country human remains occur in so many different contexts that interpretation becomes very difficult. Human remains are found as inhumations, cremations and small isolated fragments, and on many occasions are associated with animal remains. They are found in ditches, pits, mounds, houses, hillforts, and cemeteries (Whimster 1981; Wilson 1981; Craig *et al.* 2005). This extreme complexity in the archaeological record has led to the tendency for scholars to overlook important information that can be gleaned from human remains, even when found in isolated contexts. Attempts to provide a synthesis of burial practices only highlighted the extreme diversity of burial contexts (Whimster 1981; Wilson 1981). Recently, however, there has been a growing realization of the value of human remains analysis in answering difficult questions with a long history of interest.

For a long time evidence from the Iron Age was taken at face value. Hillforts were assumed to be defensive and swords to be utilitarian. These automatic identifications have been questioned recently and a backlash developed against these interpretations. Debates arose surrounding artefacts and structures that were previously believed to be martial and some researchers now suggest a ritual function. Hillforts are argued, by some (e.g. Sharples 1991: 85; Hamilton and Manley 2001; Finney 2006), to be ritual centres, swords ritual symbols not tools of war, and possible combat to be an expression of a ritual cycle (Finney 2006: 89). However, not all researchers are satisfied with this conclusion (Armit 2007; James 2007).

Use-wear analysis may be able to tell if a sword was hit against another sword, but this does not exclude use in ritual dances or mock battles. In order to establish whether the function of a sword or a sling-stone was purely ritual or not, there must be direct evidence of its use against another human being. Sharp force trauma on the bones or sling-stone shaped depressed fractures of the cranium help in identifying a violent context for the artefacts. However, there needs to be a synthesis of data on the human remains present at hill-forts. There is evidence for trauma at sites like Danebury in Hampshire (Hooper 1984; Craig *et al.* 2005), Sutton Walls in Herefordshire (Kenyon 1954), and Maiden Castle in Dorset (Redfern 2006). With the exception of Redfern's work in Dorset, there has been little integration of data on a regional scale. Warfare cannot be truly understood if sites continue to be viewed in isolation. A population-level approach, is needed; an assessment of how these sites compare to each other, other hillforts, villages and burial contexts.

In order to give evidence for trauma a wider context, there must be an analysis of the burial population as a whole. Population is defined as the entire aggregation of items from which samples can be drawn. Archaeological skeletal material is only a sub-sample of the past living population, a sample that constitutes those members of a past society who entered the burial record. So even at the broadest level, it is not possible to see the actual living population; a population-level approach, therefore, refers to the recovered skeletal material and not to the living population. Using all the available material will give a more representative sample than focusing on one or two assemblages or skeletons.

## Methodological approaches

There are several directions that need to be taken for both the study of war-fare in general and for Iron Age Britain in particular. Firstly, the use of human remains in warfare studies is crucial. Human remains can provide direct evidence of interpersonal violence that can be used to assess or supplement evidence from architecture and weapons studies. There is a much greater understanding now of the processes of change in the body before, during and after death, which can contribute significant detail to such studies.

The methods of analyzing archaeological skeletal evidence for interpersonal violence stem from modern forensic work. There is a large body of data on how to identify human remains, age-at-death, sex and evidence of trauma. The underlying assumption is that bone reacts to trauma the same way, whether modern or prehistoric. Based on this assumption, we can use the same techniques to analyze archaeological samples (Novak 2000: 90; Rogers 2004).

Weapon-related trauma is the least ambiguous marker for interpersonal violence as it is less likely to come from an accidental source. Thus, defining the type and shape of the injury is important in identifying specific weapons, such as swords, spears, and sling stones. Non-weapon related injuries are also important. During life, bones can be broken during violent interactions and will not show a specific weapon involved. This can occur by fending off a large blunt instrument like a club, or even in hand-to-hand combat. A commonly cited example of this is the parry fracture, which is a fracture of the distal third of the ulna. The parry fracture is considered an indication of violence because it is caused by the raising of the forearm to protect the upper body from a blow. It is a commonly cited fracture in incidences of spousal abuse and interpersonal violence (Lovell 1997: 165; Galloway 1999; 145; Judd 2008).

Skeletal evidence must be observed critically, however, because wounds may have multiple causes. Fractures only indicate that the bone was subjected to an applied force great enough to overcome its structural integrity. A fracture does not demonstrate specific intentionality, such as an opponent attacking with the intention to kill.

Even when trauma is considered intentional, such as sharp force trauma or cut marks, it can also be attributed to ritual and mortuary practices. There are some ethnographic examples of ritual violence, such as tinku – the ritual battles of the Inca – or human sacrifice among the Inca and Aztec (Moseley 1993: 66). Such evidence is also invoked to explain some bog bodies in Europe (Aldhouse-Green 2005: 158). Ritual and violence are often closely linked, with violent events (e.g. executions) being highly ritualized and ritual events (e.g. human sacrifice) being violent (Knüsel 2005: 60).

It is important to remember that the forensic approach is just a tool-kit with which to identify signs of violence. It is up to the archaeologist to extract meaningful contextual information out of it by using other lines of evidence, such as demographic profile, burial context, and associated artefacts (Gowland and Knüsel 2006).

There must also be a broader social context of warfare and violence. When studied in isolation the knowledge gained is limited. Violent interactions must be placed within the larger social framework, so that the decisions and motivations behinds these interactions can be better understood. It is not enough to establish the presence or absence of interpersonal violence. Violence is a socially constructed phenomenon. It is a choice made by a group or groups of people in reaction to a stimulus, but it is not a foregone conclusion. How did it affect the community? Who was involved? If the evidence is substantial enough to indicate warfare, where are the warriors, and how did their society view them? Warfare is not restricted to the combatants. The rest of the community acted either as instigators, victims or even arbitrators. For instance, among the Andamanese, the women conducted the peace negotiations, and could prolong a feud as long as they remained angry (Radcliffe-Brown 1964: 85–6; Kelly 2000: 106).

Ultimately, it is the community that gives the combatant or victim special status – whatever it might be. They bury the dead and create the burial record. To understand this connection, there must be a consideration of the treatment of the dead, of mortuary behaviour surrounding victims of violence and its perpetrators. The affected individuals must be placed in context within the larger population. This is the only way to see overall trends with regard to violence and warfare and how it was experienced by the community.

When looking at one assemblage, it is important to look at all individuals present and discuss the skeletal population as a whole, not just focus on those individuals who show signs of violence. There must be an understanding of the burial practices present for everyone, or any information about the individuals involved in violence will be ambiguous and potentially misleading. Also, prevalence of violence in the skeletal population is important to consider. How many of the individuals in the population are affected and how many are unaffected? One must also look at modern and clinical data because a surprising number of injuries due to interpersonal violence may not show up on the skeleton. Even in known contexts, rates may be very low. Surprisingly, in the mass graves of Rwanda victims, only 75 percent of the remains showed evidence of trauma (Rogers 2004: 15). Considering that each individual in the pit was a victim of interpersonal violence, it shows how much can be hidden or unobservable.

When looking at the population, demography, health, evidence for trauma, burial context, and material culture should all be considered. This can give an overall context with regard to age-at-death, sex, health status, burial type, burial position and burial location at site level, which increases understanding of how the different factors are related to violent trauma. The burial context and material culture are important in understanding how the populations dealt with those who died a violent death. Where were they buried? What type of burial – barrow, pit, single, double or multiple inhumations, primary, secondary, excarnation, etc.? What position were they in? How does one burial compare with others at the site and diachronically? Are there artefacts included and, if so, what kind? When evidence for violence appears in the populations, it is important to know who is being affected. Are women and men both carrying signs of violence? Are children likely to be directly physically affected by the violence? Only by merging mortuary behaviour and physical evidence of violence can patterns emerge that allow for the distinction between different forms of violent interactions and the identification of warfare, as well as a better understanding of the social context of violent interaction.

The potential of population-wide analyses of violence has already been demonstrated by the work of Redfern and Judd. Rebecca Redfern used this approach to look at the Iron Age and Romano-British sites in Dorset. She looked at overall health and included trauma as one of its factors, and was able to assess the temporal changes over a very dynamic period for that region, showing that the Iron Age in Dorset had much higher rates of interpersonal violence, whereas the trauma dating from the Romano-British period was more likely of accidental origin (Redfern 2006). Beyond temporal change, she was also able to use a gendered perspective on the evidence to argue for direct female involvement in interpersonal violence during the Iron Age, with females being victims of attacks and showing injury recidivism, which has been associated clinically with individuals engaging in violent interactions (Judd 2002; Redfern 2008). These types of studies are successful at giving a more meaningful view of the evidence. In another study, Margaret Judd (2004) looked at a population from the ancient city of Kerma (1750–1550 BC). She completed a detailed analysis of the trauma patterns among the individuals and compared her results with modern clinical data associated with accidental injuries. She was able to demonstrate that her data did not match well with evidence for accidental trauma and that the high frequencies of trauma at Kerma were associated with interpersonal violence (Judd 2004). The injuries in isolation could not be interpreted, but by situating them in the larger population she was able to compare them to other populations and provide them with a social meaning.

# Future directions

The above is just a brief description of methods available to archaeologists the examination of trauma in human remains. These methods are extremely helpful in looking at warfare and violence in prehistory. I intend to apply these techniques to the study of warfare and violence in the Iron Age of East Yorkshire and central southern Britain in an ongoing doctoral study. To do that, I will be analyzing a cemetery population from East Yorkshire. This cemetery represents a large skeletal population from one group that covers a broad temporal range.

The cemetery population will then be compared with populations from a diversity of sites and contexts in central southern England so that differences and patterns across regions, periods and contexts can be examined.

The archaeological group known as the "Arras Culture" in north eastern England is an example of a local adoption of the La Tène culture. This group is mainly characterized by its burial practices, as they are the most obvious features on this landscape, and the settlements are more difficult to find. The cemeteries seem to be associated with settlements and cover a long period of time (Stead 1979; Cunliffe 2004: 215). At Wetwang and Garton Slacks, in the Yorkshire Wolds, there is some evidence for habitation structures or perhaps ritual houses and granaries. These settlements seem to be occupied for much of the Iron Age, in some cases being turned into Roman villas after Roman occupation (Stead 1979: 16; Dent 1982: 449; Cunliffe 2004: 215). The East Yorkshire cemeteries are characterized by distinctive relatively small, square burial mounds, which most often contain only one inhumation. Similar square barrows are found in some areas of Scotland (though from a much later date) and at some La Tène sites on the continent. The burials are inhumations, which in most cases, are flexed or semi-flexed lying on their left side, which differs from the continental style of extended burials. Most of the burials are arranged with the head to the north with a few exceptions that have the head to the south, east or west. The direction of the burial is clustered through time and may indicate changing styles (Stead 1979: 14).

These sites are important because the cemeteries were in use for a long time and cover a cross-section of the population. They can show us temporal changes in a single community, as well as continuity that is more difficult to see in the other cultural areas where burial rites seem restricted to single events. These cemeteries also contain, in rare cases, chariot burials that are similar to those in Northern France (Brewster 1971; Dent 1985a; 1985b; Cunliffe 2004: 549). In such burials the chariots were generally dismantled and placed around the body, and in some instances weapons and shields were also included (Dent 1985a). They may represent elite burials and therefore have gained a lot of attention from archaeologists in the past (see Dent 1982; Selkirk 1984; Denison 2001; Hill 2001, 2002).

Wetwang Slack was excavated in the late nineteen-seventies and early eighties by John Dent. The site is located on the Yorkshire Wolds in a shallow valley or slack. Newly obtained radiocarbon dates place the range of the cemetery from the early fourth century cal BC to the first century cal AD (Jay, pers comm.). It is made up of over 450 burials placed as individual inhumations, many covered by small square mounds. The barrows were built close enough to each other that many of them overlap, making it possible to order the burials in a chronological sequence independent of grave goods. A road dating to the same broad period bisects the cemetery along an approximately northeast-southwest axis. The primary grave goods are brooches of the La Tène style (Dent 1982: 439).

Despite the site containing one of the largest groups of Iron Age burials found in England, and retrieved using good excavation methods, this collection has been greatly neglected in the archaeological literature despite the quality of preservation of the skeletons. These are ideal for the kind of a population-level analysis proposed above. The population consists primarily of young to old adults most of who died past the age of puberty and before the age of 45. Some children have been found as satellite burials in the ditches of earlier mounds or in flat graves. The burials all lie in a north-south direction as seen in other East Yorkshire burials, with 75 percent lying on their left side. The grave goods show that most of the brooches are a distinctive native form of the continental La Tène style (Stead 1979).

The re-analysis of this material will provide a broader social context for the evidence of interpersonal violence found at this site, and a basis for comparison for sites in different regions during the same period. By integrating the skeletal data with the burial context, I will seek to establish whether the victims of interpersonal violence were given special treatment in burial and whether the artefacts of violence, such as swords and spears, show any relationship to the individuals who may have used them. By analyzing the patterns between violence and burial choices, it will be possible to apply the evidence to Ferguson's (1984) definition of warfare and establish whether it existed for this period, to what degree and how it may have affected the community.

## Conclusions

The unique position of Iron Age Britain as a bridge between prehistory and history makes it an excellent arena in which to examine the cultural dimensions of warfare. It was a period of rapid change truncated by the arrival of a large colonizing power. Due to the importance of the Iron Age in gaining a stronger comprehension of warfare and cultural change, it must be studied critically without assumptions based on classical sources or broad generalizations. What is needed, therefore, is a population-based method of documenting evidence for violence. Sites should be considered both in and of themselves, and how they compare to other sites across broad regions. Studies must integrate skeletal analysis with archaeological context to provide an overall view of the social contexts of warfare during the Iron Age of Britain. It is not enough to report the presence or absence of violence; it is necessary to develop an understanding of how violence was constructed, maintained or avoided by the people during this period. In this way, warfare will be seen as a dynamic negotiated force, a social decision, not an inevitable outcome.

# Acknowledgements

I am very grateful to my supervisors Chris Knüsel (University of Exeter), Ian Armit (University of Bradford), and Jo Buckberry (University of Bradford) for guidance and providing comments on this manuscript. I also thank Mandy Jay (Durham University), Fiona Tucker (University of Bradford), Susan Wyche, Karen King and the anonymous reviewer for their insightful comments on previous drafts of this paper. The re-analysis of Wetwang Slack is made possible by the Hull and East Riding Museum and by the Biological Anthropology Research Centre (BARC) at University of Bradford. S.S. King is currently funded by the Overseas Research Student Awards Scheme.

# Bibliography

*Ancient:*

Caesar, *The Gallic Wars*, translated by C. Hammond (Oxford World's Classics). Oxford: Oxford University Press. 1996.

*Modern:*

Aldhouse-Green, M. (2005). Ritual bondage, violence, slavery and sacrifice in later European prehistory. In M. Parker Pearson and I. J. N. Thorpe (eds.) *Warfare, Violence and Slavery in Prehistory: proceedings of a Prehistoric Society conference*: 155–163. Oxford: British Archaeological Reports, International Series 1374.

Armit, I. (2007). Hillforts at war: Maiden Castle to Taniwaha Pa. *Proceedings of the Prehistoric Society* 73: 25–37.

Armit, I., C. J. Knüsel, J. Robb and R. Schulting (2006). Warfare and violence in Prehistoric Europe: an introduction. *Journal of Conflict Archaeology* 2: 1–11.

Bishop, N. A. and C. J. Knüsel (2005). A palaeodemographic investigation of warfare in Prehistory. In M. Parker Pearson and I. J. N. Thorpe (eds.) *Warfare, Violence and Slavery in Prehistory: proceedings of a Prehistoric Society conference*: 201–216. Oxford: British Archaeological Reports, International Series 1374.

Brewster, T. C. M. (1971). The Garton Slack chariot burial, East Yorkshire. *Antiquity* 45: 289–292.

Brothwell, D. (1999). Biosocial and bio-archaeological aspects of conflict and warfare. In J. Carman and A. Harding (eds.) *Ancient Warfare, Archaeological Perspectives*: 25–39. Wiltshire: Sutton Publishing.

Craig, C. R., C. J. Knüsel and G. C. Carr (2005). Fragmentation, mutilation and dismemberment: an interpretation of human remains on Iron Age sites. In M. Parker-Pearson and I. J. N. Thorpe (eds.) *Warfare, Violence and Slavery in Prehistory: Proceedings of a Prehistoric Society Conference*: 165–180. Oxford: British Archaeological Reports, International Series 1374.

Cunliffe, B. (1993). *Wessex to AD 1000*. Harlow: Longman.

Cunliffe, B. (2004). *Iron Age Communities in Britain: an account of England, Scotland and Wales from the seventh century BC until the Roman conquest*. London: Routledge.

Denison, S. (2001). Another chariot. *British Archaeology* 59: 6.

Dent, J. S. (1982). Cemeteries and settlement patterns of the Iron Age on the Yorkshire Wolds Iron Age. *Proceedings of the Prehistoric Society* 48: 437–457.

Dent, J. S. (1985a). Three cart burials from Wetwang, Yorkshire. *Antiquity* 59: 85–92.

Dent, J. S. (1985b). Wetwang: a third chariot. *Current Archaeology* 8: 360–361.

Ferguson, R. B. (1984). Introduction: studying war. In R. B. Ferguson (ed.) *Warfare, Culture and Environment*: 1–81. Orlando: Academic Press.

Finney, J. B. (2006). *Middle Iron Age Warfare of the Hillfort Dominated Zone c. 400 BC to c. 150 BC*. Oxford: British Archaeological Reports, British Series 423.

Galloway, A. (ed.) (1999). *Broken Bones: anthropological analysis of blunt force trauma*. Springfield Illinois: Charles C. Thomas.

Gowland, R. and C. Knüsel (2006). Introduction. In R. Gowland and C. Knüsel (eds.) *Social Archaeology of Funerary Remains*: ix–xiii. Oxford: Oxbow Books.

Hamilton, S. and J. Manley (2001). Hillforts, monumentality and place: a chronological and topographic review of first millennium BC hillforts of south-east England. *European Journal of Archaeology* 4: 7–42.

Hill, J. D. (2001). A new cart/chariot burial from Wetwang, East Yorkshire. *Past* 38: 2–3.

Hill, J. D. (2002). Wetwang chariot burial. *Current Archaeology* 15: 410–412.

Hooper, B. (1984). Anatomical considerations. In B. Cunliffe (ed.) *Danebury an Iron Age Hillfort in Hampshire: vol. 2 the excavations 1969–1978: the finds*: 463–474. London: Council for British Archaeology.

James, S. (2007). A bloodless past: the pacification of Early Iron Age Britian. In C. C. Haselgrove and R. E. Pope (eds.) *The Earlier Iron Age in Britain and the Near Continent*: 160–173. Oxford: Oxbow Books.

Judd, M. (2002). Ancient injury recidivism: an example from the Kerma Period of ancient Nubia. *International Journal of Osteoarchaeology* 12: 89–106.

Judd, M. (2004). Trauma in the city of Kerma: ancient versus modern injury patterns. *International Journal of Osteoarchaeology* 14: 34–51.

Judd, M. (2008). The parry problem. *Journal of Archaeological Science* 35: 1658–1666.

Keeley, L. H. (1996). *War Before Civilization: the myth of the peaceful savage*. Oxford: Oxford University Press.

Kelly, R. C. (2000). *Warless Societies and the Origin of War*. Ann Arbor: University of Michigan Press.

Kenyon, K. M. (1954). Excavations at Sutton Walls, Herefordshire, 1948–1951. *The Archaeological Journal* 110: 1–85.

Knüsel, C. J. (2005). The physical evidence of warfare – subtle stigmata? In M. Parker-Pearson and I. J. N. Thorpe (eds.) *Warfare, Violence and Slavery in Prehistory: proceedings of a Prehistoric Society conference*: 49–65. Oxford: British Archaeological Reports, International Series 1374.

Lee, R. B. (1979). *The !Kung San: men, women and work in a foraging society*. Cambridge: Cambridge University Press.

Lovell, N. C. (1997). Trauma analysis in paleopathology. *Yearbook of Physical Anthropology* 40: 139–170.

McOmish, D. S. (2001). Aspects of prehistoric settlement in western Wessex. In J. Collis (ed.) *Society and Settlement in Iron Age Europe*: 73–81. Sheffield: Sheffield Academic Press.

Moseley, M. E. (1993). *The Incas and their Ancestors*. London: Thames and Hudson.

Novak, S. (2000). Battle-related trauma. In V. Fiorato, A. Boylston and C. Knüsel (eds.) *Blood Red Roses: the archaeology of a mass grave from the Battle of Towton AD 1461*: 90–103. Oxford: Oxbow Books.

Parker Pearson, M. (2005). Warfare, violence and slavery in later prehistory: an introduction. In M. Parker Pearson and I. J. N. Thorpe (eds.) *Warfare, Violence and Slavery in Prehistory: proceedings of a Prehistoric Society conference*: 19–33. Oxford: British Archaeological Reports, International Series 1374.

Radcliffe-Brown, A. R. (1964). *The Andaman Islanders*. New York: Free Press of Glencoe.

Redfern, R. (2006) *A gendered analysis of health from the Iron Age to the end of the Romano-British period in Dorset, England (mid to late 8th century B.C. to the end of the 4th century A.D.)*. Unpublished PhD dissertation. University of Birmingham.

Redfern, R. (2008). A bioarchaeological analysis of violence in Iron Age females: a perspective from Dorset, England (fourth century BC to the first century AD). In O. Davis, N. Sharples and K. Waddington (eds.) *Changing perspectives on the first millennium BC*: 139–161. Oxford: Oxbow Books.

Rogers, T. (2004). Recognizing inter-personal violence: a forensic perspective. In M. Roksandic (ed.) *Violent Interactions in the Mesolithic: evidence and meaning*: 9–21. Oxford: British Archaeological Reports, International Series 1237.

Selkirk, A. (1984). Two chariot burials at Wetwang Slack. *Current Archaeology* 8: 302–306.

Sharples, N. M. (1991). Warfare in the Iron Age of Wessex. *Scottish Archaeological Review* 8: 79–89.

Stead, I. M. (1979). *The Arras culture*. York: Yorkshire Philosophical Society.

Tierney, J. J. (1960). The Celtic ethnography of Posidonius. *Proceedings of the Royal Irish Academy* 60: 189–275.

Walker, P. L. (1997). Wife beating, boxing, and broken noses: skeletal evidence for the cultural patterning of interpersonal violence. In D. L. Martin and D. W. Frayer (eds.) *Troubled Times: violence and warfare in the past: (War and Society, vol. 3)*: 145–181. Amsterdam: Gordon and Breach Publishers.

Walker, P. L. (2001). A bioarchaeological perspective on the history of violence. *Annual Review of Anthropology* 30: 573–596.

Whimster, R. (1981). *Burial Practices in Iron Age Britain: A discussion and gazetteer of the evidence, c. 700 BC–AD 43*. Oxford: British Archaeological Reports, British Series 90.

Wilson, C. E. (1981). Burials within settlements in southern Britain during the Pre-Roman Iron Age. *Bulletin of the Institute of Archaeology* 18: 127–170.

## CHAPTER 10

# A Land of Ghosts: the treatment of human remains in Iron Age Atlantic Scotland

*Fiona Tucker*

(University of Bradford)

## Abstract

The long Iron Age of the far north and west of Scotland, stretching through the Roman period and up to the Viking incursions, provides an opportunity to look at long-term changes in society and identity in later prehistory. Particularly relevant to this should be the physical remains of the inhabitants of this region; how they were treated after death, and where they were placed in the landscape. As in much of Iron Age Britain, however, formal burials are extremely rare during the first millennium BC in Atlantic Scotland, and archaeologists must look beyond inhumation to gain a true understanding of treatments of, and attitudes toward, the dead in this period. The occurrence of human remains in domestic contexts in southern England has been the focus of growing study, and similar deposits of human bodies and body parts have been found in settlements in Atlantic Scotland. Later in the Iron Age, moving into the first millennium AD, formal burial also reappears in this region, though as yet examples are few, dispersed and poorly understood. These human remains must be looked at as a group, and on a regional scale, to gain an insight into changing patterns of funerary behaviour during the long Iron Age, and the possible fate of the majority of the dead.

## Introduction

Atlantic Scotland encompasses the island groups of Orkney, Shetland and the Western Isles, as well as the north and west coast of mainland Scotland that lies opposite them, north of the Firth of Clyde (Figure 10.1). This dispersed geographic area can, of course, not be assumed to have been a single cultural

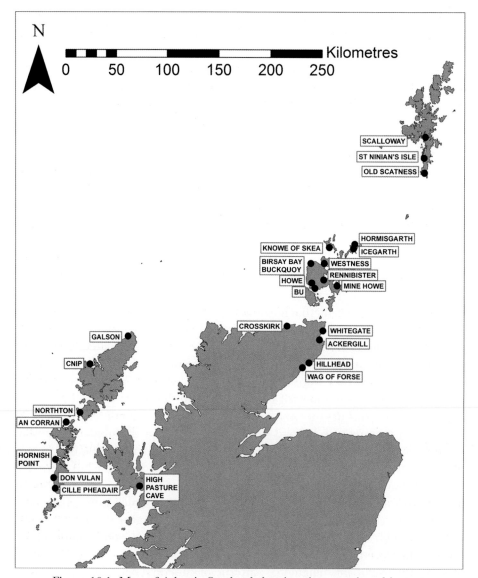

Figure 10.1: Map of Atlantic Scotland showing sites mentioned in text

entity at any time in its history. However, the archaeological record shows considerable similarities between these areas in architecture and material culture in the period under study, the long Iron Age of 800 BC to AD 800. It seems inevitable that the inhabitants of these communities would have relied on each other for trade and cultural contact, and that considerable maritime interaction would have been necessary for their basic survival.

The Iron Age of Atlantic Scotland has for most of the last two centuries been studied almost as a separate entity from the rest of Iron Age Britain and

Europe. Partly this divide has been caused by chronology: the limited Roman impact on any part of northern Scotland means that the Iron Age in this area can be defined as running up until the Viking incursions in around AD 800, 750 years longer than in lowland Britain (Harding 2004: 4). The stone architecture of this region, though sharing the predominant roundhouse form of much of Iron Age Britain, has also often been examined as an isolated tradition.

Nineteenth and early twentieth century antiquarians and archaeologists were guilty of viewing Atlantic Scotland as a marginal and therefore backward area, cut off from the more civilized south by the highlands. This perspective led to the plentiful evidence for complex cultures in this area, manifested most dramatically by the extraordinary architecture of the Atlantic roundhouses and brochs, being assigned to migrants from the south or invaders from the north (e.g. Mackie 1974: 103–5; Childe 1944: 94). The last fifty years, however, have seen a huge advance in our understanding of Iron Age Atlantic Scotland. The ever-better dating of archaeological materials has allowed the dates of the earliest Atlantic roundhouses to be pushed back beyond even the most hardened diffusionists' grasp (Harding 2004: 123). Further, the recognition that the waterways of the Atlantic and Irish seas could have acted as a link with the rest of Britain, Ireland and the continent rather than a barrier (Henderson 2007: 307) has allowed this area to begin to be studied as an integral part of Iron Age Europe.

Most research to date has focused almost exclusively on the domestic architecture of this region. This is perhaps unsurprising, due to the undeniably impressive nature of the standing remains of this area, but it has tended to overshadow the study of other, equally vital, aspects of the archaeology such as material culture, and the physical evidence for the inhabitants of this region. Human remains have been recovered from a range of Iron Age contexts in Atlantic Scotland. Treated in a wide variety of ways, from inhumation and cremation to dismemberment and modification, and deposited in many different types of features from graves to wall-fills and middens, these remains provide a rich resource for analysis. This study sets out to examine this material as a group for the first time, to elucidate patterns of treatment of human remains throughout Atlantic Scotland from 800 BC to AD 800, and to consider the possible meanings behind this complex web of treatments.

## The Iron Age burial gap and the excarnation hypothesis

The reason for the lack of study of human remains in Iron Age Atlantic Scotland may seem obvious; most authors simply state that there is little or no evidence for formal burial in the Atlantic province in the first millennium BC (e.g. Harding 2004: 7). Whimster's map of burial in Iron Age Britain for example, assigns just a single grave to Atlantic Scotland (1981: 168). This will come as no surprise to most who study Iron Age Britain, as large areas of the country are devoid of formal burial during this period (Cunliffe 1991: 498). In Atlantic Scotland, as in much of Iron Age Britain, it seems we must look for an alternative, less archaeologically visible, method of disposal for the majority of the dead.

Early archaeologists often seemed happy with the idea of the Iron Age inhabitants of Britain casually discarding their dead, and finds of human remains in ditches and middens were often interpreted in this way (Whimster 1981: 4). However, given our current knowledge of the complexity of Iron Age societies, the discarding of the dead with little ceremony or care must be regarded as unlikely, if not impossible. A more convincing suggestion is that of cremation of the dead and scattering of the ashes; cremation had been the predominant practice in the preceding Bronze Age (Brück 1995: 252), and scattering of the ashes could result in no trace of the skeleton being left for archaeologists to find. Yet it should still be possible to find traces of cremation sites, assuming that a set location was used. So far, little trace of these sites has been found, although the site of Hermisgarth in Orkney provides one likely case (Downes and Morris 1997). Another possibility, perhaps particularly tempting for Atlantic Scotland due to its coastal environment, is that bodies were sent out to sea, although this remains impossible to prove archaeologically. Human bones or cremated remains may also have been placed into rivers; Bradley has suggested that this practice could be linked to the deposition of metalwork in rivers in the late Bronze Age and Early Iron Age (Bradley 1998: 107–9).

The practice of excarnation, in which bodies are left in an exposed location to skeletonise with the help of the elements, scavengers or carrion birds, has frequently been suggested as the solution to the Iron Age burial gap. Perhaps the main strength of the excarnation hypothesis for Iron Age Britain is that it could explain both the rarity of formal burials and the disarticulated human remains that are frequently found on settlement sites. Carr and Knüsel, who looked at the evidence from both hilltop and open settlement sites in southern Britain, argued that exposure is the most likely source of the human bones found on these sites (1997: 167–9). They point out that other practices which involve the complete loss of the skeleton, such as cremation or sending bodies out to sea, would provide no such opportunity for the recovery of human remains.

Several authors have brought up the fact that carrion birds are prominent in the 'Celtic' mythology derived from early medieval Irish sources (e.g. Luff 1996: 7). Some of the pits at Danebury that produced intriguing and apparently ritual human and animal deposits also contained the skeletons of ravens

– a carrion bird particularly associated with death (*ibid.*: 8). If the raven was an integral part of Iron Age ritual life, as this may suggest, the disposal of the dead would seem to be the most natural sphere for their involvement.

Clearly, the excarnation hypothesis requires more proof than this. Evidence can be sought in the form of weathering and gnaw marks on human bones, which suggest they were left unprotected while enough meat remained on them to tempt scavengers (Carr and Knüsel 1997: 167–8). Such marks have now been found on human bones from a few Scottish sites, such as Whitegate broch in Caithness and MacArthur Cave in Oban (Heald pers. comm.; Tucker forthcoming), but remain relatively rare. More recent studies of human remains from southern British sites (Madgwick 2008; Redfern 2008) have also found only limited evidence for excarnation, though Madgwick discusses the possibility that remains were protected in some manner during primary burial treatment (2008: 107).

Brück has argued that one of the strengths of excarnation as a ritual practice is that it makes public and visible the process of death and decay, and so lends increased ritual power to the remains themselves (Brück 1995: 261–2). This might help to explain the frequent deposition of disarticulated human remains on Iron Age settlement sites in Atlantic Scotland, and adds some weight to the idea of excarnation as the predominant mode of dealing with the dead in this area.

# Human remains in domestic contexts in Iron Age Atlantic Scotland

Human remains have so far been recovered from over thirty settlement sites in Atlantic Scotland. At the paired wheelhouse at Cnip, Lewis, several fragments of human bone were found, one of which, the frontal part of an adult skull, was buried in a scoop dug into the wheelhouse floor along with fragments of pottery (Armit 2006a: 36). At the Wag of Forse, Caithness, two long bones were buried under the entrance to the roundhouse, one of which, judging by polishing and wear to one end, had been used as an awl or other tool before deposition (Curle 1947: 21). At Hillhead, a cranial fragment with three holes drilled into it was found in the roundhouse entrance passage (Barry 1902). Other examples include a whole skeleton buried in a seated position in a stone cist in one of the outbuildings at Crosskirk roundhouse (Fairhurst 1982: 86), a human arm deposited under the outer skin of the roundhouse at Bu (Hedges 1987: 124), skulls deposited in a souterrain at Rennibister (Marwick 1927: 296–301), a jaw bone placed in a drain at Dun Vulan (Parker Pearson and Sharples 1999: 139), two individuals buried in a large drain at Howe (Ballin Smith 1994: 260–1), and many more.

Perhaps the most widely discussed example of human remains being deposited in a domestic context from Iron Age Atlantic Scotland, however, is that of the Hornish Point boy. Under one of the piers of a wheelhouse at Hornish Point four pits had been dug. Into them had been placed animal bones bearing signs of normal butchery, and most of the skeleton of a young boy, divided into four. The skeleton appears to have been partially decomposed upon deposition, as epiphyses are still in articulation but few bones bear any sign of purposeful dismemberment (Barber 2003: 773–8). The only possible marks of violence are two peri-mortem chop-marks to the vertebrae, delivered by an extremely sharp instrument from behind (*ibid.*: 775). This injury could conceivably be the cause of death, or could have occurred during funerary treatment.

What does the inclusion of these human remains in domestic contexts signify? A diagram such as the one by Armit (Figure 10.2) suggests possible scenarios by which human remains might find their way into a settlement: cannibalism, headhunting, human sacrifice, ancestor veneration or funerary treatment. Unfortunately, the lack of any 'normal' comparative population in Iron Age Atlantic Scotland means that it is impossible to know whether the individuals deposited in settlements were members of an in-group or an out-group: shamed enemies or loved relatives. Examination of skeletal traits and perhaps, in the future, isotope analysis might help to identify any obvious differences within this unusual group.

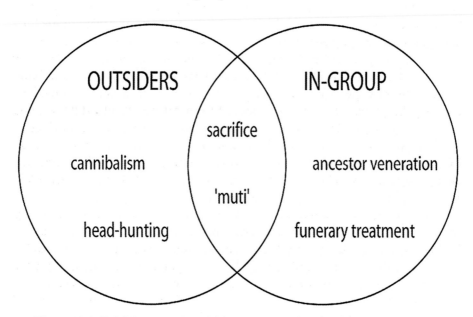

Figure 10.2: Possible routes by which human remains might enter a domestic context (after Armit and Ginn 2007: 127).

Of the possible explanations in Armit and Ginn's diagram (Figure 10.2), the one that it seems we can most easily discard based on current information is that of cannibalism. Though this was the conclusion leapt to by many early excavators upon discovering human remains in middens and floor deposits, none of the recognized signs of cannibalism – cut marks at muscle attachments, burning, breaking for marrow and so on (see White 1992: 62) – have been noted in human remains from Iron Age Atlantic Scotland. Nor are the remains normally treated in a similar way or deposited in the same contexts as animal remains. Hill and others have in any case argued that many unusual deposits of animal bone on Iron Age settlements may represent ritual rather than gastronomic activity (Hill 1995: 13–19).

Headhunting and human sacrifice are practices for which more evidence exists in Iron Age Europe. Headhunting has traditionally been associated with 'Celtic' societies due to descriptions by classical authors such as Strabo (*Geographia* IV.4.5), although of course these authors, even if considered reliable, are only referring to late first millennium BC France. Southern France has also produced statuary which seems to depict the taking and displaying of heads, and southern French sanctuaries such as Roquepertuse and Entremont contained skull niches and, in some cases, actual human skulls. It does therefore seem that a 'head-hunting complex' existed in this area during the Iron Age (Armit 2006b: 8–11).

Human sacrifice is also mentioned by classical authors, and fairly unarguable evidence of this practice exists in Iron Age Europe in the form of bog bodies, many of which seem to have been violently killed in a highly ritualised manner before deposition in uninhabited wetlands (Van der Sanden 1996: 165–174). Scandinavia has produced the majority of these Iron Age bog bodies, but Britain has also produced examples such as Lindow Man, found in the Cheshire peat (Stead *et al.* 1986). To date, however, no definitely Iron Age bog bodies have been recovered from Atlantic Scotland (Cowie and Wallace 2002). An image on the Gundestrup cauldron, an extraordinary artefact found in Denmark and thought to date to the second or first century BC, has also been argued to depict ritual sacrifice by drowning, although an alternative possibility is that it depicts a mythical scene (Green 2001: 10–11).

The evidence for either headhunting or human sacrifice in Iron Age Atlantic Scotland is unfortunately much less convincing. Unlike southern France or Denmark, Atlantic Scotland has not produced even a possible artistic depiction of either practice, and written sources on this area, which the Romans barely reached, are few and silent on this as on many subjects.

This leaves the human remains to speak for themselves. The only signs of violent injury occur on the Hornish Point boy, whose injuries may have been inflicted post-mortem, and a single individual deposited in a midden at Mine

Howe who seems to have been killed by multiple wounds inflicted with a sharp instrument. This man may have been an isolated case of human sacrifice, or he may have simply been a victim of murder or even a particularly brutal execution, practices which we have no reason to think were not present in Iron Age society. Overall, the evidence for human sacrifice in Atlantic Scotland is weak.

There does appear to be a preponderance of cranial fragments on Iron Age sites in Atlantic Scotland (Armit and Ginn 2007: 127). This phenomenon, perhaps exaggerated in the past by antiquarians who were most interested in this part of the human skeleton themselves, has been shown to be real by modern excavations. It is possible that these cranial fragments were retrieved from enemies, and that the modifications made to some of them – such as the holes drilled into the Hillhead skull fragment – were intended to aid in the display or use of these crania as trophies. However, it is equally possible that these skulls could have belonged to ancestors or other members of the in-group. Again, these cranial fragments provide very little clue as to the cause of death, and we have no more reason to think that they were obtained by violence than that they were retrieved from excarnation grounds for ritual use in the home.

Whatever their origin, it is clear that human remains were being actively used by Iron Age communities. The depositional context of many of these disarticulated human bones seems particularly significant. The placing of some in, under or around entrances might have been intended to emphasise and enhance the liminality of these areas, the transition from the wild outside world to the ordered inside (Brück 1995: 247). In his discussion of the Wag of Forse and Cnip fragments, Hingley suggests that the placement of human bones in entranceways may have been to designed to demonstrate rights of access, claims to the house based on ancestry and identity (1992: 16–17). Human remains buried under floors and walls have often been interpreted as foundation deposits, blessing, protecting or adding power to the building raised above them (Bradley 2007: 52); the Hornish Point boy can perhaps most easily be interpreted in this way. It is clear in any case that the proximity of the dead to the living within the household was in Iron Age Atlantic Scotland something that was thought normal, desirable and beneficial.

This idea accords well with current ideas about the ritual nature of everyday life in the Iron Age, and the lack of a clear division between the two. Parker Pearson in particular has focused on the ways in which roundhouse space may have been imbued with meaning and governed by rules that structured everyday activity and movement round the building (Parker Pearson 1999: 44–50; 2005: 534) (Figure 10.3). Pope (2007) has rightly pointed out that we must not ignore the practical concerns that must have influenced house construction and daily activity in this period; but the very presence of

206

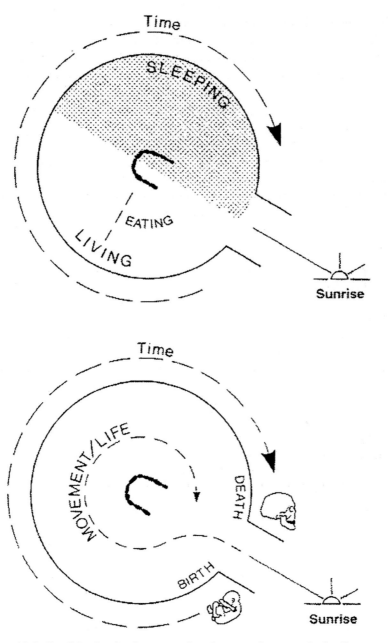

Figure 10.3: Possible ritual rules governing the everyday use of wheelhouse space
(Parker Pearson and Sharples 1999: 22)

human remains in the roundhouses of Iron Age Atlantic Scotland does infer that these buildings combined ritual and domestic functions.

To what extent human remains were used for ritual activities around the house or elsewhere before their deposition is much harder to quantify, although it may seem intrinsically likely if such items were thought to contain magical power or properties. The modification of human bones for display or into artefacts, as evidenced at Hillhead, Cnip, and the Wag of Forse among other sites, may seem initially to show a disregard or disrespect for these remains; it is assumed that these bones were not viewed as the remains of individuals but simply a useful raw material. However, it may instead be the case that the use of human remains for these items meant that they were considered magical or powerful, and revered.

## The use of caves

Human remains have also been found in non-domestic contexts in Iron Age Atlantic Scotland. Unusual deposits of human bone have been found in caves in Argyll and Skye. MacArthur Cave in Oban was unfortunately excavated in the late nineteenth century, and although the rough context of the human remains was recorded it is unclear whether they represented articulated burials or mixed remains. The surviving remains appear to represent four individuals (Saville and Hallen 1994: 715–23), and gnaw marks on some of the bones suggest that these bodies must have lain exposed, making this one of the few possible examples of an excarnation site (Tucker forthcoming).

At High Pasture Cave in Skye a quite different event seems to have taken place. Shortly before the sealing of the cave, the bodies of a woman, a neonate and a foetus were placed at the top of the stairs – the woman's skeleton appears to have been articulated but the neonate and foetus were deposited in multiple contexts and were probably already disarticulated. Further neonatal and foetal bones have been found, along with pig bones, on the steps of the cave (Sinfield, pers. comm.). There is no evidence that these depositions, which may have occurred in a single event, represent human sacrifice, but a ritual offering or closing deposit of human remains is implied.

Outside of Atlantic Scotland there are further examples of the deposition of human remains in caves during the Iron Age. At Sculptor's cave in Moray, human remains dating to the Roman Iron Age represent multiple individuals, some of whom seem to have been decapitated, suggesting that this was either an execution or a sacrificial site (Shepherd 1995; Armit and Schulting 2007: 1–3). At Alveston cave in Gloucestershire, human bones representing at least seven individuals were found, several of which bore marks of violence and, possibly, rare evidence of Iron Age cannibalism (Horton 2001). These examples start to suggest that some caves may have been the site of violent ritual activity during the Iron Age.

## The return of formal burial

Looking at a long Iron Age, up to AD 800, also allows the question of when formal burial returned to Iron Age Atlantic Scotland to be properly addressed. For a long time it was assumed that inhumation would have reappeared as a result of the appearance of Christianity in western Scotland from the end of the sixth century AD. However, the welcome modern trend to radiocarbon date human remains has revealed that many isolated burials and small cist cemeteries in Atlantic Scotland are actually much earlier than previously thought, dating as far back as the last few centuries BC.

The Western Isles have so far produced the earliest inhumation burials in this study area. Human remains have been found at several sites eroding out of the machair, and seem to represent a long-lived tradition of simple isolated burial from the late first millennium BC (Dunbar and Thoms 2008; Hunter Blair 2004; MacGregor 2001; Sharples 2005). Many of these eroding burials must have gone unrecorded in the past. Small 'cemeteries' dating to the first few centuries AD have been found at An Corran, Boreray, where three flexed inhumations were found within stone cists, and at Galson on Lewis, where fourteen skeletons were found laid supine inside stone cists, oriented west/east (Mulville *et al.* 2003: 24). Although further examples of formal burial in the Western Isles can be dated to between the sixth and eighth centuries AD, such as those at Northton, Harris (Murphy *et al.* 2004) and Cille Pheadair, South Uist (Mulville *et al.* 2003), there appears to be no noticeable increase in inhumations towards the end of the long Iron Age.

In the Northern Isles, the Knowe of Skea on Orkney represents by far the largest site of deposition of Iron Age human remains so far discovered in Atlantic Scotland, with over 150 burials, some dating back to the last few centuries BC (Moore and Wilson 2006); however, true understanding of this site must await post-excavation analysis and publication. Other small groups of cist or cairn inhumations at Hermisgarth, Buckquoy, Westness and Birsay Bay have been dated to between the third and seventh centuries AD (Downes and Morris 1997; Ritchie 1979; Kaland 1993; Morris 1989), again preceding the arrival of Christianity in this area, which is currently thought unlikely to have occurred much before the eighth century AD (Foster 2004: 87). Only at St. Ninian's Isle on Shetland can an association between inhumations and an early church building be supported (Barrowman 2003).

Turning to the mainland, two very early cairn burials, dating to around the turn of the first millennium, have been excavated in Sutherland at Loch

Borralie (MacGregor *et al.* 2003) and Sangobeg (Batey 2005). It has been argued that inhumations under kerbed cairns may represent a 'Pictish' burial rite of the first millennium AD (Close-Brooks 1984: 105), and a cemetery of this type at Ackergill, Caithness, is now thought to date to around the fourth century AD (Heawood 2005).

Cremation was previously thought to have entirely disappeared by the early first millennium BC, and most of the Iron Age cremations identified so far were at first taken to be Bronze Age; indeed, one was placed in a re-used Bronze Age vessel (Cook 1999; Graham Ritchie and Thornber 1988; Sheridan 2003). Worryingly, this raises the prospect not only that cremation might have persisted in at least some areas into the late Iron Age in Atlantic Scotland, but that many more undated cremations assigned to the Bronze Age may in fact date to the Iron Age.

There is clearly no simple change from exposure and use of human remains on settlement sites to formal inhumation in the early first millennium AD. Only a minority of individuals are represented in these generally small inhumation cemeteries, cremations and individual burials, and human remains continue to be deposited on settlement sites up until at least the seventh century in the Western Isles at sites such as Dun Vulan (Parker Pearson and Sharples 1999) and until the ninth century in the Northern Isles at Scalloway and Old Scatness (Sharples 1998; Tucker *et al.* forthcoming). The post-mortem removal of the sternum from a female seventh century burial at Cille Pheadair in the Western Isles (Mulville *et al.* 2003: 26) (Figure 10.4) also suggests that human remains were still being recovered and used in this period. The evidence so far, therefore, is of the adoption of formal, unaccompanied inhumation in some areas of Atlantic Scotland from the last few centuries BC, alongside the continuing deposition of human remains on settlement sites and a still unknown majority rite or rites, up until the end of the Iron Age.

The reason for the re-adoption of formal burial by certain individuals, centuries before Christianity is known to have influenced these areas is unclear, but worthy of more study than it has received to date. One of the most convincing explanations so far propounded is that it may have been driven by an increasing focus on individual identity from the early first millennium AD. Personal ornamentation seems to have become much more common in this period, and less effort was put into building impressive structures in late Iron Age Atlantic Scotland (Armit 1996: 180; 1990: 195–7). As the power structures that were eventually to form the late Iron Age Pictish kingdom started to spread across Atlantic Scotland in the early centuries AD, it may be that societies in the north witnessed a move from power being focused on the household and the local community to a culture in which for some members of society individual identity, and the body itself, was considered more important, in life and in death.

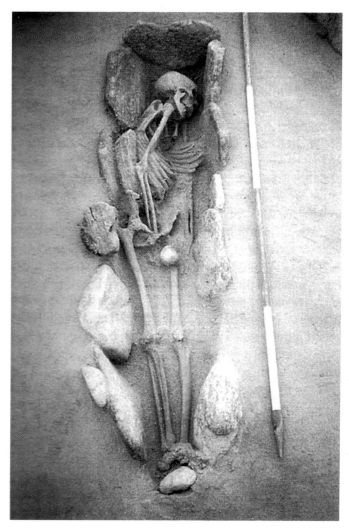

Figure 10.4: The female burial at Cille Pheadair, disturbed
and with the sternum removed after initial burial
(Mulville *et al.* 2003: 26)

## Conclusion

By looking at all finds of human remains dating to the Iron Age, rather than
simply dismissing this area as lacking in formal burials, we can start to at least
partially re-people the map of Atlantic Scotland. As more research is done
and more remains are dated this map should be filled in still further.
Radiocarbon dating has so far revealed many more human remains from a
variety of contexts to fall within the Iron Age than previously imagined, and

the number of other skeletons that may have in less thoughtful days been mistakenly assigned to the Bronze Age or Medieval period is a fascinating, if slightly worrying, thought.

Human remains are found in Iron Age Atlantic Scotland in a variety of contexts. Though still only a tiny minority are represented, these remains do start to suggest the variety of methods for dealing with the dead in this period: the extent of regional variation and changes through the Iron Age, the importance of human remains in domestic ritual, and the fate of the rest of the dead. From the evidence we have now, it seems likely that the majority of individuals in Iron Age Atlantic Scotland were left exposed, or possibly sent out to sea, with only a few individuals being selected for inclusion in domestic rituals, turned into artefacts, placed in caves, cremated, or buried individually or in small cemeteries. The reason certain individuals were treated in these very different ways remains a ripe subject for research.

It seems worth considering what this new picture of the treatment of human remains in Iron Age Atlantic Scotland can add to wider studies of burial and the treatment of the dead in Iron Age Britain and Europe. Firstly, it suggests that is important to focus on what we have, in the form of human remains deposited in domestic contexts and other apparently unusual locations, rather than mourning the lack of formal burials. Human remains clearly formed an important part of daily life in many Iron Age societies, and the complexities of their treatment may reveal fascinating insights into ritual life in this period, an ever tricky subject to approach.

The apparent co-existence of different methods for dealing with the dead is an interesting phenomenon, and must remind us of the possibility that there were different identities and beliefs in the past even within a local area, just as there are today. Finally, the changing treatment of the dead through the Iron Age in Atlantic Scotland raises the question of how we can use burial practice to look at changes in society, religious belief, and changing attitudes to the human body. Iron Age Europe, with its fascinating mixture of methods for dealing with the dead, provides the perfect environment for examining these issues.

## Acknowledgements

I would like to thank first and foremost my supervisor, Ian Armit, for the inspiration for this project and his constant support and advice throughout. I am grateful to Vicky Ginn of Queens University, Belfast, for sharing with me her knowledge of this subject, to Andrew Heald of AOC whose research on past excavations in Caithness has brought to light such treasures as the notebooks of Tress Barry, and to Steve Dockrill (University of Bradford) and Chris Knüsel

(University of Exeter) for their help and advice on many aspects of this research. I must also thank Alison Sheridan at the National Museums of Scotland, Sally-Anne Coupar and Jeff Liston at the Hunterian Museum, Glasgow, the staff at GUARD, Neil Curtis at the Marischal Museum, Aberdeen, Keith Jones at Dunrobin Castle, Sutherland, Laura Sinfield of the University of Edinburgh and Vicky Ewens of the University of Bradford for access to the skeletal collections I have examined so far, and for their time and frequently vital information on the remains under their care. Also Anne Brundle of Tankerness House Museum, Kirkwall and Mark Elliot at the Museum nan Eilean, Stornoway.

# Bibliography

## Ancient Sources:

Strabo. *The Geography of Strabo* (Translated by H.L. Jones). London: Heinemann, (1927).

## Modern Sources:

Armit, I. (1990). Epilogue: the Atlantic Scottish Iron Age. In I. Armit (ed.) *Beyond the Brochs*: 194–210. Edinburgh: Edinburgh University Press.

Armit, I. (1996). *The Archaeology of Skye and the Western Isles*. Edinburgh: Edinburgh University Press.

Armit, I. (2006a). *Anatomy of an Iron Age Roundhouse*. Edinburgh: Society of Antiquaries of Scotland.

Armit, I. (2006b). Inside Kurtz's Compound: headhunting and the human body in prehistoric Europe. In M. Bonogofsky (ed.) *Skull Collection, Modification and Decoration*: 1–14. Oxford: British Archaeological Reports, International Series 1539.

Armit, I. and V. Ginn (2007). Beyond the grave: human remains from domestic contexts in Iron Age Atlantic Scotland. *Proceedings of the Prehistoric Society* 73: 113–134.

Armit, I. and R. Schulting (2007). An Iron Age decapitation from the Sculptor's Cave, Covesea, Northeast Scotland. *Past: Newsletter of the Prehistoric Society* 55: 1–3.

Ballin Smith, B. (1994). *Howe: four millennia of Orkney prehistory, excavations 1978–1982*. Edinburgh: Society of Antiquaries of Scotland.

Barber, J., P. Halstead, H. James and F. Lee (1989). An unusual Iron Age burial at Hornish Point, South Uist. *Antiquity* 63: 773–78.

Barrowman, R. (2003). A decent burial? Excavations at St Ninian's Isle in July 2000, in J. Downes and A. Ritchie (eds.) *Sea Change: Orkney and northern Europe in the later Iron Age AD 300–800*: 51–61. Balgavies: Angus.

Barry, T. (1902) Unpublished notebook, National Museum of Scotland.

Batey, C. (2005). Sangobeg in 'radiocarbon dates'. *Discovery and Excavation in Scotland* 6: 181.

Bradley, R. (1998). *The Passage of Arms*. (2nd edition). Oxford: Oxbow Books.

Bradley, R. (2007). *The Prehistory of Britain and Ireland*. Cambridge: Cambridge University Press.

Bruck, J. (1995). A place for the dead: the role of human remains in Late Bronze Age Britain. *Proceedings of the Prehistoric Society* 61: 245–277.

Carr, G. and C. Knüsel (1997). The ritual framework of excarnation by exposure as the mortuary practice of the Early and Middle Iron Ages of central and southern Britain. In A. Gwilt and C. C. Haselgrove (eds.) *Reconstructing Iron Age Societies*: 167–173. Oxford: Oxbow Books.

Childe, V. G. (1944). *Scotland Before the Scots*. London: Methuen.

Close-Brooks, J. (1984). Pictish and other burials. In J. G. P. Friell and W. G. Watson (eds.) *Pictish Studies*: 87–111. Oxford: British Archaeological Reports, British Series 125.

Cook, M. (1999). Excavation of two cairns, a cist and associated features at Sanaigmhor Warren, Islay, Argyll and Bute. *Proceedings of the Society of Antiquaries of Scotland* 129: 251–279.

Cowie, T. and C. Wallace(2002). Bog Bodies from Scotland: redrawing the map. *Newswarp* 30: 14–22.

Cunliffe, B. (1991). *Iron Age Communities in Britain*. London: Routledge.

Curle, A. O. (1947). The excavation of the 'wag' or prehistoric Cattlefold at Forse, Caithness, and the relation of 'wags' to brocks, and implications arising therefrom. *Proceedings of the Society of Antiquaries of Scotland* 80: 11–25.

Downes, J. M. and C. D. Morris (1997). Hermisgarth, Sanday: the investigation of pyre settings and Pictish burials in Orkney. *Proceedings of the Society of Antiquaries of Scotland* 127: 609–626.

Dunbar, L. and J. Thoms (2008). *Vallay, Noth Uist*. Unpublished Data Structure Report.

Fairhurst, H. (1982). *Excavations at Crosskirk Broch, Caithness*. Edinburgh: Society of Antiquaries of Scotland.

Foster, S. M. (2004). *Picts, Gaels and Scots: early historic Scotland*. London: BT Batsford Ltd

Graham Ritchie, J. M. and I. Thornber (1988). Cairn 3, Acharn, Morvern, Argyll. *Proceedings of the Society of Antiquarians of Scotland* 118: 95–8.

Green, M. (2001). *Dying for the Gods: human sacrifice in Iron Age and Roman Europe*. Stroud: Tempus.

Harding, D. W. (2004). *The Iron Age in Northern Britain*. Abingdon: Routledge.

Heawood, A. (2005). Ackergill, Caithness. *Discovery and Excavation in Scotland* 6: 74.

Hedges, J. W. (1987). *Bu, Gurness and the Brochs of Orkney. Part I: Bu*. Oxford: British Archaeological Reports, British Series 163.

Henderson, J. C. (2007). The Atlantic West in the Early Iron Age. In C. C. Haselgrove and R. E. Pope (eds.) *The Earlier Iron Age in Britain and the Near Continent*: 307–324. Oxford: Oxbow Books.

Hill, J. D. (1995). *Ritual and Rubbish in the Iron Age of Wessex*. Oxford: British Archaeological Reports, British Series 242.

Hingley, R. (1992). Society in Scotland from 700 BC to AD 200. *Proceedings of the Society of Antiquarians of Scotland* 122: 7–53

Horton, M. (2001). *Cannibalistic Celts discovered in South Gloucestershire*. http://www.bristol.ac.uk/news/2001/cannibal.htm. Date of last access: September 2008.

Hunter Blair, A. (2004). Scarista, Harris (Harris Parish), inhumation. *Discovery and Excavation in Scotland* 5: 136.

Kaland, S. H. H. (1993). The settlement of Westness, Rousay. In C. E. Batey, J. Jesch, and C. D. Morris (eds.) *The Viking age in Caithness, Orkney and the North Atlantic*: 312–17. Edinburgh: Edinburgh University Press.

Luff, R. (1996). The 'bare bones' of identifying ritual behaviour in the archaeological record. In S. Anderson and K. Boyle (eds.) *Ritual Treatment of Human and Animal Remains*: 1–10. Oxford: Oxbow Books.

MacGregor, G. (2001). Swainbost, Ness, Lewis, Western Isles (Barvas parish), burial. *Discovery and Excavation in Scotland* 2: 101.

MacGregor, G., J. Mackenzie, D. Perry and P. Sharman (2004). 'Excavation of an Iron Age burial mound, Loch Borralie, Durness, Sutherland'. *Scottish Archaeological Internet Reports* 9.

Mackie, E. (1974). *Dun Mor Vaul*. Glasgow: University of Glasgow Press.

Madgwick, R. (2008). Patterns in the modification of animal and human bones in Iron Age Wessex: revisiting the excarnation debate. In O. Davis, N. Sharples and K. Waddington (eds.) *Changing perspectives on the first millennium BC*: 99–118. Oxford: Oxbow Books.

Marwick, H. (1927). Underground galleried building at Rennibister, Orkney. *Proceedings of the Society of Antiquaries of Scotland* 61: 296–303.

Moore, H. and G. Wilson (2006). Knowe of Skea, Orkney (Westray parish), eroding multi-period funerary complex. *Discovery and Excavation in Scotland* 7: 127.

Morris, C. D. (1989). *The Birsay Bay Project: coastal sites beside the Brough Road, Birsay, Orkney: excavations 1976–1982, 1.* Durham: University of Durham.

Mulville, J., M. Parker Pearson, N. Sharples, H. Smith and A. Chamberlain (2003). Quarters, arcs and squares: human and animal remains in the Hebridean Iron Age. In J. Downes and A. Ritchie (eds.) *Sea Change: Orkney and northern Europe in the later Iron Age AD 300–800*: 23–28. Balgavies: Angus.

Murphy, E., R. Gregory and D. Simpson (2004). Post-Beaker period death and burial at Northton, Isle of Harris, Scotland. *Environmental Archaeology* 9(2): 163–171.

Parker Pearson, M. (1999). Food, sex and death: cosmologies in the British Iron Age with particular reference to East Yorkshire. *Cambridge Archaeological Journal* 9: 43–69.

Parker Pearson, M. (2005). *The Archaeology of Death and Burial.* Stroud: Tempus.

Parker Pearson, M. and Sharples, N. (1999). *Between Land and Sea: excavations at Dun Vulan, South Uist.* Sheffield: Sheffield Academic Press.

Pope, R. (2007). Ritual and the roundhouse: a critique of recent ideas on the use of domestic space in later British prehistory. In C. C. Haselgrove and R. E. Pope (eds.) *The Earlier Iron Age in Britain and the Near Continent*: 204–228. Oxford: Oxbow Books.

Redfern, R. (2008). New evidence for Iron Age secondary burial practice and bone modification from Gussage All Saints and Maiden Castle (Dorset, England). *Oxford Journal of Archaeology* 27: 281–301.

Ritchie, A. (1979). Excavation of Pictish and Viking-Age farmsteads at Buckquoy, Orkney. *Proceedings of the Society of Antiquaries of Scotland* 108: 174–227.

Saville, A. and Y. Hallen (1994). The 'Obanian Iron Age': human remains from the Oban cave sites, Argyll, Scotland. *Antiquity* 68: 715–23.

Sharples, N. (1998). *Scalloway: a broch, Late Iron Age settlement and Medieval cemetery in Shetland.* Oxford: Oxbow Books.

Sharples, N. (2005). Pollochar, South Uist, Western Isles, human burial. *Discovery and Excavation in Scotland* 6: 148.

Shepherd, I. A. G. (1995). The Sculptor's Cave, Covesea, Moray: from Bronze Age ossuary to Pictish shrine? *Proceedings of the Society of Antiquaries of Scotland* 125 Lecture Summaries.

Sheridan, A. (2003). Uyea, Shetland (radiocarbon date). *Discovery and Excavation in Scotland* 4: 169.

Stead, I.M., J.B. Bourke and D. Brothwell (1986). *Lindow Man: the body in the bog.* London: Guild Publishing.

Tucker, F. (forthcoming). *The Use and Treatment of Human Remains in Iron Age Atlantic Scotland.* Unpublished PhD thesis.

Tucker, F., A. Ogden and A. Boylston (forthcoming). The human skeletal material. In S.J. Dockrill, J. M. Bond, L. D. Brown, V. E. Turner, D. Bashford, J. E. Cussans and R. A. Nicholson. *Excavations at Old Scatness, Shetland Volume 1: the Pictish village and Viking settlement.* Lerwick: Shetland Heritage Publications.

Van der Sanden, W. (1996). *Through Nature to Eternity: the bog bodies of north west Europe.* Amsterdam: Batavian Lion International.

Whimster, R. (1981). *Burial Practices in Iron Age Britain.* Oxford: British Archaeological Reports, British Series 90.

White, T. D. (1992). *Prehistoric Cannibalism at Mancos 5MTUMR-2346.* Princeton: Princeton University Press.

## CHAPTER 11

# OLD BONES, NEW IDEAS.
# $^{14}$C-DATING OF CREMATED BONES FROM LATE BRONZE AGE AND EARLY IRON AGE URNFIELD CEMETERIES IN FLANDERS

## Guy De Mulder

### (Universiteit Ghent)

## Abstract

Recently a method has been developed and tested to date cremated bones using bioapatite. By using the cremated bones the human element is properly dated. From some cremations charcoal dates were also obtained to confirm the validity of the $^{14}$C-dates on bone. The traditional chronological framework for this period in Western Belgium was based on the study of the funerary pottery alone, since metalwork was scarce in the cemeteries. The typochronology was worked out in a comparison with the framework of the neighbouring regions and especially Central Europe.

At the moment $^{14}$C-dates of five urnfield cemeteries are available. The dated graves were selected on the basis of the cremation type, their position in the cemetery and their relation to funeral monuments. The traditional ideas about the urnfield period in the region have been challenged. First, the chronological framework based on the pottery studies is open for discussion and needs to be reworked. Second, the occupational history of some of the urnfields can be revised, especially the long term existence of the sites. The transition from the Middle Bronze Age to the Late Bronze Age and the appearance of the urnfield cemeteries starts earlier than expected before now. Also, the end of this phenomenon is not limited to the transition of the Early Iron Age – Late Iron Age.

## Research history

Since the late 1990s the possibility of using bioapatite from cremated bones for radiocarbon dating has been recognized and studied. Before then bioapatite from bone was not considered as a dating material because of possible sample contamination by groundwater or secondary calcium carbonate (Hassan *et al.* 1977). However, bioapatite can be used as a reliable dating material. Certain environmental conditions favour the conservation of the bioapatite above bone collagen, which is mostly used for dating. Good bioapatite dates from bone were obtained from samples from the Sahel (Saliège *et al.* 1998). Recently, a cave burial site on the island of Menorca (Spain) showed a remarkable conservation of leather, plant material (wood and ropes) and human tissue (Fullola *et al.* 2007). Hair and a bioapatite sample from the same human burial gave dates that were in excellent agreement (Van Strydonck *et al.* 2009: 554). Both areas showed ideal environmental conditions for bioapatite preservation: a dry context without rain and groundwater and a soil free of carbonates.

Lanting and his colleagues started with the first tests on bioapatite from cremated bones and showed good results (Lanting and Brindley 1998). This method uses structural carbonate from the bioapatite in bone, which survived the cremation process and was available for dating the remnants of the deceased. These dates were further confirmed by charcoal dates from the same graves (Lanting *et al.* 2001). These promising results prompted further research into the chemical mechanism or process behind it and the quality of the incinerated bone necessary to have a reliable date. Van Strydonck *et al.* (2005) have demonstrated that the changes in crystallinity, the combustion of the organic material and the compaction of the bone are preserving the structural carbonate in the cremated bone and are forming a barrier preventing the penetration of the bicarbonate into the bone, which can influence the radiocarbon date. Another aspect of the ongoing research was a laboratory intercomparison study on Iron Age and early medieval bones from the Netherlands and Belgium, which confirmed again the validity of the dating method. An assessment of the sample quality of the cremated bone was not made during this project. It was assumed that the samples were well cremated (temperature above 600°C) and that there was no, or only easy to remove, contamination by secondary carbonate (Naysmith *et al.* 2007). An important factor to distinguish the good quality of a cremated bone to obtain a reliable date was its colour. This criterion has been recognised by different researchers. The difference between charred (burnt) and cremated bone depends on the colour which is scientifically supported by a colour index. Research had been conducted on this subject and criteria established by Shipman *et al.* (1984), Mays (1998) and Munro *et al.* (2007). Cremated bones that have been burned above 600°C have a greyish-white to white colour (Lanting *et al.* 2001; Van Strydonck *et al.* 2005). Research on a human individual, who had been affected by low temperatures as well as high cremation temperatures, came up with more objective parameters to make this discrepancy (Olsen *et al.* 2007).

Recent testing of the quality of cremated bones and of the problems with eventual contamination by secondary carbonate on bone samples from Belgian and Spanish urnfield sites delivered some new insights about the advisable selection of cremated bone. The geological condition of the burial site and the degree of cremation plays an important role in this process. It is favorable to select bones which have been cremated at a temperature above 725°C. These all show a white colour at the outside as well as on the inside of the bone. If bones are white on the outside, but grey on the inside, then the inside has not reached the same degree of cremation as the outside. Although, according to the crystallinity index, grey coloured bone must be considered well cremated (temperature above 600°C), it is much more vulnerable to contamination than white coloured bone. This can influence the $^{14}$C-date in a negative way (Van Strydonck *et al.* 2009).

Two methods were used for pre-treating the selected bone samples. In the first method, the bones were first inspected to see if they were completely cremated; then the surface of the bone samples was leached away with 1% HCl. Finally the bones were ground. The $CO_2$ was extracted with phosphoric acid. Before graphitisation the $CO_2$ gas was cleaned by heating for 30 min. at 1000°C in the presence of Ag. Targets were prepared at the Royal Institute for Cultural Heritage in Brussels (Belgium) and measured at the Leibniz Labor für Altersbestimmung und Isotopenforschung in Kiel (Germany) (De Mulder *et al.* 2007). Another option was to remove secondary carbonate by an acetic acid treatment following Lanting *et al.* (2001). After testing both methods the following steps to obtain reliable radiocarbon dates were proposed: First, there is a visual inspection to see if the bone is completely cremated. Then the surface is removed. After drying the bone was ground and treated with acetic acid to remove secondary carbonate (Van Strydonck *et al.* 2009: 566–567). The charcoal samples were treated by using the common alkali-acid-alkali (AAA) method. For the calibration the program OxCal v3.10 was used (Bronk Ramsey 1995; 2001) together with the IntCal 04 terrestrial calibration curve (Reimer *et al.* 2004).

The success of this dating technique lies in the fact that an absolute date now can be attributed to archaeological phenomena that previously were only datable indirectly. When archaeological artefacts were present, the cremation burials were dated based on the typology of ceramics and/or metals. An absolute date could be attributed if charcoal from the pyre was present. Charcoal, however, can have an 'old wood' offset resulting in an age difference between the $^{14}$C date and the real cremation date (De Mulder *et al.* 2004: 51). Furthermore, charcoal was not always present on the burial sites due to selection processes after the cremation. Sometimes only the cremated bones from the deceased were selected from the pyre for deposition in a grave pit. As a result of this, sites were dated by means of the few datable burials. This implies that the internal chronology of the site could not always be studied. Furthermore, the typochronology of the ceramics and the metals remains questionable in the study region of the Scheldt basin. The typochronological framework for the urnfield cemeteries was largely based on the study of the pottery in the graves which consisted mostly of the urn and the occasionally accompanying funeral gift. These funeral goods were mostly also limited to a single cup or beaker. Metalwork is scarce during the Late Bronze Age in a funeral context. Only at the end of the Late Bronze Age and during the Early Iron Age do a few graves with metalwork appear sporadically in the region.

## Chronological framework

The chronological framework for the Late Bronze Age and Early Iron Age on the continent is mainly based on the German and French typochronologies. The base for the German chronology was established by Müller-Karpe, who studied the Bavarian urnfields in southern Germany (Müller-Karpe 1959). Hatt proposed a system for the Late Bronze Age and Early Iron Age in France (Hatt 1961) (Figure 11.1). Although regional changes have been introduced and refined this framework, it still represents the main phases for the studied period.

   A new interpretative concept of the urnfield culture was proposed by Brun in the 1980s (Brun 1984; Brun 1988). This shifted the emphasis from migrations to a socio-economic explanation for the changes in the Late Bronze Age. Brun introduced the concept of the 'Rhin-Suisse-France orientale (RSFO) group', which is situated in the northern Alpine area of the continental techno-complex covering a part of southern Germany, Switzerland

| Müller-Karpe (Germany) | Hatt (France) | Brun | British Isles | Years BC |
|---|---|---|---|---|
| Bronzezeit D | Bronze final I | Etape 1 | Middle Bronze Age | 1300–1200 |
| Hallstatt A1 | Bronze final IIa | | Late Bronze Age | 1200–1100 |
| Hallstatt A2 | Bronze final IIb | Etape 2 | | 1100–1000 |
| Hallstatt B1 | Bronze final IIIa | | | 1000–900 |
| Hallstatt B2/3 | Bronze final IIIb | Etape 3 | | 900–800 |
| Hallstatt C | Hallstatt ancien | | Early Iron Age | 800–600 |
| Hallstatt D | Hallstatt moyen/ final | Hallstatt moyen/final | | 600–450 |

Figure 11.1: The chronological sequence of the Late Bronze Age and Early Iron Age in Central Europe, Western Europe and the British Isles based primarily on typology.

and northeastern France. A new chronological framework for this period was proposed based on the socio-economic processes in this region. Brun distinguishes a first phase (*etape* 1) which groups the periods Bronzezeit D (Bz D) and Hallstatt A1 (Ha A1). The second phase (*etape* 2) is characterised by the expansion in the direction of western Europe from the 'RSFO group'. This phase 2 covers the periods of Ha A2 and Ha B1. The last phase (*etape* 3) is a period of economic problems, social changes and regression in the 'RSFO group'. This process happened during the final phase of the Late Bronze Age (Ha B2/3) and the beginning of the Early Iron Age (Ha C).

The regional framework for Belgium was first published in the 1950s by De Laet and the Seminar for Archaeology at Ghent University, who studied the urnfields in western Belgium (De Laet *et al.* 1958). The chronological scheme they proposed was adapted from the German typochronological classification and based on the ceramics from the urnfield cemeteries (De Laet *et al.* 1958). In 1968 the typochronological framework of the cemeteries in the region between the North Sea and the lower Rhine was further refined by Desittere who established a chronology for the Late Bronze Age based on comparison with central European pottery from this period (Desittere 1968). The revision of the concept of urnfields in the 1980s and the introduction of the 'RSFO group' and its cultural influences during the Late Bronze Age in the Scheldt basin resulted in a new evaluation of the excavated sites. This revision was focused on confronting the regional archaeological information with the proposed three-phased chronology of Brun (Bourgeois 1989a).

In central Europe the 'RSFO group' starts around 1300 BC (*etape* 1), according to the traditional chronology, with the appearance of the first urnfield cemeteries. The urnfield phenomenon in Flanders, which is part of the Atlantic world, starts later around 1100 BC when the first of these new style cemeteries appear in the archaeological record. Next to the urnfields the influence of the 'RSFO group' is also visible in the appearance of pottery shapes and decoration styles, imitating examples from the 'RSFO group', in western Belgium. Bronze objects with a continental origin were also becoming frequent in the Late Bronze Age in wet deposits from Atlantic Europe, but they are, in general, not associated with the funeral sphere. In the Scheldt area the bronze objects come almost exclusively as dredging finds, recovered from the meandering riverbed in the late nineteenth and early twentieth centuries (Verlaeckt 1996). A connection between the typochronologies of the pottery and the metal objects is difficult to establish in the studied area due to the rather occasional appearance of both types of artifacts in the same archaeological contexts of the urnfield period.

As a result of the first successful dating outcome on cremated bones a proposal of a slightly modified chronology for the Late Bronze Age and Early Iron Age in central and northwestern Europe has been put forward (Figure

| Lanting & van der Plicht (2001/2002) | Calibrated calendar years | Radiocarbon years |
|---|---|---|
| Bronzezeit D | 1325–1200 BC | 3100–3000 BP |
| Hallstatt A1 | 1200–1125 BC | 3000–2950 BP |
| Hallstatt A2 | 1125–1025 BC | 3000–2875 BP |
| Hallstatt B1 | 1025–925 BC | 2875–2800 BP |
| Hallstatt B2 | – | |
| Hallstatt B3 | 925–800 BC | 2800–2650 BP |
| Hallstatt C | 800–625 BC | 2650–2450 BP |
| Hallstatt D | 625–480 BC | 2500–2400 BP |

Figure 11.2: The chronological sequence of the Late Bronze Age and Early Iron Age in Southern Germany and neighbouring areas based on absolute dates (after Lanting and van der Plicht 2001/2002).

11.2). The new archaeological information from the cremated bones has been confronted with the existing work on typochronologies and regional dendrochronological datasets to produce a new revised chronology (Lanting *et al.* 2001/2002).

## Funeral rites

The Scheldt basin, which covers part of northern France, Belgium and the southwestern Netherlands, belongs during the Bronze Age to the 'Atlantic region'. The tradition of erecting round barrows was a typical feature of the burial tradition in this region during the Early and Middle Bronze Age. The barrow was normally constructed above a primary grave. Secondary burials were added later. The available information points to a dominant tradition of cremation burials in the Flanders region. These funeral sites tended to be made up of a limited number of monuments forming a small cemetery (Bourgeois and Cherretté 2005: 48–57).

Following the traditional chronology from 1300 BC onwards the 'RSFO group' develops in the central European region. One of the characteristics is the dominant appearance of cremations, which had been collected in an urn and deposited in flatgraves, replacing inhumation. These cremation burials tend be grouped in large cemeteries, the so-called urnfields (Brun 1988: 601). The 'RSFO group' spreads its influence from 1100 BC onwards in a western direction incorporating regions which belonged to the Atlantic zone, such as central France. The southern part of Belgium, in the river Meuse area, also falls under the expansion zone of the 'RSFO group' in this period (Warmenbol 1988). However, the western part of Belgium is only partially affected by these central European influences (Bourgeois 1989a: 49–50). It is in this period that we see the spread of the tradition of the urnfield cemeteries over the study region. Cremation and the deposit of the remains in flat graves becomes a dominant feature in most of western Europe. The urnfield cemeteries are constructed on sites away from the traditional barrow cemeteries.

In Flanders two different regional groups are apparent during the Late Bronze Age, although they share a lot of characteristics in common. The so-called 'Flemish' group covers western Belgium, which includes the western part of Flanders and the southern province of Hainaut. The tradition of erecting barrows disappears from the archaeological image in this period and monuments have been excavated at only two sites. The other urnfield cemeteries consist only of flat graves (De Mulder 1994: 98–103, 109–113). To the east of the Scheldt region in the environs of Antwerp the 'Northwestern group' is located. The cemeteries of this group are spread over the eastern part of Flanders, the southern Netherlands and part of western Germany (Desittere 1968: 30). Here funerary monuments are still frequently found in the cemeteries of this period. The barrows are quite small in comparison with their Early and Middle Bronze Age predecessors, normally measuring from 3 to 10m in diameter (De Laet 1982: 533). Another type of monument that appears is the long barrow (*langebed*). This type of barrow is frequently found in the urnfield cemeteries of this region (Roymans and Kortlang 1999b: 36).

In the core area the socio-economic changes from 900 BC onwards (phase 3) are reflected in some of the cemeteries. Inhumation again becomes popular and slowly replaces the cremation graves. At the same time the dominant cultural influence of the 'RSFO group' on the Atlantic region is disappearing due to this internal socio-economic crisis (Brun 1988: 609–611). In the urnfields of both regional groups these changes are less visible. In western Belgium the archaeological record testifies that several urnfields stay in use during the Early Iron Age. A shift to the south, away from the river Scheldt is evident in the area of the 'Flemish group'. By Ha D some urnfields are already deserted and those still in use show a diminishing number of cremations (De Mulder 1994: 113–116). The cemeteries in the part of the 'Northwestern group' also show continuity in their use and burial practices. Next to the existing funerary sites, numerous new urnfields were started during the Early Iron Age. During the Early Iron Age the number of funeral sites almost doubles in comparison with the Late Bronze Age (Roymans and Kortlang 1999b: 38–39).

In the 'Flemish group' the urnfield tradition is considered to end before the start of the Late Iron Age. The complete absence of typical Early La Tène pottery in the cemeteries is an indication that they were given up as funerary sites (De Mulder 1994: 115–116; Bourgeois and Cherretté 2005: 69). The 'Northwestern group' reveals a somewhat different pattern – There are archaeological indications that some urnfields came to a finish during the

Early Iron Age. The Dutch urnfield at Beegden is estimated to end around 625 BC, while the Weert urnfield was used until about 550 BC (Gerritsen 2003: 131). Others stayed in use until at the latest 400 BC. The carinated pottery at the site of Lommel/Kattenbosch was an indication that some cemeteries survived into the Early La Tène period (De Laet and Mariën 1950). The urnfield of Rijkevorsel/Hellehoeksheide also covers the period between the Early Iron Age and the Early La Tène until 400 BC on the basis of the excavated pottery (Theunissen 1993).

In both regional groups cremation was the dominant tradition, although there were some differences. Five different types of cremation grave are recognisable; two types use an urn as a container for the deposition of the cremated bone. Type A is an urngrave which contains only selected bones from the pyre. In type B charcoal fragments from the pyre have also been deposited in, but mostly around the urn. The other types can be classified as urnless graves. Type C is a so-called *Knochenlager* ('bone-pack-grave'), which can be described as a selection of the cremated bones deposited in a perishable container. Type D is called the 'Destelbergen style' cremation-grave because it was recognised for the first time at this site. It resembles a *Knochenlager* ('bone-pack-grave') with a concentration of cremated bones, but is covered by remains from the funeral pyre. Finally, type E is a kind of cremation-grave that can be identified as a gravepit, which contains a limited part of the cremated bones and the pyre, deposited without distinction in the pit (German *Brandgrubengrab*). It is clear that not all the cremated bones from the deceased are deposited in this structure. Sometimes only some 10 to 100 grams is found (De Mulder 1994: 98; De Mulder and Bourgeois forthcoming).

Regional differences are visible in the chronological appearance of certain types of cremation grave. In the western part of Belgium there is during the Late Bronze Age a predominance of urngraves. During the Early Iron Age burials without an urn are becoming more popular, especially the 'bone-pack-grave' and the cremation-grave style Destelbergen (Bourgeois 1989b: 88–89). However, the opposite phenomenon is visible in the 'Northwestern group'. During the Late Bronze Age urnless graves prevailed but the Early Iron Age saw a change to a predominance of deposition in an urn (Roymans and Kortlang 1999a: 286).

The Destelbergen style cremation-grave was, until recently, only recognised in the urnfield of the same name. In the other cemeteries in western Belgium it is missing entirely in the archaeological record. However, during a re-evaluation of older excavated urnfields in the eastern part of the studied area new examples were discovered. One cremation has been identified in the cemetery of Aarschot (Mertens 1951: 15–16) and two other examples were found in a neighbouring urnfield at Herk-de-Stad/Donk (Van Impe 1980: 13, 22). The youngest Destelbergen style cremations were excavated at the site of

Tessenderlo, situated to the northeast of both aforementioned cemeteries where seven graves could be attributed to this type.

# $^{14}$C-dating of urnfields

For the moment several sites have yielded new information on the basis of $^{14}$C-dating of cremated bones (Figure 11.3). Both urnfields at Velzeke/Paddestraat and Velzeke/Provinciebaan as well as Blicquy have been the subject of different $^{14}$C-dating projects financed respectively by the Provincial Archaeological Museum-Velzeke and the Free University Brussels (VUB) (De Mulder *et al.* 2007). These sites are situated in the area of the 'Flemish' group. The results to be discussed further in the paper are part of a new dating project sponsored by a grant of the Flemish Foundation for Scientific Research (FWO-Flanders nr. 1.5.029.07). The cemeteries of Destelbergen and Tessenderlo have been selected for a series of new dates on cremations (Figure 11.4). The selection for this dating project was based on the combination of the following archaeological parameters: grave type, typochronological information, grave monuments and internal distribution. Concerning the scientific criteria for the bones, only samples were selected that had been cremated above 725° C and which had a white colour inside as well as outside. Another point of choice was the use of only large thick fragments of bone, because the outside is removed before dating to eliminate potential contamination.

The site of Neerharen-Rekem, in the 'Northwestern' group has also been subjected to a series of $^{14}$C-datings on cremated bone, but the results are not yet published (pers. comm. Luc Van Impe). To finish this overview, there

| Site | Total $^{14}$C-dates | Cremated bones dated | Charcoal dated | Inhumation |
|------|------|------|------|------|
| **Belgium** | | | | |
| Beerse | 2 | 2 | – | – |
| Blicquy | 19 | 15 | 4 | – |
| Couvin | 3 | – | – | 3 |
| Destelbergen | 20 | 16 | 4 | – |
| Kontich | 2 | 1 | 1 | – |
| Neerharen-Rekem | 15 | 15 | – | – |
| Tessenderlo | 17 | 12 | 5 | – |
| Velzeke/Paddestraat | 26 | 21 | 5 | – |
| Velzeke/Provinciebaan | 10 | 8 | 2 | – |

Figure 11.3: Overview of the number of $^{14}$C-dates on cremated bone, charcoal and inhumations in Belgium.

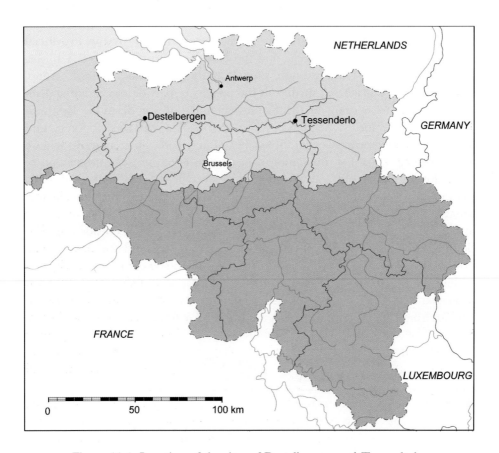

Figure 11.4: Location of the sites of Destelbergen and Tessenderlo.

exist a limited set of other dates in the eastern part of Flanders. An urngrave at Kontich has tested cremated bone as well as charcoal (De Mulder and Van Strydonck 2008). The site at Beerse was only recently excavated and the only two cremations were dated on cremated bone (Delaruelle *et al.* 2008: 34). It is interesting to remark that although cremation was dominant, there are indications of other practices with deceased human remains. In one room of the cave La Roche Alberic in Couvin (southern Belgium) three human skulls were found. They have been interpreted as a ritual deposition in a sacred place instead of funerary remains. Three radiocarbon measurements have been made on these skulls. Surprisingly all three dates belong to the Late Bronze Age (Robertz 2008: 108–9).

## Tessenderlo/Engsbergen

Tessenderlo is located in the area of the 'Northwestern' group. The first archaeological reference to an urnfield goes back to 1879 when during construction activities an urn and a small cup were discovered. In 1971 a second urn was discovered by chance. The urnfield cemetery of Tessenderlo was excavated between 1992–1993 and 1995–1996. The excavations were limited to the plots of land that were threatened by new buildings (Figure 11.5). The site has for the moment not been completely uncovered. During these rescue excavations, 49 cremation graves were discovered together with a circular structure and a long barrow (so-called '*langebed*'). Most of the cremations are *Knochenlager* (type C) and the two other urnless types (types D and E) whilst the two types of urngraves (types A and B) represent only 27.45% of the funeral finds (Figure 11.6), the two older discoveries included. The preliminary study of the site, dated on the basis of the typochronology of the urns, situates the cemetery in the Early Iron Age (Creemers 1994; 1997). A full excavation and study report is not yet published.

After a visual quality control of obtained temperature level of the cremated bones 17 samples were dated using bone (12 samples) and charcoal (5 samples) (Figure 11.7). For the charcoal dates only single pieces were used. It is also necessary to remark that the type of wood of the charcoal samples has not been identified. Five of the cremations were double dated to test again the validity of the method. The results from the charcoal and cremated bone of grave 14 were exactly the same. Both samples from grave 13 fall in the same chronological time span. There is a difference in the results on the charcoal and the cremated bone from grave 35, but this is still acceptable. Both cremations 43 and 19 have a much older charcoal date then the cremated bone date. It seems plausible to interpret this difference as the result of 'old wood' effect due to the own lifespan of wood.

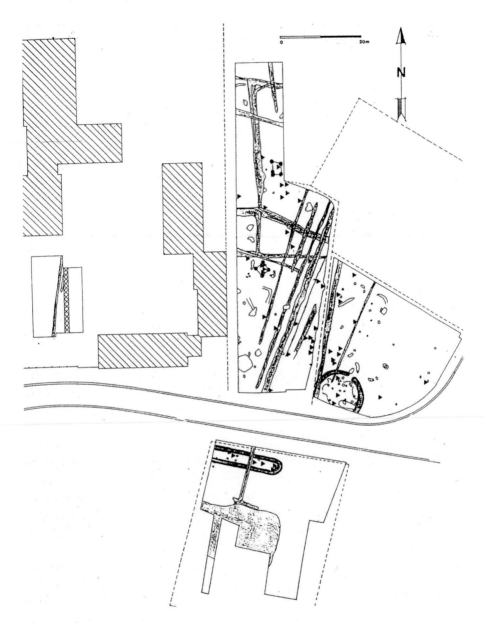

Figure 11.5: Excavation plan of the urnfield at Tessenderlo/Engsbergen
(after Creemers).

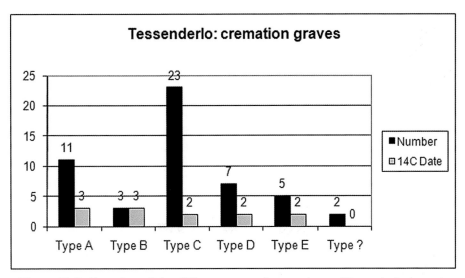

Figure 11.6: Overview of the different types of cremation at Tessenderlo (type A: urngrave, type B: urngrave with charcoal fragments, type C: bonepackgrave; type D: cremationgrave style Destelbergen, type E: cremationgrave with mixed remnants).

The [14]C-dates give a completely different picture in comparison with the established ceramic chronology (Figure 11.8). None of the dates belong to the expected Early Iron Age. Instead they are all situated in the Bronze Age, most of them in the Late Bronze Age. The oldest [14]C-date on the site of Tessenderlo goes back to the twentieth-eighteenth centuries BC (KIA-33844: 3500±35BP). This date is too old to accept. The cremated bone sample in question was recovered from an urngrave and the technical characteristics and form of this urn do not fit with the known pottery manufacturing style for the proposed absolute date. It seems plausible that the cremated bone sample was contaminated by secondary carbonate (Van Strydonck *et al.* 2009) and it is hoped a new [14]C-date will bring more clarity in this case.

In the southeastern sector a ring ditch with a diameter of 11m and an opening on the NNE-side was found. Within this structure three graves were registered (Creemers 1994). Only one cremation (type E) delivered a good bone sample. The supposed central grave (14) of the ring ditch was chronologically located between 1530–1410 cal BC (see Figure 11.7). This result places the barrow in the Middle Bronze Age. The date is a lot older than is traditionally accepted for the start of the urnfield cemeteries. There is a chronological gap between this funerary monument and the installation in this zone of the urnfield cemetery. If it is assumed that the two charcoal dates are too old due to the 'old wood' effect, then the first cremation graves of the urnfield go back to the late twelfth-eleventh century BC. All the [14]C-dates point

| Grave nr. | Lab. nr. | Material | Age BP | Calibrated date (2σ) |
|-----------|----------|----------|--------|----------------------|
| 2 | KIA-34153 | Cremated bone | 2710±30BP | 920BC (95.4%) 800BC |
| 13 | KIA-33612 | Cremated bone | 2795±30BP | 1020BC (95.4%) 840BC |
| 13 | KIA-33631 | Charcoal | 2790±30BP | 1010BC (95.4%) 840BC |
| 14 | KIA-33814 | Charcoal | 3210±30BP | 1530BC (95.4%) 1410BC |
| 14 | KIA-33618 | Cremated bone | 3210±30BP | 1530BC (95.4%) 1410BC |
| 15 | KIA-34145 | Cremated bone | 2790±30BP | 1010BC (95.4%) 840BC |
| 19 | KIA-33614 | Charcoal | 2890±30BP | 1210BC (95.4%) 970BC |
| 19 | KIA-33616 | Cremated bone | 2715±30BP | 980BC (95.4%) 800BC |
| 20 | KIA-33830 | Cremated bone | 2835±30BP | 1120BC ( 1.4%) 1100BC<br>1090BC (94.0%) 910BC |
| 27 | KIA-34146 | Cremated bone | 2695±30BP | 905BC (95.4%) 800BC |
| 32 | KIA-33831 | Cremated bone | 2780±30BP | 1010BC (95.4%) 840BC |
| 34 | KIA-33844 | Cremated bone | 3500±35BP | 1930BC (95.4%) 1730BC |
| 36 | KIA-33619 | Cremated bone | 2850±30BP | 1120BC (95.4%) 920BC |
| 36 | KIA-33617 | Charcoal | 2800±30BP | 1040BC (91.1%) 890BC<br>880BC ( 4.3%) 840BC |
| 43 | KIA-33813 | Charcoal | 3010±30BP | 1390BC (95.4%) 1120BC |
| 43 | KIA-33615 | Cremated bone | 2825±25BP | 1050BC (95.4%) 910BC |
| 45 | KIA-33845 | Cremated bone | 2710±35BP | 920BC (95.4%) 800BC |

Figure 11.7: Overview of the $^{14}$C-results on cremated bone and charcoal from the urnfield at Tessenderlo.

to an occupation in the Late Bronze Age. The functioning of the site stops in the ninth century BC, before the start of the Early Iron Age. To the south of the ring ditch a long barrow (*langebed*) is located in which six cremations had been deposited. Only one cremation in the central axis of this funerary structure could be dated (KIA-33845: 2710±35BP). It situates the functioning of this monument in the latest occupation phase of the site at the end of the Late Bronze Age.

## Destelbergen/Eenbeekeinde

The urnfield cemetery of Destelbergen, located close to Ghent in western Belgium, was discovered by a local amateur archaeologist in 1927–1928 during sand digging although it remained largely unknown until the late 1950s. The first excavation took place in 1960 under direction of prof. De Laet and Ghent University (De Laet *et al.* 1958 (1961)). Work continued on the site until 1984. During this period 106 graves of an urnfield were uncovered

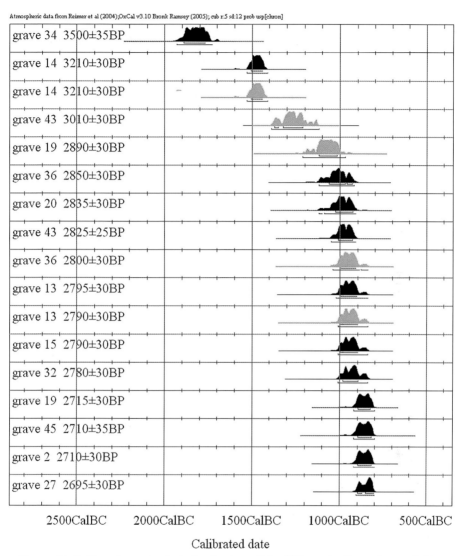

Figure 11.8: The chronological distribution of the [14]C-results from the urnfield at Tessenderlo. The charcoal samples are in grey.

together with a series of funeral monuments (Figure 11.9). It was assumed that during the sand digging activities about 40 other cremations were lost (De Laet *et al.* 1986: 11–21). Among the 106 cremations the *Knochenlager* (type C) represent the largest group. The ' Destelbergen style' cremations (Type D) form *c.* 10% of the cemetery. Urngraves were more frequent on this site then in Tessenderlo (Figure 11.10). On the site was not only an urnfield but also an important Gallo-Roman settlement.

Figure 11.9: The urnfield cemetery of Destelbergen/Eenbeekeinde

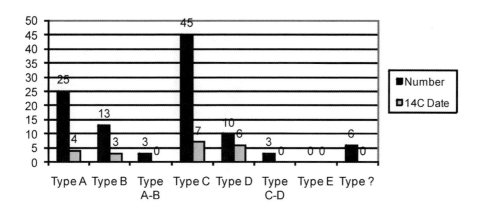

Figure 11.10: Overview of the different cremation types at Destelbergen: (type A: urngrave, type B: urngrave with charcoal fragments, type C: bonepackgrave; type D: cremationgrave style Destelbergen, type E: cremationgrave with mixed remnants).

The evolution of the site was based on the typochronoogical study from the pottery. Other datable objects like metal were rather scarce. The number of cremation graves that could be dated typochronologically by the urns themselves or by associated funeral gifts is limited in comparison with the group of cremations that were not datable (Figure 11.11) – the dated cremations represent only 38.67% of the total number of graves. The group of cremations belonging to the Late Bronze Age (Ha A2–B2/3) are less well represented than the dated Early Iron Age cremations. Central in the layout of the urnfield was a round barrow, about 10m in diameter, which was hypothetically dated to the beginning of the Late Bronze Age (Ha A2) due to its form. This barrow was interpreted as a reminder of the Early and Middle Bronze Age funeral tradition. The modest size was an argument to date this monument rather late in the Bronze Age. According to the excavators this round barrow had to be the starting point of the cemetery. To the East of it was the Late Bronze Age area of the cemetery with some long barrows (*langebed*). These ovular structures had rather limited sizes. They measured about 7.5 to 11m (length) by 3.4 to 5.2m (width). The old finds from 1927–1928 were also dug up in this sector. This pottery displayed the typical shapes and decoration patterns of the Late Bronze Age. The western sector housed the Early Iron Age area with the quadrangular monuments. They can be divided into two subgroups on the basis of their measurements: the first had sizes of 8 to 11m, the second group was larger and varied

233

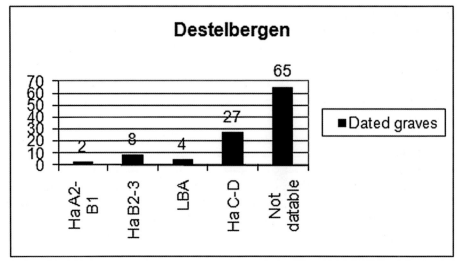

Figure 11.11: Overview of the dated cremations on basis of typochronology and the non-datable graves at Destelbergen.

between 16 to 19m. It was possible to date typochronologically four of the central graves within the ditches to the Ha C phase. The two others were assumed to belong to the same period. Among the cremations in this sector there was a clear dominance of the *Knochenlager* (De Laet *et al.* 1986: 74–78, 87–90).

For the moment 20 cremations are $^{14}$C-dated (Figure 11.12). The results from 10 more samples are expected. There are 22 $^{14}$C-dates available for the site of Destelbergen: six on charcoal and 16 on cremated bone. Only two graves (18 and 75) have been double dated on charcoal and on cremated bone. Both dates from grave 75 match and reflect the same age span. The age difference between the cremated bone and charcoal samples from grave 18 is too large. This difference is probably to be ascribed to the 'old wood' effect.

The first results were surprising for the understanding of the site (Figure 11.13). Only a limited number of $^{14}$C-dates of the Late Bronze Age have been realized. Two graves are dated in the Late Bronze Age. The oldest absolutely dated grave (68) in the site fits in the phase Ha A2–B1 (KIA-34157: 2875±30 BP). It has been obtained using charcoal. The second $^{14}$C-date (KIA-34923: 2755±30 BP) comes from an urngrave that had been disturbed by one of the later Iron Age quadrangular monuments. It is the only Late Bronze Age cremation that is located in the Early Iron Age area of the cemetery.

Most dates are situated in the Early Iron Age period, but cannot be refined due to the problem of the so-called Hallstatt plateau. The majority of the cremations are chronologically situated in the expected Early Iron Age period. Surprisingly, some cremations belong to the Late Iron Age. This period was not recognized in the former study of the site based on a typochronological analysis from the funerary pottery. The pottery of the beginning of the Late Iron Age (Early La Tène I) is characterised by typical biconical shapes. Because of the lack of this kind of ceramics, the cemetery was assumed to stop at the end of the Early Iron Age around 500 BC. Some of the younger dates belong to the Late Iron Age, especially the fourth-third century BC. One single date has even a possible chronological range until the first half of the first century BC (KIA-34909: 2120±30BP). These dates prove that the urnfield at Destelbergen was in use longer than was initially supposed. It contradicts the current opinion that the urnfield cemeteries of the 'Flemish' group stop at the end of the Early Iron Age before 500/450 BC

The $^{14}$C-dates have also shed a new light on the dating of the funeral monuments of Destelbergen. The hypothesis that the circular monument represent the oldest phase of the site was tested by dating the central grave (91). This 'bone-pack-grave', has been dated to the Early Iron Age (KIA-34179: 2400±30 BP). This cremation can be situated from the mid eight century until the beginning of the fourth century BC. This monument belongs also to the Early Iron Age occupation of the site. Three of the quadrangular monuments have their central grave dated on cremated bone (Figure 11.14). The structures at Destelbergen are believed to be the oldest known examples of this type in Europe. One date corresponds with the assumed chronological attribution to the Early Iron Age (grave 12: KIA-34892: 2495±30 BP), although the typochronological date points to Ha C. The results for the two other cremations are later. Both grave 71 (KIA-34887: 2320±30 BP) and grave 57 (KIA-30042: 2215±30 BP) can be situated in a time span from the fifth to the third century BC.

The basic idea about the horizontal stratigraphy and chronological evolution at Destelbergen can be preserved in a slightly modified version. The eastern sector is predominantly used during the Late Bronze Age. The round barrow does not belong to the beginning of the Late Bronze Age but needs to be integrated in the Early Iron Age funerary landscape of the site.

# New ideas about the urnfields

To sum up the results of this dating project on Destelbergen and Tessenderlo the absolute dates, obtained by dating the cremated bones, do not always match with the 'classical typochronology' of the urnfield pottery, which had already been assessed by dating other cemeteries in the Flemish group (De Mulder *et al.* 2007: 508–511). A review of this chronology is necessary but

| Grave nr. | Lab. nr. | Material | Age BP | Calibrated date (2σ) | |
|-----------|----------|----------|--------|----------------------|---|
| 9 | KIA-34178 | Cremated bone | 2360±30BP | 530BC (95.4%) | 380BC |
| 10 | KIA-34923 | Cremated bone | 2755±30BP | 980BC (95.4%) | 820BC |
| 12 | KIA-34892 | Cremated bone | 2495±30BP | 790BC (95.4%) | 510BC |
| 18 | KIA-35797 | Charcoal | 2440±30BP | 760BC (22.2%) | 680BC |
| | | | | 670BC ( 8.7%) | 610BC |
| | | | | 600BC (64.5%) | 400BC |
| 18 | KIA-34910 | Cremated bone | 2330±35BP | 520BC (90.3%) | 350BC |
| | | | | 290BC ( 5.1%) | 230BC |
| 26 | KIA-35363 | Cremated bone | 2590±30BP | 820BC (87.5%) | 750BC |
| | | | | 690BC ( 6.3%) | 660BC |
| | | | | 620BC ( 1.6%) | 590BC |
| 32 | KIA-35353 | Cremated bone | 2370±30BP | 540BC (95.4%) | 380BC |
| 33 | KIA-34154 | Charcoal | 2460±30BP | 760BC (26.5%) | 680BC |
| | | | | 670BC (68.9%) | 410BC |
| 35 | KIA-comb | Cremated bone | 2500±60BP | 800BC (87.3%) | 480BC |
| | | | | 470BC ( 8.1%) | 410BC |
| 36 | KIA-30041 | Cremated bone | 2480±30BP | 770BC (90.9%) | 480BC |
| | | | | 470BC ( 4.5%) | 410BC |
| 65 | KIA-35364 | Cremated bone | 2515±30BP | 790BC (95.4%) | 530BC |
| 68 | KIA-34157 | Charcoal | 2875±30BP | 1190BC ( 1.4%) | 1170BC |
| | | | | 1160BC ( 1.7%) | 1140BC |
| | | | | 1130BC (88.1%) | 970BC |
| | | | | 960BC ( 4.2%) | 930BC |
| 71 | KIA-34887 | Cremated bone | 2320±30BP | 490BC ( 1.0%) | 460BC |
| | | | | 420BC (87.3%) | 350BC |
| | | | | 290BC ( 7.2%) | 230BC |
| 75 | KIA-35796 | Charcoal | 2490±30BP | 750BC (15.7%) | 680BC |
| | | | | 670BC ( 4.0%) | 640BC |
| | | | | 560BC (75.8%) | 400BC |
| 75 | KIA-34922 | Cremated bone | 2420±30BP | 750BC (15.7%) | 680BC |
| | | | | 670BC ( 4.0%) | 640BC |
| | | | | 560BC (75.8%) | 400BC |
| 83 | KIA-34893 | Cremated bone | 2435±35BP | 760BC (20.8%) | 680BC |
| | | | | 670BC ( 8.7%) | 610BC |
| | | | | 600BC (65.9%) | 400BC |
| 84 | IRPA-476 | Charcoal | 2430±50BP | 760BC (20.1%) | 680BC |
| | | | | 670BC (75.3%) | 400BC |
| 86 | KIA-34180 | Cremated bone | 2390±30BP | 730BC ( 5.5%) | 690BC |
| | | | | 550BC (89.9%) | 390BC |
| 87 | IRPA-477 | Charcoal | 2410±55BP | 760BC (17.9%) | 680BC |
| | | | | 670BC (77.5%) | 390 BC |
| 91 | KIA-34179 | Cremated bone | 2400±30BP | 740BC ( 8.2%) | 690BC |
| | | | | 660BC ( 1.2%) | 650BC |
| | | | | 550BC (85.9%) | 390BC |

Figure 11.12: Overview of the [14]C-results on cremated bone and charcoal from the urnfield at Destelbergen.

236

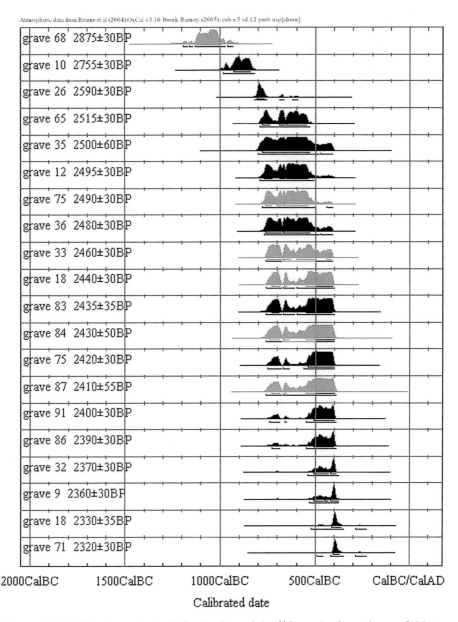

Figure 11.13: The chronological distribution of the $^{14}$C-results from the urnfield at Destelbergen. The charcoal samples are in grey.

Atmospheric data from Reimer et al (2004);OxCal v3.10 Bronk Ramsey (2005); cub r:5 sd:12 prob usp[chron]

grave 68  2875±30BP

grave 10  2755±30BP

grave 26  2590±30BP

grave 65  2515±30BP

grave 35  2500±60BP

grave 12  2495±30BP

grave 75  2490±30BP

grave 36  2480±30BP

grave 33  2460±30BP

grave 18  2440±30BP

grave 83  2435±35BP

grave 84  2430±50BP

grave 75  2420±30BP

grave 87  2410±55BP

grave 91  2400±30BP

grave 86  2390±30BP

grave 32  2370±30BP

grave 9  2360±30BP

grave 18  2330±35BP

grave 71  2320±30BP

2000CalBC        1500CalBC        1000CalBC        500CalBC        CalBC/CalAD

Calibrated date

Figure 11.13: The chronological distribution of the $^{14}$C-results from the urnfield at Destelbergen. The charcoal samples are in grey.

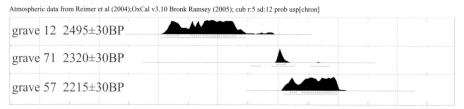

Atmospheric data from Reimer et al (2004);OxCal v3.10 Bronk Ramsey (2005); cub r:5 sd:12 prob usp[chron]

grave 12  2495±30BP

grave 71  2320±30BP

grave 57  2215±30BP

1200CalBC  1000CalBC  800CalBC  600CalBC   400CalBC  200CalBC  CalBC/CalAD

Calibrated date

Figure 11.14: ¹⁴C-dates of the quadrangular monuments at Destelbergen.

more dates on pottery from the cremation graves are necessary to establish a new typochronology.

The available absolute dates for the urnfields in Flanders make it possible to review the phenomenon of the appearance of these cemeteries in the region. A majority of the barrows in the Middle Bronze Age are constructed between 1800–1500 BC. Afterwards they are still being used as is shown by their secondary burials (Bourgeois and Cherretté 2005: 56; Toron 2006: 74–75). It is traditionally supposed that the urnfield cemeteries represent a cultural rupture with the preceding period because they are created in new areas away from the barrow cemeteries. The ring ditch structure at Tessenderlo is dated at the transition period of the barrow tradition around 1500 BC. The other ¹⁴C-dates of the site suggest that there is a chronological gap between this burial and the functioning from the site as an urnfield cemetery. The urnfield seems to start around 1100–1000 BC. At Haps in the Netherlands the development of an urnfield around a Middle Bronze Age funerary site is also witnessed (Verwers 1972: 143–145, Lanting and van der Plicht 2001/2002: 195, 221). One of the cremations in Blicquy can be situated in the same period (KIA-23752: 3185±30 BP). The majority of the ¹⁴C-dates indicate that the site was in use from the fourteenth to the tenth century BC. This suggests an early start of the urnfield cemetery at Blicquy (De Mulder *et al.* 2007: 511). The urnfield of Neerharen-Rekem was believed to start around the traditional date of 1100 BC, although some urns still reflected the influence from the Middle Bronze Age Hilversum/Drakenstein pottery (De Boe *et al.* 1992: 482). Here ¹⁴C-dates have also proved an early beginning. The urnfield started in the second half of the Middle Bronze Age and stayed in use during the whole period of the Late Bronze Age and Early Iron Age as assumed by the typochronology of the urns (Van Impe pers. comm.).

Other available ¹⁴C-dates are later, but point to a possible start of the urnfield phenomenon in the period of Ha1 or the transition to Ha A2. The two cremations at Beerse, found in connection with a long barrow surrounded by a triple row of postholes, were dated around 2945±35 BP (KIA-33613) and 2935±35 BP (KIA-32362) (Delaruelle *et al.* 2008: 34). While some of the oldest graves at Velzeke/Paddestraat do not exclude a start of the site as an urnfield before 1100 BC (De Mulder *et al.* 2007: 511).

This hypothesis is further supported by sites from the southern Netherlands. Some of these dates were obtained using cremated bone from graves in urns of the type Laren or related forms like at Haps and Sint-Oedenrode (Lanting and van der Plicht 2001–2002: 221). At Lent 'Smitjesland a small cemetery with 10 cremation-graves was excavated. The urns still resemble a Middle Bronze Age tradition, but are of a better quality. Radiocarbon dates on three cremated bone samples place it in the twelfth- first half of the eleventh century BC (van den Broeke 2001: 135–136).

As already mentioned the tradition of the urnfields stops generally around the end of the Early Iron Age. In the area of the 'Northwestern' group some cemeteries stayed in use longer, until around 400 BC. For the first time in the western part of Flanders the use of an urnfield cemetery beyond the end of the Early Iron Age has been proven. According to the available dates an occupation until the fourth-third century BC is clearly attested for the cemetery of Destelbergen; one date suggests an even later existence until the second-first century BC. Two of the quadrangular funeral monuments were also of a later period. They can be dated between 400–200 BC. Both are located in the southern part of the cemetery and belong to the subgroup with larger sizes. Related indirect information for later period quadrangular monuments was found on other sites. At the Bronze Age cemetery of Oedelem in western Flanders a date on charcoal from the bottom of the ditch of a rectangular monument situated it in the period between 390–220 cal BC (KIA-14815: 2240±30 BP) (Cherretté and Bourgeois 2005: 30). This is also confirmed by different radiocarbon dates from the southern Netherlands which locates this type of monument in the Early Iron Age and also in the beginning of the Late Iron Age (Lanting and van der Plicht 2005/2006: 300–303).

# Conclusion

The possibility of dating cremated bone offers new insights in the evolution of the urnfield cemeteries. The supposed chronology of the use of some cemeteries needs correction. Due to the $^{14}$C-dates it becomes possible to document the transition between 1500–1100 BC from the main barrow building period to the full blossoming of the urnfields in the Late Bronze Age. It has been shown that some of these sites start earlier then previously thought, placing them in the Middle Bronze Age instead of the Late Bronze Age. The present picture thus points to a complex and diverse scheme of regional and local evolution of the funeral ritual.

This work shows that some ideas about the regional cultural-historical processes of the Late Bronze Age and Iron Age will have to be modified and further work on controlling and correcting the existing typo-chronology will be necessary. However, we must take into account some of the limitations: it is still difficult on the basis of $^{14}$C-dates to establish a fine chronology as has been done with the typo-chronological studies of pottery and metalwork. Also, the Hallstatt plateau limits the potential of chronological work for the Early Iron Age.

These new insights change our ideas about the Iron Age funerary landscape of western Flanders. It has been proven that at least one urnfield existed into the Late Iron Age helping to fill the gap in our knowledge of funerary ritual and sites.

# Bibliography

Bourgeois, J. (1989a). De ontdekking van nieuwe grondstoffen en de eerste metaalbewerkers in Temse en in het Waasland. In H. Thoen (ed.) *Temse en de Schelde. Van IJstijd tot Romeinen*: 44–68. Brusssel: Gemeentekrediet.

Bourgeois, J. (1989b). Grafrituelen in de ijzertijd in de provincie Oost-Vlaanderen. Nieuwe gegevens uit de opgravingen van Ursel en Kemzke. In *XLIX^e Congres van de Federatie van Kringen voor Oudheidkunde en Geschiedenis van België. Congrès de Namur. 18–21 VIII 1988. Handelingen II*: 79–92. Namur.

Bourgeois, J. and B. Cherretté (2005). L'âge du Bronze et le premier âge du Fer dans les Flandres occidentale et orientale (Belgique): un état de la question. In J. Bourgeois and M. Talon (eds.) *L'âge Bronze du Nord de la France dans son contexte européen* : 43–81. Paris: CTHS/APRAB.

Bronk Ramsey, C. (1995). Radiocarbon calibration and analysis of stratigraphy: the Oxcal program. *Radiocarbon* 37(2): 425–30.

Bronk Ramsey, C. (2001). Development of the radiocarbon calibration program. *Radiocarbon* 43(2A): 355–363.

Brun, P. (1984). *La Civilisation des Champs d'Urnes, étude critique dans le Bassin parisien*, Documents d'Archéologie Française 4. Paris: Editions MSH.

Brun, P. (1988). L' entité «Rhin-Suisse-France orientale»: nature et évolution. In P. Brun and C. Mordant (eds.) *Le groupe Rhin-Suisse-France oriëntale et la notion de la civilisation des Champs d'Urnes*: 599–620. Mémoires du Musée de Préhistoire d'Ile-de-France 1. Nemours: Editions A.P.R.A.I.F.

Cherretté, B. and J. Bourgeois (2005). Circles for the dead. Early and Middle Bronze Age funerary practices in Western Flanders – Belgium (2000–1100 BC). In R. Laffineur, J. Driessen and E. Warmenbol (eds.) *Actes du XIVème Congrès UISPP, Université de Liège, Belgique, 2–8 septembre 2001. Section 11 L'âge du bronze en Europe et en Méditerranée. Sessions générales et posters*: 25–31. Oxford: British Archaeological Reports, International Series, 1337.

Creemers, G. (1994). Noodonderzoek van een urnenveld te Tessenderlo-Engsbergen (Limb.). *Lunula. Archaeologia protohistorica* 2: 27.

Creemers, G. (1997). Het urnenveld van Tessenderlo-Engsbergen (Lb.). *Lunula. Archaeologia protohistorica* 5 : 13.

De Laet, S. J. (1982). *La Belgique d'avant les Romains.* Wetteren: Editions Universa.

De Boe, G., M. De Bie, and L. Van Impe (1992). Neerharen-Rekem. Die komplexe Besiedlungsgeschichte einer vor den Kiesbaggern geretteten Fundstatte. In *Spurensicherung. Archäologische Denkmalpflege in der Euregio Maas-Rhein*: 477–496. Mainz: Philipp von Zabern Verlag.

De Laet, S. J and M. E. Marien (1950). La nécropole de Lommel-Kattenbosch. *L'Antiquité Classique* 19: 309–366.

De Laet, S. J., J. A. E. Nenquin and P. Spitaels (1958). *Contributions à l'étude de la civilisation des champs d'urnes en Flandre*, Dissertationes Archaeologicae Gandenses 4. Brugge: De Tempel.

De Laet, S. J., J. A. E. Nenquin P. Spitaels and A. Van Doorselaer (1958(1961)). Het urnenveld van Destelbergen. *Nieuwe Oudheidkundige Opgravingen en Vondsten in Oostvlaanderen* II: 38–52.

De Laet, S. J., H. Thoen and J. Bourgeois (1986). *Les fouilles du Séminaire d'Archéologie de la Rijkuniversiteit te Gent à Destelbergen-Eenbeekeinde (1960–1984) et l'histoire la plus ancienne de la région de Gent (Gand). I. La période préhistorique*, Dissertationes Archaeologicae Gandenses 23. Brugge: De Tempel.

Delaruelle, St., B. De Smaele and J. Van Doninck (2008). Ovalen voor de doden. Opgraving van een grafmonument uit de bronstijd aan de Mezenstraat in Beerse (provincie Antwerpen, België). *Lunula. Archaeologia protohistorica* 16: 31–38.

De Mulder, G. (1994). Aspects of the funeral ritual in the Late Bronze Age and the Early Iron Age in the western part of the Flemish region. *Helinium* 34(1): 94–133.

De Mulder, G. and J. Bourgeois (forthcoming). Les tombes à restes de bûcher dans les nécropoles du Bronze final et premier Âge du Fer dans le province de la Flandre orientale (Belgique). *Revue du Nord.*

De Mulder, G. and M. Van Strydonck (2008). Een [14]C-datering van het urnengrafveld te Kontich/Duffelsesteenweg (provincie Antwerpen, België), *Lunula. Archaeologia protohistorica* 16: 61–63.

De Mulder, G., M. Van Strydonck and M. Boudin (2004). [14]C-dateringen op gecremeerd menselijk bot uit de urnengrafvelden te Velzeke (O.-Vl.). *Lunula. Archaeologia protohistorica* 12: 51–58.

De Mulder, G., M. Van Strydonck, M. Boudin, W. Leclercq, N. Paridaens and E. Warmenbol (2007). Re-evaluation of the late Bronze Age and early Iron Age chronology of the western Belgian urnfields based on [14]C dating. *Radiocarbon* 49(2): 499–514.

Desittere, M. (1968). *De Urnenveldenkultuur in het gebied tussen Neder-Rijn en Noordzee (Periodes Ha A en B)*, Dissertationes Archaeologicae Gandenses 11. Brugge: De Tempel.

Fullola, J. M, V. M. Guerrero, M. À. Petit, M. Calvo, A. Malgosa, N. Armentano, P. Arnau and S. Cho (2007). La Cova de Pas (Ferreries, Menorca): un avanç. In *L'Arqueologia à Menorca: eina per al coneixement del passat.* Llibres del patrimoni històric i cultural: 95–110. Menorca: Consell Insular de Menorca.

Gerritsen, F. (2003). *Local identities. Landscape and community in the late prehistoric Meuse-Demer-Schelde-region*, Amsterdam Archaeological Studies 9. Amsterdam: Amsterdam University Press.

Hassan, A. A., J. D. Termine and C. V. Haynes (1977). Mineralogical studies on bone apatite and their implications for radiocarbon dating. *Radiocarbon* 19(3): 364–374.

Hatt, J. J. (1961). Chronique de protohistoire V: une nouvelle chronologie de l'âge du Bronze final. Exposé critique du système chronologique de H. Müller-Karpe. *Bulletin de la Société Préhistorique Française* 58: 184–195.

Lanting, J. N. and A. L. Brindley (1998). Dating cremated bone: the dawn of a new era. *Journal of Irish Arcaeology* 9: 1–7.

Lanting, J. N., A. T. Aerts-Bijma and J. van der Plicht (2001). Dating of cremated bones. *Radiocarbon* 43 (2A): 249–254.

Lanting, J. N. and J. van der Plicht (2001/2002). De [14]C-chronologie van de Nederlandse pre- en protohistorie IV: bronstijd en vroege ijzertijd. *Palaeohistoria* 43–44: 117–262.

Lanting, J. N. and J. van der Plicht (2005/2006). De [14]C-chronologie van de Nederlandse pre- en protohistorie V: midden en late ijzertijd. *Palaeohistoria* 47–48: 241–427.

Mays, S. (1998). *The Archaeology of Human Bones*. London: Routledge.

Mertens, J. (1951). *Een urnengrafveld te Aarschot-Langdorp*. Archaeologia Belgica, 5. Brussel: Nationale Dienst voor Opgravingen.

Müller-Karpe, H. (1959). *Beiträge zur Chronologie der Urnenfelderzeit nördlich und südlich der Alpen*. Römisch-Germanische Forschungen XXII. Berlin: Verlag Walter de Gruyter.

Munro, L. E., F. J. Longstaffe and C. D. White (2007). Burning and boiling of modern deer bone: effects on crystallinity and oxygen isotope composition of bioapatite phosphate. *Palaeogeography, Palaeoclimatology, Palaeoecology* 249: 90–102.

Naysmith, P., E. M. Scott, G. T. Cook, J. Heinemeier, J. van der Plicht, M. Van Strydonck, C. Bronk Ramsey, P. M. Grootes and S. P. H. T. Freeman (2007). A cremated bone inter-comparison study. *Radiocarbon* 49(2): 403–408.

Olsen, J., J. Heinemeier, P. Bennike, C. Krause, K. M. Hornstrup and H. Thrane (2007). Characterisation and blind testing of radiocarbon dating of cremated bone. *Journal of Archaeological Science* 35(3) : 791–800.

Robertz, A. (2008). La grotte de la "Roche Alberic" à Couvin (province de namur, Belgique; âge du Fer): contribution par l'étude du matériel céramique. *Lunula. Archaeologia protohistorica* 16 : 107–116.

Reimer, P. J., M. G. L. Baillie, E. Bard, A. Bayliss, J. Warren Beck, C. J. H. Bertrand, P. G. Blackwell, C. E. Buck, G. S. Burr, K.B. Cutler, P. E. Damon, E. Lawrence Edwards, R. G. Fairbanks, M. Friedrich, T. P. Guilderson, K. A. Hogg, B. Kromer, G. McCormac, S. Manning, C. Bronk Ramsey, R. W. Reimer, S. Remmele, J. R. Southon, M. Stuiver, S. Talamo, F. W. Taylor, J. van der Plicht and C. E. Weyhenmeyer (2004). IntCal 04 terrestrial radiocarbon age calibration, 0–26 cal kyr BP. *Radiocarbon* 46 (3): 1029–1058.

Roymans, N. and F. Kortlang (1999a). Urnfield symbolism and social organization in the Lower Rhine region: the Beegden cemetery. In *Eliten in der Bronzezeit. Ergebnisse zweier Kolloquien in Mainz und Athen*. Monographien des römischen-germanischen Zentralmuseums, 43: 277–317. Bonn: Rudolf Habelt Verlag.

Roymans, N. and F. Kortlang (1999b). Urnfield symbolism, ancestors and the land in the Lower Rhine region. In F. Theuws and N. Roymans (eds.) *Land and Ancestors. Cultural dynamics in the Urnfield period and the Middle Ages in the Southern Netherlands*. Amsterdam Archaeological Studies, 4: 33–61. Amsterdam: Amsterdam University Press.

Saliège, J.-F., A. Person, and F. Paris (1998). Datation du carbonate-hydroxylapatite d'ossements Holocenes du Sahel (Mali, Mauritanie, Niger). In *Pré-actes du 3ème Congrès International [14]C et Archéologie*, Lyon : 172–173.

Shipman, P., G. F. Foster and M. Schoeninger (1984). Burnt bones and teeth: an experimental study of colour, morphology, crystal structure and shrinkage. *Journal of Archaeological Science* 11: 307–325.

Theunissen, M. (1993). Het grafveld van Rijkevorsel/Hellehoekheide (A.) 700–400 BC. *Lunula. Archaeologia protohistorica* 1: 41–42.

Toron, S. (2006). De la Picardie aux Flandres belges: une approche comparative des enclos circulaires de l'âge du Bronze ancien et moyen. *Lunula. Archaeologia protohistorica* 14: 71–76.

van den Broeke, P.W.(2001). Een gordel van macht en pracht. Het Midden-Nederlandse rivierengebied in het 1[ste] millennium v. Chr. In J. Bourgeois, Ph. Crombé, G. De Mulder and M. Rogge (eds.) *Een duik in het verleden. Schelde, Maas en Rijn in de pre- en protohistorie.* Publicaties van het Provinciaal Archeologisch Museum van Zuid-Oost-Vlaanderen – site Velzeke. Gewone reeks 4: 131–156. Zottegem: Provinciaal Archeologisch Museum van Zuid-Oost-Vlaanderen – site Velzeke.

Van Impe, L. (1980). *Urnenveld uit de Late Bronstijd en de Vroege IJzertijd te Donk. I Beschrijvende inventaris.* Archaeologia Belgica, 224. Brussel: Nationale Dienst voor Opgravingen.

Van Strydonck, M., M. Boudin, M. Hoefkens and G. De Mulder (2005). $^{14}$C-dating of cremated bones, why does it work? *Lunula. Archaeologia protohistorica* 16: 61–63.

Van Strydonck, M., M. Boudin and G. De Mulder (2009). $^{14}$C-dating of cremated bones: the issue of sample contamination. *Radiocarbon* 51(2): 553–568.

Verlaeckt, K.(1996). *Between River and Barrow. A reappraisal of Bronze Age metalwork found in the province of East-Flanders (Belgium)*, Oxford: British Archaeological Reports, International Series 632.

Verwers, G. J. (1972). *Das Kamps Veld in Neolithikum, bronzezeit und Eisenzeit*, Analecta Praehistorica Leidensia V. Leiden: Leiden University Press.

Warmenbol, E. (1988). Le groupe Rhin-Suisse-France orientale et les grottes sépulcrales du Bronze final en Haute Belgique. In P. Brun and C. Mordant (eds.) *Le groupe Rhin-Suisse-France oriëntale et la notion de la civilisation des Champs d'Urnes*: 153–158. Mémoires du Musée de Préhistorie d'Ile-de-France 1. Nemours: Editions A.P.R.A.I.F.

## CHAPTER 12

# HUMANS AND ANIMALS: A DEADLY COMBINATION? THE IDENTIFICATION OF BOVINE TUBERCULOSIS IN ARCHAEOLOGICAL FAUNAL MATERIAL. WORKING TOWARDS DIFFERENTIAL DIAGNOSTIC CRITERIA

*Jeanette Wooding*

*(University of Bradford)*

## Abstract

Tuberculosis is a disease of considerable antiquity. The fact that the bovine strain (*M. bovis*) is anthropozoonotic provides the ideal opportunity to study both the human and animal populations of the past, through the medium of disease. The opportunity is therefore afforded to gain a better understanding of the socio-economic environment in which humans and animals first came into prolonged contact with each other. This close interdependent relationship became established over time and has ultimately resulted in the society in which we live today; however, it came at a price – zoonotic disease. This paper provides a succinct review of the history of *M. bovis* in both archaeological human and faunal remains and emphasises the need for comprehensive skeletal criteria within a standardised recording framework. The primary aim of the doctoral research from which this paper derives is centred upon the production of differential diagnostic criteria for the identification of tuberculous lesions in faunal material (specifically cattle and pig bone). This further expands upon the postgraduate research of Roha (2005). Basic skeletal lesion patterning maps for cattle and pig are presented as a starting point for the further understanding of lesion patterning and predilection sites. These are intended to provide the first step to potentially identifying this disease in disarticulated archaeological faunal remains. The ability to recognise and record the manifestation and aetiology of tuberculosis in faunal material will provide a better understanding of disease prevalence and its impact on past society – in particular the Iron Age in southern Britain.

# Introduction

Tuberculosis (TB) is one of the most prolific infectious diseases in human history. Having plagued past populations for thousands of years, it is still a leading cause of death due to infectious disease in the world today (Thoen *et al.* 2009: 136). However, TB is not just a disease of humans. It is a highly adaptable, opportunistic disease possessing several strains of *mycobacteria* that have the ability to infect all types of mammal and bird, both wild and domesticated (Belschner 1967: 54), a fact that has been alluded to from at least the Roman Period, if not earlier (see Meinecke 1927). The dynamics of the human/animal relationship is a topic of research that evokes much interest and debate. Animals form an integral part of human life and have done since the first humans began to hunt them. However, this relationship was to change forever with the advent of domestication, when humans began to dominate animals, become their masters and in some cases mismanage them. This change in relationship dynamic was central to the development of civilisation and society; however, it came at a price – *zoonotic disease*. This research seeks to study and further explore the human/animal relationship through the analysis of arguably one of the most infamous zoonotic diseases, bovine tuberculosis (bTB).

# Bovine tuberculosis: a zoonotic disease

The 'Mycobacterium Tuberculosis Complex' (MTB) consists of several species of *mycobacteria*, but it is the bovine strain in particular that forms the main focus of the author's research. *Mycobacterium bovis* possesses 'one of the broadest host ranges of all known pathogens' (O'Reilly and Daborn 1995: 1). Many different species of mammal, including humans can contract this strain (Vincent and Gutierrez Perez 1999: 139). However, it is cattle along with both bison and buffalo that are the natural hosts for this pathogen (DEFRA 2008) hence the name 'bovine tuberculosis'. Bovine tuberculosis is not only a disease that can be contracted by humans and other mammals, but is also transmissible between them (Bathurst and Barta 2004: 917). This type of disease is zoonotic or as some prefer 'anthropozoonotic' (*ibid.*).

The transmission of zoonotic diseases like bTB between animals and humans makes their aetiology heavily intertwined with the history, development and subsequent establishment of agriculture and settled societies. This makes for an interesting avenue of research especially from an archaeological and anthropological viewpoint. Inevitably, however, there are a number of obstacles to research incorporating zoonoses, particularly where archaeological assemblages are concerned. A pivotal problem is the differential diagnosis of osseous lesions in disarticulated, co-mingled and more often than not highly fragmented archaeological faunal material. A second is the difficulty faced when attempting to study the impact of this disease in past human populations when it is impossible to distinguish macroscopically which strain of the disease was ultimately responsible for the osseous lesions present in the bones (Moda *et al.*1996: 103), if indeed they are present in the first place. This latter point lends itself to the third problem. Even if bTB is successfully identified in faunal assemblages, it will unfortunately be impossible to gain an accurate indication of its true prevalence in the human and domestic animal populations of the past because not all humans and animals afflicted with the disease would have survived long enough for osseous lesions to develop, either as a result of acute illness or because in the case of domestic livestock, the animal was slaughtered prior to the skeleton becoming affected. It also has to be emphasised that bones that display no lesions may also indicate disease free animals. Therefore, we are faced with a further complication to our understanding.

If these impediments can be tackled, then the implications are profound. Not only would a greater insight as regards the aetiology and pathogenesis of this disease be provided, but also the beginnings of an improved understanding of potential frequency and prevalence. Added to this, the prospect of a better perception of husbandry regimes and agricultural intensification as well as a more informed grasp of the effect of disease in animals and if and/or how it influenced the treatment and deposition of infected animals. Finally, being able to identify the markers for bTB in particular could provide information on the movement and spread of chronic disease with humans and their animals. The result of such research has value for both Iron Age studies and for modern attempts to combat the spread of this disease. Thereby following the example of '*mortui vivos docent*' – let 'the dead teach the living'.

## Tuberculosis: a disease of considerable antiquity

Up until relatively recently the general consensus (see for example Vincent and Gutierrez Perez 1999; Hershkovitz and Gopher 1999) was that the human strain of TB (*M. tuberculosis*) evolved from the bovine strain (*M. bovis*) at the time of cattle domestication during the Neolithic period. This was a plausible hypothesis considering the newfound closeness of humans and animals at this point in time. However, contrary to this, it was demonstrated in 2002 that *M. tuberculosis* did not evolve from *M. bovis*, in fact, the two species evolved independently of each other from a common ancestor some 15–20,000 years ago (Brosch *et al.* 2002: 3688). Therefore, tuberculosis and more importantly bovine tuberculosis (bTB), pre-dates the domestication of plants and animals and is, consequently, a disease of considerable antiquity. Animals were not the vectors responsible for the appearance of human strain of this disease. In reality, it was the act of adopting a sedentary lifestyle which resulted in a new-found closeness with animals that not only provided ideal conditions for the human strain to thrive (still described in the present day as a 'global emergency' (TB Alert 2005)) but also opened up the flood gates for a whole new disease threat: zoonoses, including most notably bTB.

## Tuberculosis in the Archaeological Record

Lesions characteristic of TB have been identified in human skeletal remains dating as far back as the Neolithic in Italy (Canci *et al.* 1996), the Iron Age in England (Mays and Taylor 2003) and the Pre-Columbian period in the Americas (see Buikstra 1981). There is an abundance of evidence for TB where human remains are concerned, but this is unfortunately not the case for the faunal record. The inability to differentiate between the strains of *M. bovis* and *M. tuberculosis* macroscopically (Moda *et al.* 1996: 103) in human skeletal remains makes it very difficult to gain a true understanding of the prevalence of *M. bovis* in the past. Having said this, people undoubtedly suffered from and died as a result of the bovine strain (see Taylor *et al.* 2007); therefore, a high proportion of domestic animals (particularly cattle, sheep/goat and pig) must also have suffered from the disease, but where is the evidence for this?

# Bovine tuberculosis (bTB) in humans: historical, archaeological and scientific evidence

Accurate figures relating to the prevalence of bTB in humans is difficult to determine even today, so attempting to calculate its prevalence in the more distant past would appear impossible. However, the use of historical evidence as well as the application of ancient DNA (aDNA) analyses on archaeological material can provide broad indications of its general prevalence in past populations/communities. However, when consulting historical records, it is essential that caution be applied to their interpretation, especially where descriptions of disease are involved. These are ultimately subjective accounts and more often than not incorrect due to a combination of lack of knowledge and lack of scientific analytical options.

## Historical Evidence

Tuberculosis has been alluded to in many different guises (Consumption, Scrofula, The White Plague, The King's Evil, Phthisis etc.) over time.

References made by Hippocrates, Aristotle, Aretaeus of Cappadocia and Galen to name but a few, as well as writings within the Susruta and Aynrveda (ancient Hindu texts) (Castiglioni 1933: 8), reveal a detailed insight into the presence of this disease in the past. These sources are unfortunately open for debate as regards their accuracy but nonetheless are supported by the fact that both archaeological and scientific evidence demonstrate that TB is indeed a disease of considerable antiquity. Therefore, some of the written sources maybe accurate and are, as a result, potentially extremely insightful.

It is not until literary sources from ancient Greece are consulted that one begins to see a more consistent, thorough and clinical approach to the diagnosis and treatment of disease. This can be largely attributed to the Greek physician Hippocrates (460–370 BC), who transformed the status of medicine and its study. Dominating the early classical literature, Hippocrates, founded the Hippocratic School of Medicine from which emerged a number of medical texts referred to as the *Hippocratic Corpus*. The pulmonary form of tuberculosis predominates in these texts but there is also mention of the non-pulmonary form, scrofula (Meinecke 1927: 383). Scrofula, derived from the Latin term '*scrofa*' meaning pig or sow (Kiple 1997: 44), commonly resulted in the swelling of the neck lymph glands (Cartwright and Biddiss 2004: 154). It is now known that scrofula represented the non-pulmonary manifestation of TB (tuberculous *adentis*) (Chalke 1962: 304), most likely of bovine origin, having been transmitted through the ingestion of contaminated meat and milk (Kiple 1997: 44). In later times some believed that the touch of a king could cure scrofula, hence it became referred to in the Middle Ages as 'The King's Evil' (Kiple 1997: 44). Those afflicted waited in vast numbers to be touched by the monarch, with Charles II reported to have touched at least 92,107 people up until his death in 1683 (Cartwright and Biddiss 2004: 154). Although these statistics cannot be relied upon as definitive, they do at least provide some indication of the potentially high prevalence of the non-pulmonary form of this disease in the Middle Ages and Early Modern Period (Renaissance) (Dormandy 1999: 4). Unfortunately, in prehistoric times we have no way of knowing the true prevalence of this disease in the human population. However, the avenues of infection in prehistory remain the same as they were in the Middle Ages and even in the present day, indicating the potential for infection.

*Archaeological and Scientific Evidence*

As highlighted previously, the skeletal lesions characteristic of TB in humans have been identified in skeletal remains the world over. However, in order to identify the causative strain responsible for the lesions, scientific analyses in the form of aDNA are necessary. The field of palaeomicrobiology, in particular the application of aDNA analyses to archaeological material, has proved extremely valuable when the impact of 'ancient pathogens' in past populations is concerned. It has been reported that the study of TB is '...the most successful application of the technology...' (Donoghue *et al.* 2004: 584), thus moving beyond the boundaries of macroscopic analysis and opening the door to identifying the specific causative strains of tuberculosis responsible for illness in past human populations. The use of aDNA as a tool to gaining a better understanding of the prevalence of *M. bovis* in the past is invaluable, a fact that is well demonstrated in a recent study by Taylor *et al.* (2007). Five Iron Age human skeletons recovered from a cemetery in southern Siberia were subjected to aDNA analysis (Taylor *et al.* 2007: 1243). Three of the five skeletons possessed skeletal lesions characteristic of TB, with the remaining two displaying new bone formation on a number of vertebrae suggestive of gastro-intestinal tract infection (*ibid.*: 1245). Of these, four yielded the first positive identifications of *M. bovis* in human remains to date (*ibid.*: 1247). The results of this study are extremely promising, particularly as there appears to be a notable lack of *M. bovis* identified from past human and faunal material (Donoghue *et al.* 2004: 588), an observation that is hard to comprehend considering that both people and animals in the past (as attested to by historical and literary evidence) suffered from the disease.

The reasons for the lack of identified *M. bovis* in archaeological human remains has been suggested as being due to two main reasons: 1) it was not a pathogen present within past populations (a fact that has now been refuted with the most recent scientific results as presented by Taylor *et al.* (2007) – see above) and 2) the pathogen was present but only at low levels (Donoghue *et al.* 2004: 588), a much more plausible explanation. As Taylor *et al.* emphasise, *M. bovis* is not a disease that is natural to humans and hence is not 'self maintaining' (Taylor *et al.* 2007: 1243). For *M. bovis* to be present in the human population there has to be a reservoir animal population providing a continual source of infection – as was most likely the case in Siberia where the people were believed to be 'semi-nomadic', employing a pastoralist economy as some still do in the present day (*ibid.*: 1245), whereby they were living/working closely with their animals.

It is important to note, however, that not all cases of TB identified in human skeletal remains from rural farming communities will necessarily be bovine in origin, as a study by Mays *et al.* (2001) demonstrates. During the excavation of a medieval churchyard at the rural site of Wharram Percy, nine cases of skeletal TB were identified. Instead of the expected identification of *M. bovis* as the causative strain, PCR analysis revealed that *M. tuberculosis* was responsible in all nine cases (Mays 2005: 131). Similar analyses on three cattle ribs from the same site displaying pleural lesions were negative. Either the disease was not present in the domestic livestock being reared at this site or the complex taphonomic history of the faunal remains rendered the aDNA too degraded for analysis (*ibid.*). The latter again emphasises the need for a better understanding of the morphology and location of tuberculous osseous lesions in the faunal skeleton.

# Bovine tuberculosis (bTB) in animals: historical, archaeological and scientific evidence

Due to the disarticulated and fragmented nature of archaeological faunal assemblages, it is difficult to identify the aetiology of pathologies, which require the analysis and recording of characteristic lesion patterning. As a consequence, there has been limited research concerning infectious disease and, regrettably, the knowledge concerning bTB as a malady of animals, in terms of skeletal evidence is patchy at best. However, this does not mean that it was not a problem in past animal populations; on the contrary, there is a wealth of historical evidence to suggest that it posed as much a problem for animals as it did for humans. Finding similar evidence in the archaeological record is challenging but definitely not beyond the realms of possibility as a number of case studies have demonstrated.

## *Historical Evidence*

Tuberculosis is referred to in its bovine form by Columella in *c.* AD 50, clearly illustrating that bovine consumption or at the very least pulmonary disorders that resembled consumption was being identified in animals (Meinecke 1927: 395; Pease 1940: 386). Columella writes:

> '...*Ulceration of the lungs is also a source of great destruction to cattle...Thence arise cough and emaciation and finally consumption attacks them.' (De Re Rustica, VI, 14, I, cited in Meinecke 1927: 395–6).*

More detailed descriptions that appear to refer to bovine tuberculosis are contained within the '*Mulomedicina Chironis*' written by Claudius Hermerus in *c.* AD 400 (Meinecke 1927: 398). This text represents the oldest veterinary literary resource and clearly illustrates a full awareness of a disease believed to be bTB in animals (*ibid.*). Claudius Hermerus outlined the symptoms as follows:

> '*At first no fever, but a wasting condition growing steadily worse, till the bones protrude everywhere; the animal chews and eats abnormally because it is constantly hungry; a hard excrement is evacuated and the diseased animal lives for a long time; eventually it can no longer regain its feet and consequently eats lying*

*down, as if resting. The disease consumes the marrow which is not benefited by food taken in; the liver becomes smaller and finally wastes away; by degrees the whole body is consumed like a tree which has been deprived of its larger roots, though sustained temporarily by the smaller ones, but in the end it gradually withers up.' (Mulomedicina (Oder), 47, 48, cited in Meinecke 1927: 398).*

This quote forms an extremely detailed account of a chronic wasting disease afflicting cattle. However, in reality, although the account appears to fit the documented pathogenesis of bTB, there are many diseases whose symptoms could be made to fit this description, including infectious disease and neoplasia (Knüscl pers. comm.). Later in AD 420, Vegetius adds to Claudius Hermerus's description by demonstrating that TB was seen as a disease that could affect both humans and animals. 'Animals suffer with consumption just like men' (Meinecke 1927: 399). Although, the use of 'consumption' cannot be taken to be definitive evidence of the presence of bTB, it clearly illustrates that the concept of zoonotic disease was beginning to take its root in human consciousness, if it had not done so before (*ibid.*). The acknowledgement of the zoonotic nature of TB is also demonstrated in the writings of the *Mosaic Laws* within the *Talmud*. According to the entries within the *Talmud* dating to the second and fifth centuries AD (Steele and Ranney 1958: 908), if an animal upon slaughter displayed lesions that were located between the pleura and lungs, then they were deemed unfit for consumption (Wight 1942: 237). As Wight states 'Since pleural adhesions often accompany tuberculosis of the lungs, the possibility of transmission of the disease from animal to man may have been recognised at that time' (Wight 1942: 237). It is important to highlight that pleural lesions are not solely diagnostic of TB in humans (figure 12.1) or animals. They can be indicative of a chronic respiratory infection that could ultimately have been as a result of a primary TB infection, but equally could also have been as a result of any number of chronic respiratory infections including for example, pneumonia and bronchitis (see Boden 2005). Here in, lesions on the visceral surface of animal ribs must not be viewed as definitive evidence for bTB in fragmentary and co-mingled faunal remains. In articulated material, they can be seen as supporting evidence for a possible diagnosis of pulmonary bTB but only when there is other evidence of the disease present.

## Archaeological and Scientific Evidence

Apart from a case of *M. tuberculosis* identified in a Iroquoian dog dating to the sixteenth century (Bathurst and Barta 2004), and evidence for MTB Complex in a number of mammoth bones (Rothschild *et al.* 2001), there have been no confirmed and subsequently published macroscopic identifications of TB,

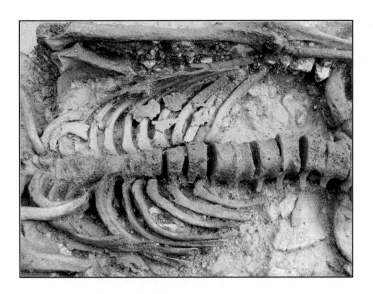

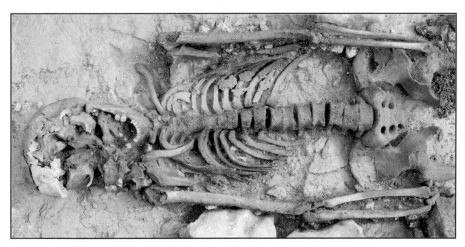

Figure 12.1: Calcified pleural lesions within the left rib cage
(photo: Author with permission from P. Vidal).

specifically bTB in the faunal archaeological record of which the author is
aware. Bathurst and Barta (2004) reported the identification of *M. tuberculosis*
in an articulated dog skeleton recovered from the excavations of a Neutral
Iroquoian site in Canada. The dog displayed pathological alterations associated with 'hypertrophic osteopathy' (HPO), a pathological condition that has
been linked on a number of occasions to a primary infection of tuberculosis,
both in dogs and humans (Bathurst and Barta 2004: 922). Rothschild *et al.*
(2001) describes the successful identification of *M. tuberculosis* complex DNA

from the metacarpal of a fossil mammoth. The mammoth bones, amongst others, were excavated from Natural Trap Cave, Wyoming, and were reported as displaying a rare but 'characteristic' lesion associated with tuberculosis, namely 'granulomatous infection, involving undermining of subchondral surfaces' (Rothschild *et al.* 2001: 2). Independent tests conducted at two laboratories were able to identify *M. tuberculosis* Complex DNA, however, upon spoligotyping, the specific causative strain was unable to be identified, but was found to most closely resemble modern *M. africanum and M. tuberculosis*. It was postulated by the authors that the reasons for the inability to identify a specific strain was due to the age of the sample (17,000 BP), and the fact that at this point in the evolution of the *M. tuberculosis* Complex, speciation of differing strains may not yet have occurred (*ibid.*: 5). This explanation would appear to fit with the research presented by Brosch *et al.* (2002).

Bendrey *et al.* (2008) report the presence of pathological lesions within two Iron Age horse skeletons from southern Britain. Upon differential diagnosis, these lesions were thought to be bacterial in origin and due either to TB or Brucellosis. Unfortunately, as often appears to be the case with archaeological faunal remains, the aDNA analysis was inconclusive and no definitive diagnosis could be entertained. However, this does not mean that the horses did not suffer from TB, but it does suggest that its identification both macroscopically and microscopically in fragmented animal remains may prove extremely difficult. Even when articulated examples are examined – with no definitive scientific confirmation of the causative agent and no modern specimens or differential diagnostic criteria from which to compare, the pathology exhibited is in danger of becoming another 'interesting specimen' as highlighted by Thomas and Mainland (2005: 2). This is where description as emphasised by Bendrey *et al.* (2008) and publication of findings is paramount and upon which this research aims to build.

## The Iron Age in southern Britain

The Iron Age in southern Britain (*c.* 800/700 BC – AD 43), was a period in history dominated by change. As Cunliffe stated, '....the Iron Age marked a turning point in British History' (Cunliffe 2004: 117). The roots of this change originated within the preceding Bronze Age and predominantly stemmed from the division of the surrounding landscape through organised farming and the appearance of a more permanent settlement pattern (*ibid.*). These changes, however, were not conducted in isolation. Britain may be an island separated from the rest of continental Europe by the English Channel, but a trade and communication network – although fluctuating over time – none the less existed from the Neolithic onwards (Mays and Taylor 2003: 194), most evident along the southern and eastern coasts (Haselgrove 1999: 131; Cunliffe 2004: 16). This contact and exchange is supported by the discovery of various prestige-bearing metal artefacts (weapons, jewellery) and pottery demonstrating affiliations with both the La Tène and Hallstatt cultures of France and Germany (Haselgrove 1999: 131). An unavoidable consequence of this long-standing contact with the European continent would undoubtedly have been the introduction and spread of infectious diseases. These diseases (including TB) would have been perfectly suited to the newly adopted and more permanent sedentary lifestyle of the period. As Mays and Taylor stated in relation to the existing trade networks 'These contacts would doubtless have facilitated the spread of disease' (Mays and Taylor 2003: 195), and TB is known to have been present in continental Europe as early as the Neolithic (see Canci *et al.* 1996).

The Iron Age in southern Britain was therefore a period in time that not only instigated change through agriculture and settlement but also witnessed a change in social organisation and cultural identity, leading to the demarcation of tribal zones and the development of tribal elites as witnessed and recorded by the invading Julius Caesar (Bewley 1994: 93). However, was the Iron Age also a period of change in terms of disease prevalence?

## The Presence of TB in Iron Age Britain

Whether TB was indigenous to the native population of Britain or not, it was most definitely present in the Iron Age. Cremation and excarnation appear to have dominated the burial rite during this period (Haselgrove 1999: 123); however, there are a number of notable exceptions that have helped to elucidate information as regards the health of these past peoples. The Iron Age site of Tarrant Hinton in Dorset has yielded the earliest case of this disease identified in Britain to date (Mays and Taylor 2003). The skeleton, one of fifteen inhumations excavated, dates to the Middle Iron Age (400-230 BC) and was associated with a 'small agrarian settlement' (*ibid.*: 189). Ancient DNA analysis using PCR methods identified the causative strain as *M. tuberculosis* (Taylor *et al.* 2005:2239). This illustrates the presence of this disease prior to the arrival of the Romans and predates similar finds by at least 300 years (Mays and Taylor 2003: 193). The present doctoral research has included in its study the faunal assemblage associated with Tarrant Hinton, amongst others, in the hope of identifying osseous lesions potentially indicative of this disease in the corresponding animal population.

Although, the specific strain of TB identified at Tarrant Hinton was *M. tuberculosis* and not *M. bovis*, the very identification of TB in this Iron Age community would suggest that the bovine form of the disease was also most likely present in both the human and animal populations of Iron Age Britain (the potential for which is discussed in the following section 'Settlement and animal husbandry: the human/animal relationship'). Other than the recently identified cases of *M. bovis* in Iron Age human remains from Siberia (see Taylor *et al.* 2007; Murphy *et al.* 2009) as far as the author is aware, there have been no such identifications of the bovine strain within the human or contemporary animal populations from this period within the UK. The reason for its lack of identification to date particularly in archaeological faunal remains is most likely a result of the disarticulated and fragmented nature of the assemblages and the lack of standardised recording of animal palaeopathology up until recently. Having said this, the Iron Age is also characterised by the presence of articulated animal burials. Complete animal burials have been excavated at Garton Slack (Noddle 1979), as well as at Danebury (Grant 1984) and at Viables Farm (Millett and Russell 1982) to name but a few. Some burials are complete, with others just represented by a limb or a cranium (Hill 1995: 14). Debate as regards the nature of these animal deposits continues with some referring to them as 'special animal deposits' and associating them with ritual, whereas others appear inclined to believe they were just rubbish (Hill 1995: 13-15) (see Morris 2008). This is not the venue for a detailed discussion concerning the ritual and beliefs of the Iron Age, but the presence of these animal burials does provide the rare opportunity to study complete remains and, in some instances, study animal remains that were potentially buried due to disease. If articulated animal skeletons are found to be pathological then the rare opportunity is afforded to analyse the patterning of those pathological lesions and differentially diagnosis them. This could lead to future identifications of bTB, leading to a better understanding of this strain of the disease in the domesticated animals of Iron Age Britain.

## Settlement and Animal Husbandry: The Human/Animal Relationship

The settlement evidence is extremely rich for southern Britain in the Iron Age. There is an abundance of archaeological remains attributable to many different types of settlement, both surviving as cropmarks and as upstanding structures (Haselgrove 1999: 113). The overwhelming majority of settlements excavated from this period are related to habitation; they differ in morphology, size, agricultural intensity and function both regionally and over time, however, they all share a common theme. From large-scale highly populated hillforts down to the less densely populated farmsteads containing one or more family groups, the emphasis is clearly on the close inter-dependant relationship shared between humans and their animals. There is no direct evidence to suggest that humans and animals were living under the same roof, but due to the evidence associated with the Iron Age economy and the animal husbandry employed, it is safe to say that humans and animals shared a very close relationship. Small ancillary roundhouse structures may well have functioned as animal pens (Hambleton 1999: 1) located within close proximity to the living areas. In addition to this, the distinctively shaped 'banjo' enclosures identified within the Iron Age landscape have been postulated as having had an agricultural function related to the corralling of animals (*ibid*.: 1).

The evidence for animal husbandry in the Iron Age, as with the settlement evidence, also appears to follow certain trends, being dependent upon geographical region, geology, topography, environmental conditions, settlement type and date as outlined by Hambleton (1999: 41–60). From the archaeozoological research conducted, the Iron Age animal economy on the whole appears to have been centred upon sheep/goat and cattle, with pig also raised but to a lesser extent (Maltby 1996: 20; Haselgrove 1999: 115). The overall frequency of sheep/goat in comparison to cattle rises over time, a trend particularly evident in the southern regions. This is associated with an increase in arable farming (Hambleton 1999: 87). Mortality profiles suggest that sheep/goat and cattle were used for both their primary and secondary products throughout the Iron Age in varying frequencies dependant on region and those geographical/environmental factors highlighted earlier (*ibid*.: 90). Sheep appear to have been highly valued for their wool in preference to meat production in the earlier Iron Age, according to Maltby (1996: 22, 23) with cattle displaying more variation (*ibid*.: 21).

Faunal analysis is not the only avenue of research that provides evidence related to the types of animal husbandry practiced in the Iron Age. Copley *et al*. (2005) provides definitive evidence of dairying at four Iron Age sites in Britain, including Danebury Hillfort, Maiden Castle, Stanwick (Northants) and Yarnton Cresswell Field (Copley *et al*. 2005: 485). Two hundred and thirty-seven pottery vessels were found to contain lipid residues, which upon further analysis were identified as dairy fats. It was concluded that milk was derived from 'a variety of ruminant sources' (*ibid*.: 489), which is supported by the fact that cattle and sheep/goat have also been found to dominate the faunal assemblages of the Iron Age (*ibid*.: 493), (see Hambleton 1999 for overview).

Evidence for dairying, whether it be through artefactual evidence, faunal assemblages or the analysis of lipid residues could potentially indicate which sites to concentrate on when trying to identify zoonotic diseases such as bTB in both human and faunal remains. As highlighted earlier, the consumption of infected milk is one of the primary avenues of infection for this disease, particularly in the young. The potential for infection in the Iron Age has been recently demonstrated in an isotope study by Jay *et al*. (2008). Thirty-four infants below the age of 6 from the Iron Age site of Wetwang Slack, East Yorkshire were sampled for a nitrogen and carbon isotope study (Jay *et al*. 2008: 2). The results illustrated that the majority of the infants were not being breast fed exclusively as would normally be expected up to a year after birth (*ibid.*: 19). In addition to breast milk, a mixture of 'animal milk and/or plant gruel' was also being consumed (*ibid.*), illustrating that at least the young at Wetwang Slack were being weaned early compared to other archaeological populations. Although not directly indicative of the presence of bovine tuberculosis, these results display the use/dependence upon animal by-products in later prehistory and also indicates the potential for this disease (if present in the animal population) to be transmitted to the young at a very early age during this period in time.

## Palaeopathology in archaeozoology: research context

The study of palaeopathology in archaeozoology is an area of research that is still very much in its infancy. The need for a more systematic approach to the recording of pathology in faunal remains was highlighted by Siegel amongst others in the 1970s, 'While faunal analyses of archaeological sites are, with greater frequency, now including some mention of such pathology, this still is not the rule....' (Siegel 1976: 349). A few years later, in 1980, the publication of Baker and Brothwell's *'Animal Diseases in Archaeology'* formed a pioneering text emphasising the importance of pathological analyses in archaeozoology whilst providing a hitherto unavailable point of reference for the faunal analyst. Nearly 30 years on and the study of palaeopathology in archaeozoology has significantly developed in recent years with the formation of the International Council for Archaeozoology (ICAZ) 'Animal Palaeopathology Working Group' (APWG). From surveying the literature this increased awareness and growing interest is immediately evident with the wealth of recent research published (see Davies *et al.* 2005). However, the need for more standardised recording is still a point of contention (see Vann and Thomas 2006; Vann 2008; Bendrey 2007; Bendrey *et al.* 2008), as unfortunately, there remains a very noticeable lack of structure in analysis and recording protocols. This is a problem that has recently been addressed by Vann in her doctoral thesis (Vann 2008). In addition to this, although interest has undoubtedly grown in the analysis and documentation of pathology in faunal remains, the emphasis has been placed more often than not upon localised and unusual pathological case studies, for example, trauma, oral pathology and traction-work related pathologies (see Davies *et al.* 2005; Thomas and Mainland 2005). Although interesting and informative, these isolated studies do little to address the broader picture of animal health in the past, resulting in the presence of a very prominent 'grey area'.

This is a problem that is undoubtedly rooted within and exacerbated by the very nature of archaeozoological faunal assemblages. Taphonomy along with diagenesis heavily modifies a faunal bone assemblage, resulting in the accumulation of disarticulated, often highly fragmented bones from multiple animals. Not only does this make it extremely difficult to gain an accurate indication of the original 'death' assemblage (see Reitz and Wing 1999: 110–141) but it also precludes the ability to observe the characteristic patterning of skeletal lesions that are routinely recorded in human remains – a vital stage in the diagnostic process for disease as emphasised by a number of different authors (Mays 2005: 139; Roberts and Buikstra 2003: 118; Knüsel and Ogden 2007). With this in mind, it is obvious why only cursory attention has been paid to the study of infectious diseases such as bTB. Most notable publications that provide overviews of the potential for identification of this disease in faunal remains (see Lignereux and Peters (1999) and Mays (2005)) only go so far as to present general reviews of the veterinary literature in relation to the skeletal manifestation of tuberculosis in non-human mammals. Mays concluded that '…little work has been carried out to identify tuberculosis among archaeo-faunal material.' (Mays 2005: 131). This lack of work is understandable given the factors outlined above, however, the need for a reliable guide/set of differential diagnostic criteria for the identification of bTB in archaeological faunal material has also been voiced elsewhere in the literature: 'Because adequate palaeopathological diagnostic criteria are lacking, it is difficult to determine whether tuberculosis was present in early animal herds using conventional palaeopathological examination' (*ibid.*: 128) and '…archaeozoologists unfortunately have not produced very much evidence at all for tuberculosis in wild or domesticated animals from archaeological sites…' (Roberts and Manchester 2005: 185). These statements very succinctly sum up the necessity that both governs and drives the current author's research.

## Working towards a skeletal criterion: where should we be looking?

A survey of the literature has reaffirmed what other authors (Lignereux and Peters 1999; Mays 2005) have stated. There is an unfortunate paucity of information as regards the morphology of tuberculous skeletal lesions in animals and a notable lack of known tuberculous faunal skeletal reference material from which to compare, contrast and differentially diagnose. There are a handful of pictures but little else to aid in our identification of the disease in archaeological faunal material.

The skeletal lesions associated with TB, as reported in the medical and human palaeopathological literature, are predominantly destructive in nature,

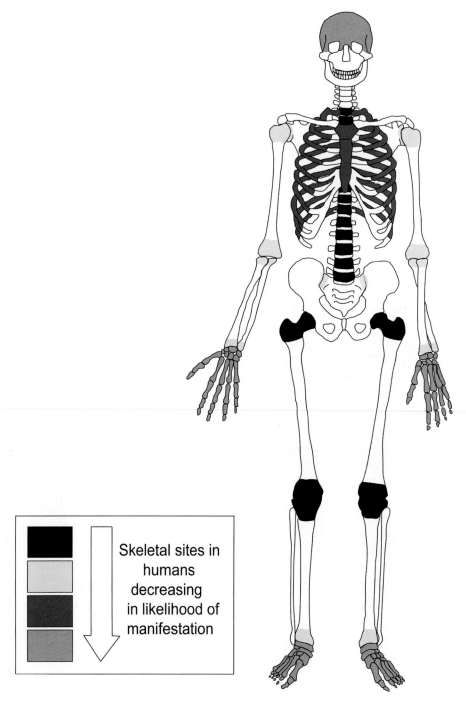

Figure 12.2: Tuberculosis: Skeletal lesion patterning in humans (redrawn from Mays 1998: figure 1.1).

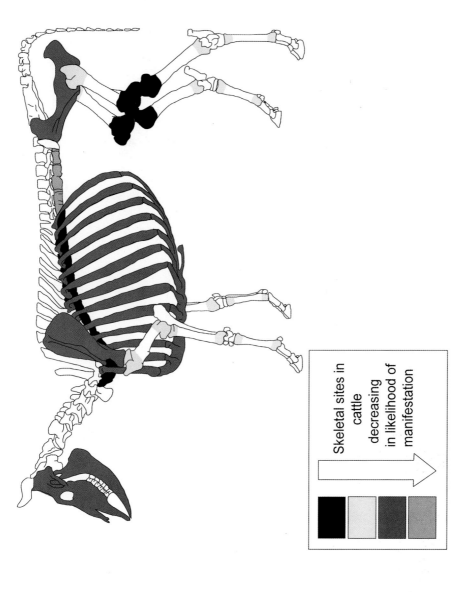

Figure 12.3: Bovine Tuberculosis: Skeletal lesion patterning in cattle (redrawn from Dyce *et al.* 1996: figure 26.1).

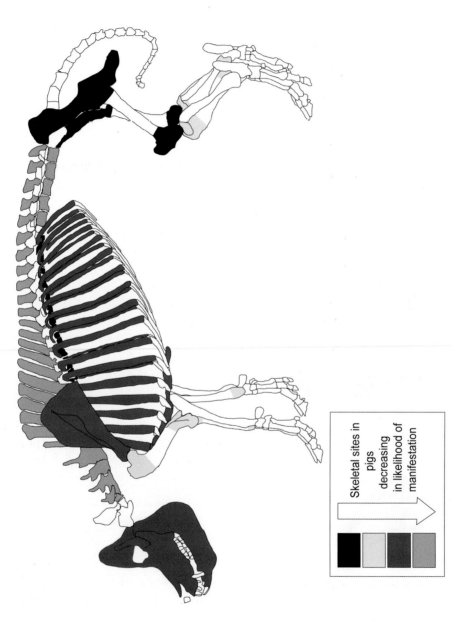

Figure 12.4: Bovine Tuberculosis: Skeletal lesion patterning in pigs (redrawn from Dyce *et al.* 1996: figure 34.1).

involving the resorption and lysis of bone, with little new bone formation (Ortner 2003: 230). In animal bone, the appearance of osseous lesions as reported by Lignereux and Peters (1999), predominantly comprise 'cold fistulized abcesses'. Arthritis, periostitis and osteomyelitis can occur as result of infection (Lignereux and Peters 1999: 342–3) leaving behind osseous lesions on the bones affected. The reality remains that these lesions could still belong to any number of diseases. This is why this research advocates the need for extensive differential diagnosis supplemented by radiography and aDNA analysis.

With reference to the medical and veterinary literature, tuberculosis of the skeletal system in both humans and animals would appear to follow a similar pattern as illustrated in Figures 12.2, 12.3 and 12.4. The skeletal maps illustrated provide a basic starting point as to the potential patterning and location of osseous lesions in cattle and pig. They are by no means definitive at this stage. These illustrations have been compiled based upon detailed descriptions in the archaeological and veterinary literature (see Cohrs 1967; Steinbock 1976; Lignereux and Peters 1999; Ortner 2003; Roberts and Buikstra 2005, and Mays 2005) along with reference to Steinbock's skeletal lesion patterning illustration for TB in humans (Steinbock 1976: fig. 69). Those bones containing high amounts of hemopoietic marrow (vertebral bodies, metaphyses and epiphyses of long bones etc.), form the primary sites of manifestation (Ortner 2003: 228–9), which also appears to be the case in animal bone (Cohrs 1967: 855).The preference for the bacilli to target areas of bone marrow results in the disease often presenting itself as *'tuberculous osteomyelitis'* (*ibid.*). In addition to this, bones located in close proximity to lymph nodes (such as the sternum and ribs) also provide potential sites for osseous manifestations. Infected lymph nodes may rupture resulting in the transfer of bacilli to surrounding tissues (*ibid.*). The veterinary literature also indicates the presence of tuberculous foci within the vertebral spinous processes of pigs (Ostertag 1922: 602 cited in Lignereux and Peters 1999: fig. 6). The occurrence of similar destructive focuses in humans is rare (Ortner 2003: 231). Therefore, this potentially highlights a crucial difference in the way in which this disease manifests itself in pigs and needs to be studied further.

## *Working Towards a Skeletal Criterion: Differential Diagnosis*

The differential diagnosis of pathological lesions is a principal component of medical and veterinary practice. In archaeological faunal assemblages, this process is compounded by the fact that the only material to survive (unless there is exceptional preservation) is bone, of which the greater part is disarticulated and fragmented. The majority of diseases that affect animals primarily affect the soft tissue (Siegel 1976: 355); therefore, with archaeological faunal assemblages a lot of information has been lost. As Siegel stated '…what we see in the way of dry bone pathology is only an indication of the bare minimum of disease processes actually at work in antiquity.' Tuberculosis (whether it be the human or the bovine strain) is by no means an exception with only a small proportion of animals and humans reportedly displaying involvement of the skeleton. In the 1960s, tuberculous lesions were reported to occur in 0.5–1% of cattle and 8–9.5% of pigs (Cohrs 1967: 855) with the estimated percentage in humans being 5–7% (Mays 1998: 135). In light of these statistics and the fact that lesions in dry bone are difficult to interpret as well as not being especially 'pathognomonic' (Lignereux and Peters 1999: 345), the likelihood of being able to identify lesions that definitively points towards bTB in terms of aetiology and more importantly differentiate them from other diseases in archaeological faunal material would appear to be a futile exercise. Having said this, archaeological faunal assemblages will always be mainly comprised of heavily modified, co-mingled, incomplete and highly fragmented osseous remains, and it is within these predetermined parameters that our efforts must be focused in order to produce a standardised methodological framework.

Lignereux and Peters outlined and described a number of potential diseases and disease categories that require consideration when attempting to identify and most importantly differentiate those osseous lesions associated with bTB. These include in no particular order; brucellosis, echinococcosis, actinomycosis, pyogenic osteomyelitis, sarcoidosis, eosinophilic granuloma, neoplasm, hypertrophic pulmonary osteoarthropathy (HPO) and mycotic infection (Lignereux and Peters 1999: 345–6). Each of these diseases manifest differently in bone and it is the emphasis of these differences that is key to the formation of a useable differential diagnostic criteria. For example, one of the main differences between tuberculosis and brucellosis is the fact that the latter is documented as producing substantial new bone formation (Baker and Brothwell 1980: 76; Lignereux and Peters 1999: 346), whereas the former is not known for this (Lignereux and Peters 1999: 346). Ultimately, the only way to be certain of a diagnosis is to subject the bone to aDNA analysis. However, as this is not always a viable option due to time, money, poor preservation and the fact that sampling involves destructive analysis, it is of paramount importance not to rely on this avenue from the offset. Differentially diagnosing the pathology macroscopically has to be the first analytical step taken.

## Conclusion

Tuberculosis is a disease of considerable antiquity. The fact that *M. bovis* is anthropozoonotic provides the ideal opportunity to study both the human and animal populations of the past, through the medium of disease. The opportunity is therefore afforded to gain a better understanding of the socio-economic environment in which humans and animals first came into prolonged contact with each other. This close interdependent relationship became established over time and has ultimately resulted in the society in which we live today; however, it came at a price – *zoonotic disease*. The more that can be done to facilitate the understanding and recognition of bovine tuberculosis in past human and animal populations is of paramount importance, not only to the further understanding of zoonotic diseases and their aetiology in general, but also to the further understanding and appreciation of the impact of the human/animal relationship over time. The ability to recognise and differentiate disease in faunal remains is the first step towards this better understanding.

In order to create a useable diagnostic criteria for the identification of those osseous lesions most likely associated with bTB in disarticulated faunal assemblages, it is essential to tackle the root of the problem i.e. gain a better understanding of the location, patterning and morphology of the skeletal changes associated with the disease in animals. This would lead to a better appreciation of what to look for and where, thus forming the first step to increased awareness. At the very least being able to differentially diagnose lesions and thus provide a short-list of possible aetiologies would provide the foundation from which further analysis could be built upon. Current and recent research within this field is beginning to realise such a methodological framework – but before this can become a successful and routine practice within archaeozoology, there needs to be detailed diagnostic criteria in place, to aid in both the recognition of pathological lesions and their differential diagnosis.

# Acknowledgements

I would like to thank my supervisors: Prof. Christopher Knüsel (University of Exeter), Dr. Julie Bond and Dr. Jo Buckberry (University of Bradford) for their help, advice and guidance in relation to this paper and the doctoral research it stems from. Thank you to Julie for providing the idea for this research and to Kristin Roha for her initial MSc research on the topic. Thanks also to Dr. Mike Taylor (University of Surrey/DEFRA) for his valuable advice and biomolecular expertise. I am grateful to the Iron Age Research Student Seminar (IARSS) for the opportunity to produce this paper, and in particular am thankful for the helpful advice provided by both Andy Tullett and Martin Sterry throughout the process. Finally, I would also like to thank the anonymous reviewer for their constructive and insightful comments on an earlier draft of this paper.

# Bibliography

*Ancient Sources:*

Claudius Hermerus – *Mulomedicina*
Columella – *De Re Rustica*

*Modern Sources:*

Baker, J. and Brothwell, D. (1980). *Animal Diseases in Archaeology.* London: Academic Press.

Bathurst, R. R. and J. L. Barta (2004). Molecular evidence of tuberculosis induced hypertrophic osteopathy in a 16th-century Iroquoian dog. *Journal of Archaeological Science* 31: 917–925.

Belschner, D. V. (1967). *Cattle Diseases.* Sydney: Angus and Robertson.

Bendrey, R. (2007). New methods for the identification of evidence for bitting on horse remains from archaeological sites. *Journal of Archaeological Science* 34: 1036–1050.

Bendrey, R., G. M. Taylor, A. S. Bouwman and J. P. Cassidy (2008). Suspect bacterial disease in two archaeological horse skeletons from southern England: palaeopathological and bio-molecular studies. *Journal of Archaeological Science* 35: 1581–1590.

Bewley, R. (1994). *Prehistoric Settlements.* London: Batsford/English Heritage.

Boden, E. (2005). *Black's Veterinary Dictionary.* London: A and C Black.

Brosch, R., S. V. Gordon, M. Marmiesse, P. Brodin, C. Buchrieser, K. Eiglmeier, T. Garnier, C. Gutierrez, G. Hewinson, K. Kremer, L. M. Parsons, A. S. Pym, S. Samper, D. van Soolingen and S. T. Cole (2002). A new evolutionary scenario for the Mycobacterium tuberculosis complex. *Proceedings of the National Academy of Sciences* 99(6): 3684–3689.

Buikstra, J. (ed.). (1981). *Prehistoric Tuberculosis in the Americas.* Northwestern University Archaeological Program Scientific Paper No. 5. Evanston, IL: Northwestern University Archaeological Program.

Canci, A., S. Minozzi and S. M. Borgognini Tarli (1996). New evidence of tuberculosis spondylitis from Neolithic Liguria (Italy). *International Journal of Osteoarchaeology* 6: 497–501.

Cartwright, F. F. and M. Biddiss (2004). *Disease and History.* Stroud: Sutton.

Castiglioni, A. (1933). History of Tuberculosis. *Medical Life* 40: 1–96.

Chalke, H. D. (1962). The impact of tuberculosis in literature, history and art. *Medical History* 6: 301–18.

Cohrs, P. (1967). *Nierberle and Cohrs Textbook of the Special Pathological Anatomy of Domestic Animals.* Oxford: Pergamon Press.

Copley, M. S., R. Berstan , S. N. Dudd, V. Straker, P. Payne and R. P. Evershed (2005). Dairying in antiquity. I. Evidence from absorbed lipid residues dating to the British Iron Age. *Journal of Archaeological Science* 32(4): 485–503.

Cunliffe, B. (2004). *Iron Age Britain.* London: Batsford.

Davies, J., M. Fabiš, I. Mainland, M. Richards and R. Thomas (2005). *Diet and Health in Past Animal Populations. Current research and future directions.* Oxford: Oxbow Books.

Department for Environment Food and Rural Affairs (DEFRA). (2008). Bovine TB: what is bovine tuberculosis? http://www.defra.gov.uk/animalh/tb/abouttb/index.htm. (Date accessed: January 2009).

Donoghue, H. D., M. Spigelman, C. L. Greenblatt, G. Lev-Maor, G. Bar-Gal, C. Matheson, A. G. Nerlich and A. Zink (2004). Tuberculosis: from prehistory to Robert Koch, as revealed by ancient DNA. *The Lancet Infectious Diseases* 4, 584–592.

Dormandy, T. (1999). *The White Death. A history of tuberculosis.* London: The Hambledon Press.

Grant, A. (1984). Animal husbandry. In B. Cunliffe (ed.) *Danebury: an Iron Age hillfort in Hampshire. Volume 2: the excavations, 1969–1978: the finds*: 496–548. London: Council for British Archaeology.

Hambleton, E. (1999). *Animal Husbandry Regimes in Iron Age Britain. A comparative study of faunal assemblages from British Iron Age sites*. Oxford: British Archaeological Reports, British Series, 282.

Hardie, R. M. and J. M. Watson (1992). Mycobacterium bovis in England and Wales: past, present and future. *Epidemiology and infection* 109(1): 23–33.

Haselgrove, C. (1999). The Iron Age. In J. Hunter, and I. Ralston (eds.) *The Archaeology of Britain. An introduction from the Upper Palaeolithic to the Industrial Revolution*: 113–134. London: Routledge.

Hershkovitz, I. and A. Gopher (1999). Is tuberculosis associated with early domestication of cattle: evidence from the Levant. In G. Pálfi, O. Dutour, J. Deák and I. Hutás (eds.) *Tuberculosis Past and Present*: 445–449. Budapest: Golden Books/Tuberculosis Foundation.

Hill, J. D. (1995). *Ritual and Rubbish in the Iron Age of Wessex. A study on the formation of a specific archaeological record*. Oxford: British Archaeological Reports, British Series 242.

Jay, M., B. T. Fuller, M. P. Richards, C. J. Knüsel and S. S. King (2008). Iron Age breast-feeding in Britain: isotopic evidence from Wetwang, East Yorkshire. *American Journal of Physical Anthropology* 136: 327–37.

Kiple, K. F. (1997). Scrofula: the King's evil and Struma Africana. In: K. F. Kiple (ed.) *Plague, Pox and Pestilence*: 44–49. London: Weidenfeld and Nicolson.

Knüsel, C. J. and A. R. Ogden (2007). Analysis of human remains: paleopathology. In D. M. Pearsall (ed.) *Encyclopedia of Archaeology*: 1795–1809. London: Elsevier.

Lignereux, Y. and J. Peters (1999). Elements for the retrospective diagnosis of tuberculosis on animal bones from archaeological sites. In G. Pálfi, O. Dutour, J. Deák and I. Hutás (eds.), *Tuberculosis Past and Present*: 339–48. Budapest: Golden Books/Tuberculosis Foundation.

Maltby, M. (1996). The exploitation of animals in the Iron Age: the archaeological evidence. In T. C. Champion and J. R. Collis (eds.) *The Iron Age in Britain and Ireland: recent trends*: 17–27. University of Sheffield: J. R. Collis Publications.

Mays, S. (1998). *The Archaeology of Human Bones*. Routledge: English Heritage.

Mays, S. (2005). Tuberculosis as a zoonotic disease in antiquity. In J. Davies, M. Fabiš, I. Mainland, M. Richards and R. Thomas (eds.) *Diet and Health in Past Animal Populations. Current research and future directions*: 125–134. Oxford: Oxbow Books.

Mays, S., G. M. Taylor, A. J. Legge, D. B. Young and G. Turner-Walker (2001). Palaeopathological and biomolecular study of tuberculosis in a medieval skeletal collection from England. *American Journal of Physical Anthropology* 113: 298–311.

Mays, S. and G. M. Taylor (2003). A first prehistoric case of tuberculosis from Britain. *International Journal of Osteoarchaeology* 13: 189–196.

Meinecke, B. (1927). Consumption (tuberculosis) in classical antiquity. *Annals of Medical History* 9: 379–402.

Millett, M. and D. Russell. (1982). An Iron Age burial from Viables Farm, Basingstoke. *Archaeological Journal* 139: 69–90.

Moda, G., C. J. Daborn, J. M. Grange and O. Cosivi (1996). The zoonotic importance of *Mycobacterium bovis*. *Tubercle and Lung Disease* 77: 103–108.

Morris, J. (2008). Associated bone groups; one archaeologist's rubbish is another's ritual deposition. In O. Davis, K. Waddington and N. Sharples (eds.) *Changing Perspectives on the First Millennium BC*: 83–98. Oxford: Oxbow Books.

Murphy, E. M., Y. K. Chistov, R. Hopkins, P. Rutland and G. M. Taylor (2009). Tuberculosis among Iron Age individuals from Tyva, South Siberia: palaeopathological and biomolecular findings. *Journal of Archaeological Science* 36: 2029–2038.

Noddle, B. (1979). *Animal Bones from Garton Slack*. Ancient Monuments Laboratory Report 2754.

O'Reilly, L. M. and C. J. Daborn (1995). The epidemiology of *Mycobacterium bovis* infections in animals and man: a review. *Tubercle and Lung Disease* 75(1): 1–46.

Ortner, D. J. (2003). *Identification of Pathological Conditions in Human Skeletal Remains*. London: Academic Press.

Ostertag, R, von. (1922). *Handbuch der fleischbeschau für Tierarzte, Ärzte und Richter*. Stuttgart: Enke.

Pease, A. S. (1940). Some remarks on the diagnosis and treatment of tuberculosis in antiquity. *Isis* 31: 380–93.

Reitz, E. J. and E. S. Wing (1999). *Zooarchaeology*. Cambridge: Cambridge University Press.

Roberts, C. A. and J. E. Buikstra (2003). *The Bioarchaeology of Tuberculosis. A global view on a reemerging disease*. Gainesville: University Press of Florida.

Roberts, C. A. and K. Manchester. (2005). *The Archaeology of Disease*. Stroud: Sutton.

Roha, K. (2005). *Tuberculosis in archaeological animal bone assemblages: an experiment in differential diagnosis*. Unpublished MSc Thesis, University of Bradford.

Rothschild, B. M., D. L. Martin, G. Lev, H. Bercovier, G. Kahula Bar-Gal, C. Greenblatt, H. Donohue, M. Spigelman and D. Brittain (2001). Mycobacterium tuberculosis complex DNA from an extinct bison dated 17,000 years before the present. *Clinical Infectious Diseases* 33: 305–311.

Siegel, J. (1976). Animal Palaeopathology: Possibilities and Problems. *Journal of Archaeological Science* 3: 349–384.

Steele, J. H. and A. F. Ranney (1958). Animal tuberculosis. *American Review of Tuberculosis* 77: 908.

Steinbock, R. T. (1976). *Paleopathological diagnosis and interpretation. Bone Diseases in Ancient Human Populations*. Springfield, Illinois: Charles C Thomas.

Taylor, G. M., D. B. Young and S. A. Mays (2005). Genotype analysis of the earliest known prehistoric case of tuberculosis in Britain. *Journal of Clinical Microbiology* 43(5): 2236–2240.

Taylor, G. M., E. Murphy, R. Hopkins, P. Rutland and Y. Chistov (2007). First report of Mycobacterium bovis DNA in human remains from the Iron Age. *Microbiology* 153: 1243–1249.

TB Alert. (2005). *Tuberculosis – A Global Emergency* http://www.tbalert.org/ worldwide/worldwide.php. (Date last accessed: August 2008).

Thoen, C. O., P. A. LoBue D. L. Enarson, J. Kaneene and I. de Kantor (2009). Tuberculosis: a reemerging disease in animals and humans. *Vet. Italiania* 45(1):135–181.

Thomas, R. and I. Mainland (2005). Introduction: animal diet and health – current perspectives and future directions. In J. Davies, M. Fabiš, I. Mainland, M. Richards and R. Thomas (eds.) *Diet and Health in Past Animal Populations. Current research and future directions*: 1–7. Oxford: Oxbow Books.

Vincent, V. and Gutierrez Perez, M.C. (1999). The agent of tuberculosis. In G. Pálfi, O. Dutour, J. Deák and I. Hutás (eds.) *Tuberculosis Past and Present*: 139–143. Budapest: Golden Books/Tuberculosis Foundation.

Vann, S. (2008). *Recording the Facts: a generic recording system for animal palaeopathology*. University of Leicester: Unpublished PhD Thesis.

Vann, S. and R. Thomas (2006). Humans, other animals and disease: a comparative approach towards the development of a standardised recording protocol for animal palaeopathology. *Internet Archaeology* 20 http://intarch.ac.uk/journal/ issue20/vannthomas_index.html.

Wight, A. E., E. Lash, H. M. O'Rear and A. B. Crawford (1942). Tuberculosis and Its Eradication. *Yearbook of Agriculture*. 237–249.

Wood, J. W., G. R. Milner, H. C. Harpending and K. M. Weiss (1992). The osteological paradox. Problems of inferring prehistoric health from skeletal samples. *Current Anthropology* 33(4): 343–370.

This series was established in 1993 to publish work related to the research interests and activities of the School of Archaeology & Ancient History, including the work of the University of Leicester Archaeological Service (ULAS). The most recently published titles are listed below and can be ordered through bookshop, or direct; more information can be found at: http://www2.le.ac.uk/departments/archaeology/research/monographs

*Debating Urbanism: Within and Beyond the Walls A.D 300–700* (2010). Edited by Denis Sami and Gavin Speed (ISBN 978-0-9560179-2-5)

*The Hemington Bridges: The excavation of three medieval bridges at Hemington Quarry, near Castle Donington, Leicestershire* (2009). By Susan Ripper and Lynden P. Cooper (ISBN 978-0-9560179-1-8)

*From Captivity to Freedom: Themes in Ancient and Modern Slavery* (2008). Edited by Constantina Katsari and Enrico Del Lago (ISBN 978-0-9560179-0-1)

*Monument, Memory and Myth, Use and re-use of three Bronze Age barrows at Cossington, Leicestershire* (2008). By John Thomas (ISBN 978-0-9538914-8-1)

*The Archaeology of the East Midlands. An Archaeological Resource Assessment and Research Agenda* (2006). Edited by Nicholas J Cooper (ISBN 978-0-9538914-7-4)

*Ethnography and Archaeology in Upland Mediterranean Spain. Manolo's world: Peopling the recent past in the Serra de L'Altmirant* (2004). By Neil Christie, Paul Beavitt, Josep A Gisbert Santonja, Joan Seguí and Maria Victoria Gil Senís (ISBN 0-9538914-6-1)

*Re-Searching the Iron Age* (2003). Edited by Jodie Humphrey (ISBN 0-9538914-5-3)

*Coins, cult and cultural identity: Augustan coins, hot springs and the early Roman baths at Bourbonne-les-Bains* (2003). By Eberhard Sauer (ISBN 0-9538914-4-5)

*The Prehistory of the East Midlands Claylands* (2002). By Patrick Clay (ISBN 0-9538914-2-9)

For further information, please contact:
Leicester Archaeology Monographs c/o School of Archaeology & Ancient History, University of Leicester, University Road, Leicester LE1 7RH, UK
Tel: +44 (0)116 252 2611; Fax: +44 (0)116 252 5005; arch-anchist@le.ac.uk